ROBERT ELMS

A LIFE IN THREADS

THE WAY WE WORE

First published 2005 by Picador
an imprint of Pan Macmillan Ltd
Pan Macmillan, 20 New Wharf Road, London N1 9RR
Basingstoke and Oxford
Associated companies throughout the world
www.panmacmillan.com

ISBN 0 330 42032 1

1 3 5 7 9 8 6 4 2

A CIP catalogue record for this book is available from
the British Library.

Printed and bound in Great Britain by
Mackays of Chatham plc, Chatham, Kent

FOR CHRISTINA

in a blue and white striped matelot top

INTRODUCTION

THE WHISTLE was correct in all details.

Closing my eyes I see it now: petrol blue, wool and mohair, Italian cut, flat-fronted, side adjusters, zip fly, sixteen-inch bottoms, central vent on the jacket, flap pockets, ticket pocket, three button (only one done up of course), high-breaking, narrow lapels, buttonhole on the left, four buttons on the cuff – claret silk lining. On the record player in the corner, one of those beige and brown jobs with a thin metal spindle to accommodate a stack of 45s, just one single: 'Too Hard to Handle' by Otis Redding, possibly on import, definitely on Stax. As the soul man punched out his deep Memphis rhythms, so the boy in the suit did a slow-motion council-estate shuffle across the floral fitted carpet we'd recently bought on HP from the Co-op. The music was his soundtrack; the dance was strictly for display. The shoes that shone out from beneath this paragon of a two-piece were Royals. I was entranced. This, as my lovably idiolectic mum said, was 'all the go'. This was what you grew up for.

The suit didn't come as a surprise. Barry had been waiting weeks for this moment and we'd been with him all the way, getting reports back, getting excited as the day approached. It wasn't so much that a suit like this was worth the wait, more that the wait was worth savouring. The process itself was sumptuous, the measurements and the fittings, meetings even, the discussion of cut, cloth and linings, with a tailor somewhere off the Edgware Road. In 1965, for a sixteen-year-old boy from Burnt Oak via Notting Dale, to have meetings and a tailor to call his own was quite something, but then Barry was something – he was a mod. He was one.

Leave school at fifteen, save for a suit at sixteen. As I watched my eldest brother, ten years my senior, display the sweet fruits of the first year of his labours, with a shimmy and a show, parading his standing and his allegiance, his status and his taste, somehow I understood that this was a path, a lineage. My dad, a dapper man when he wasn't wearing overalls, nodded approval. When he'd first asked my mum to jitterbug, he'd sported a chalk-stripe double-breasted at the Palais de Dance, looking natty with a Marcel wave in his ash-blond-hair and a carnation in his lapel. He was still with her later that night, when Al Bowley and his orchestra struck up the last waltz, and he'd been by her side ever since. As this new dance took place in our cluttered little north London living-room, I just sat mesmerized, silently enraptured by the lure of the look. I was in thrall to threads.

To this day I like clothes. I'm slightly wary of people who don't like clothes. What you wear is your interface, what you say to the world. But I admit that I'm a touch obsessive. When I was a boy I liked stamps, briefly, like most boys do, but deeply. It was the idea that you could master stamps, learn about them, own them, line them up in a book with hinges and that diaphanous paper to separate the sheets. People would look at your collection and be impressed. Stamps went away though: too fiddly, too national health spectacles. I still get a little frisson from stationery. Smythsons for example, where the paper has that weft on the surface, all crisp and sharp, edges lined precisely up, kept in a royal blue box. But really I like clothes. Clothes tell stories.

The room in which I'm writing has a wardrobe. It has a line of wardrobes, built into the wall, designed by my wife, who does that sort of thing, all smooth off-white and minimalist modern, brushed steel tubular handles, just the sort of thing she does. Sometimes, always when I'm on my own, so as to avoid charges of vanity and behaving like Richard Gere in *American Gigolo*, I open the one that contains the suits. They're soundless, these wardrobes, which is a good thing, as a creak would let everybody know that I'm 'at it' again, indulging in a spot of sartorial onanism. The suits – there's a dozen at the time of writing – are draped from identical wooden hangers in a line, and all I really see is their profile, the curve of the shoulder, the drop of the sleeve, the overlapping buttons arrayed on the cuff. The colours run through a strictly, maybe sadly limited palette of greys, blues and fawns – but they're all different. There's a muted check here, a sheen in the weave there. Occasionally I move them a little, space them out like some camply pedantic shop assistant. But mostly I just look. It makes me feel good.

Cloth is good. It's the perfect combination of the tactile and the visual: you feel cloth; it wraps itself around you. Made up into something as precisely prescribed, yet infinitely varied as a gentleman's suit, cloth becomes better than good, it becomes a piece. Leather is good too, but only for shoes. Shoes are undeniable. Shoe trees in place, the smell of wax and care. Shoes repay you. Shoes look back at you. Fantastic. Shoes are good, but suits are better.

I like clothes, and I like the fact that you're not really supposed to like clothes, that they are seen as somehow superficial, unworthy. Now that I'm a certain age, that I've arrived at a certain place, I like clothes much more than I like fashion. I like clothes for their own sake, divorced of any context or subtext. Underwear: white cotton boxer shorts please, still in the wrapping, sitting in a drawer. Having pristine, unopened two-ply white cotton underwear, made by a small, very traditional company in Derbyshire, unopened in your drawer, piled neatly, waiting – well, that's a sign to yourself. You're doing all right, you're not in a mess.

But suits are best. Each of those crafted pieces, each of those, if truth be told, damn near identical suits, has a series of little tales to relate. That's the one I was wearing when I first met her. Those two were made for that television show I presented so badly. That's the lovely Savile Row number I'd dreamed of for years and spent that windfall on. That's the suit I got married in.

I'm planning a new one now, the perfect way to celebrate doing the deal for this book. I'm in preliminary discussions with a tailor called Nick, a young Anglo-Greek guy with a good and growing reputation who's recently moved up west, got a little place in Mayfair. We've talked about an early sixties, English cut, two-button two-piece – think James Bond in *From Russia with Love* – side vents, single pleat on the strides, neat but not mannered, manly in fact. I fancy a pearl grey. When it takes its place in the wardrobe it will sit there to remind me of writing this.

But in my memory there's a far larger wardrobe, groaning and buckling under the weight of all the outfits I've ever entertained, all the ridiculous get-ups, the fads and the fashions which have taken the boy with big eyes for his brother's whistle through every step. I've been there as mod begat skinhead, begat suedehead, begat Bowie boy, begat soul boy, begat punk, until all the begatting began to go mad and I ended up in a kilt. I've worn some clothes. And just about every bit of old tat, every precious piece of the clothes designer's craft, every shape of shoe, every variety of collar has lodged itself in my brain, with a million barnacles of association clinging to its threads. I recall events by what I was wearing, a button-down, chisel-toed, fly-fronted mnemonic.

What's worse is that not only do I carry round this stupidly over-stuffed wardrobe of mine, containing just about every item I've ever worn or lusted after, but I also have a mental inventory of what others were wearing too. Name a record and I can tell you what you had on when you first heard it. All right, I might not be able to, but I can tell you what you should have had on, what was all the rage at that precise point in time. It's a party piece which has done me little good.

I was wearing one of my suits at a party recently. I'm now in that peculiar, inverted position where I loaf around in jeans and T-shirts all day, but get suited and booted to go out of an evening. This two-piece was midnight blue; Venetian gabardine, with a pearl tie-pin in the welt of the breast pocket, holding a silk hankie in place. The little band of material that runs across the top of the breast pocket is called a welt, and into that, as close to the centre as I could manage, I stuck a tie pin, with a little pearl head, and then pushed it down, so that all you could see was the pearl. The pin thus speared the hankie, thereby stopping that annoying habit silk handkerchiefs have of slipping down in your pocket. It's a very dandyish touch, I know, and my wife thinks it's a foppish affectation, but I can't help it. You see, my other brother, Reggie, the middle boy of three, wore just such a pin in the pocket of his Crombie, when he wanted to look particularly tasty. He was a skinhead, a 69 original. The idea was that the pin would keep your mandatory silk hankie – red to match the socks which sat inside the brogues, which nestled under the Levi's – in place, even if you were skanking to Toots and the Maytals or rucking on the North Bank at Highbury.

It's a neat idea and one I was sporting with undeniable vanity. I can't remember the wheres or whys of that party, my brain is far too clothes-cluttered to hold such details for long. But I distinctly recall one of the other guests, a conservatively dressed gentleman about the same age as myself, standing, looking at me, clearly focusing on my left breast. I was aware of his gaze until finally he approached and said respectfully, '1970?'

I nodded and he smiled. Then out came a litany of looks as we played a verbal game of garment ping-pong. He'd serve Sta-prest,

I'd reply with channel seams. He would smash down a pair of smooths, I'd lob up a desert boot. He'd spin me a bowling shirt and I'd have to return a cheesecloth. Cap sleeves against tulip collars, Fred Perry countered by Gola, Budgie jackets versus Harringtons; back and forth it went, back and forth in ever more gleeful rallies of long-forgotten objects of sartorial desire. Or at least I thought they'd been forgotten by everyone but me. Yet here was a Liverpudlian, a lawyer, who was every bit as bulging with motheaten old clothes as I was.

Our pleasure at expelling all this pent-up, long-buried stuff was contagious, as we fed off each other's hunger to share our passion. For what seemed like and probably was hours, we talked in this semaphore of styles, conversing in a lost code. We weren't just talking clothes, we were running through our shared youths, our communal experience of growing up as working-class urban boys in a culture where what you wore determined who you were. Every outfit was a stage we went through together, every new type of footwear or brand of jeans, every silly haircut signalling a stylistic turning-point, was a major step we shared, not just with each other, but with our many hundreds of thousands of overdressed, under-valued contemporaries, who also ran the gamut of trouser tribes and youth cults that *were* our culture.

As our conversation bounced from one look, one craze or scene, to the next, it was actually leading us through our lives. Mention a particular pair of trousers and we were really recalling street games in crumbling terraced blocks and pugnacious school playgrounds. Talk of a shoe shop or a brand of trainer and we were actually discussing our emergence into teenage gangs and groups and bonding and fighting, our discovery of music and girls and drugs, our nights in clubs and days in college, our football teams and our families, our simultaneous and at times overpowering desire to fit in and to stand out. We'd grown up in that unsettled post-war Britain where council-estate kids, while encouraged by the welfare state, were still marginalized by the class system. So the margins were bursting with creativity.

There was an energy and a passion among our young cohorts, a unique drive to excel at something, much of which manifested itself in an audacious creativity with hosiery and trousering and pins in pockets. We were talking fashion, but not fashion designers or haute couture; this was not salon style imposed from above, not a glossy magazine saga of effete clothes designers, or swanky celebrities with vast budgets and arrays of stylists. Our story was of great, unsung clothes-wearers. The restless elegance, the tribalism and dandyism of so many otherwise ordinary British kids in the second half of the twentieth century. That is what we were really celebrating with our little game. We were also lamenting a little, a nod to the knowledge that we now live in reduced times.

This contest of ours came to an end when my new-found, and I now had to admit rather well-dressed friend dug deep, and fired off a rocket from long ago. A winning shot before it even hit. With a slight grin on his face and a reverence in his tone, he said firmly and quietly, 'Salatio box-top loafers.' There was nothing I could do. You can't beat Salatio box-top loafers and we both knew it. I put out my hand, which he shook manfully. He did, though, have one last thing to impart before we both turned to return to the party. 'You know,' he said with a slight melancholy catch in his voice, 'that's an untold story.'

1

NOTTING DALE was the ea[illegible] Notting Hill [illegible] because the area has [illegible] [illegible] until even the name, [illegible] [illegible] community is all but [illegible] [illegible] always eager to exploit a qu[illegible] little villages, [illegible] and a few [illegible] the motorway. [illegible] [illegible] ancestral homeland could [illegible] [illegible]. This [illegible] [illegible] and the Westway on [illegible] Notting Hill on the [illegible] [illegible] of the[illegible] [illegible] class [illegible] [illegible] riots [illegible] in 1958.

There had been Chinese [illegible] recall, which is not all that [illegible] to go in for genealogy. Chin[illegible] [illegible] who came in the mid-ninetee[illegible] and Gray Railway, which co[illegible] were a rollcall [illegible] of [illegible] the [illegible] and [illegible]

NOTTING DALE was the rapscallion neighbour of Notting Hill. I say was, because the area has been slum-cleared and town-planned away until even the name, usually the most tenacious aspect of a city community, is all but extinct. The fact that estate agents, always eager to exploit a quaint old moniker that might add a little villagey charm and a few grand to a former council flat by the motorway, haven't tried to resurrect the traditional title of my ancestral homeland could show just how lowly and unloved it was. This misshapen triangle of W10 is bordered by the railway lines and the Westway on two sides, and posh Holland Park and Notting Hill on the third. If there is any residual memory of this forgotten enclave, it's of these three things: rag-and-bone men, mass murder and race riots. It's a good place to start. Or at least it was in 1959.

There had been Elmses in the Dale for as long as anyone can recall, which is not all that long really, as we aren't the sort of family to go in for genealogy. Chances are they arrived with the navvies who came in the mid-nineteenth century to dig the Hammersmith and City Railway, which cuts through this area. Its inhabitants were a rollicking mix of Irish and English peasants, who had left the hungry land and ended up mired in a clay pit, used to mine and fire the bricks for the grand stucco terraces up on Notting Hill and to keep a few pigs. Hence the nicknames, the piggeries and the potteries, which were still just about current when we were there.

The other traditional inhabitants of Notting Dale were gypsies. This area, which had once had a race track and horse fair, was the centre of London Romany life, and there had long been a large travelling encampment on Latimer Road, which is as close to a main thoroughfare as the Dale ever got. The gypsies gave the area its reputation for rowdiness and scruffiness and bequeathed a tradition of street trading which became our game.

There's still a contemporary gypsy camp, all spick and span caravans, broken fridges and anorexic mutts, squeezed beneath the strands of stained concrete where they entangle at the northern end of the motorway confluence that is now much of the neighbourhood. You even get the occasional horse. But the most famous testament to the Romany street-trading past is the classic television comedy series *Steptoe and Son*. It was set in this tangled warren of 'Shepherd's Bush borders', and based on a real-life Notting Dale totter, Arthur Arnold, whose stables and scrapyard on Latimer Road, yards from the house where my dad, Albert, grew up, was just one of the many that littered the area. My family weren't rag-and-bone merchants, but Nanni Elms, with her flaming auburn hair, pipe between her lips and sleeves rolled to the biceps for a Friday night fight, was a proper gypsy girl, cursing and brawling with the best.

Or so they say. She passed on shortly after I arrived, but her husband, Grandad Weenie, as small a man as his sobriquet might suggest, was still around, the head of a sprawling mob who shifted a quarter of a mile south-west and now inhabited a large, crumbling, but always tumultuous terraced house in Norland Gardens, right by the market where they kept fruit and veg stalls. On the famous Charles Booth maps of *Life and Labour of the People in London*, that's a move from 'very poor' to 'fairly comfortable', which is just about right. Grandad Weenie was a near-silent, always canny little man, an unofficial pawnbroker and street angler, who made sure his mob had a few bob. We were 'Gord blimey' London but always good for a drink in the Monkey House, the local and clan base.

There's a shoebox of portraits and holiday snaps going back to the end of the nineteenth century which substitutes for any real family record. And one of the most remarkable aspects of these yellowing black and white people is just how fiercely smart they are. Obviously, when it's a special occasion, a wedding photo or something, you'd expect them to be dolled up, but in almost every shot their sartorial brilliance shines like the Brylcreem in their hair.

There's a shot of Grandad Weenie as a young man. My mental image of Dad's dad was of a tiny old chap in a vest, or a collarless shirt, usually watching the racing with a pale ale in his lap and slippers on his feet. But here he was fifty years before, an Edwardian teenager with his four brothers standing in the street outside a pub on the Portobello Road. You can see that he's a short man, but his stature, expressed in his stance and his attire, not just smart, but almost terrifyingly sharp, is looming. Hair centre-parted and plastered down, three-piece suit with fob chain, gleaming black boots, countenance set. It was then I recalled long ago whispered tales of how Grandad Weenie, as a young man, would fight on the cobbles, take off his jacket and take on big men in the street for money. In this picture he was attired as a serious young fellow. Even further back there's one sepia shot of *his* father dressed for work, dragging a handcart through the streets, his waxed handlebar moustache preceding him, his uniform flawless.

Aunt Glad, the eldest of seven kids of whom my father was the youngest, had taken over control of the house and the family from her fiery-haired mother. Women ran things, and she was a woman and a half. Under five foot for sure and bone-juttingly thin, with a voice strangled by tar and time, and skin which looked like it had served once before as parchment in some ancient civilization. I grew up thinking that Aunt Glad, despite always being called Aunt Glad, was actually my grandma. It was as if she was everybody's grandma. She had as good as raised my dad, her beloved little brother, dragging him round the streets as a toddler like some animated rag doll, fighting his fights, after a bout of rheumatic fever had laid him low. Aunt Glad was one of those women who cannot get thirty yards down a street without getting embroiled. If she took you out to the market, and she only ever went to the market, it was like an endless shopping odyssey in other people's lives, feeling their apples, reorganizing their display and nicking a grape to taste. She knew everything, everyone, and told them so in that singed voice laden with expletives which were positively Old Testament in their vim. Aunt Glad was Notting Dale. She was my grandma.

Mum, Eileen, came from a slightly more genteel area, albeit a council estate, over the railway tracks, a mile or two away in East Acton. But the male members of her family were no less dapper. There's a fantastic picture of Uncle Fred, my mum's eldest brother, aged about nineteen or twenty, out for a night back in the early thirties with his mates, and they look splendid. Fred, with a dark, dashing resemblance to my own brother Reggie, has on a broad-shouldered, tight-fitting double-breasted suit, high-collared shirt, kipper tie with pin, handkerchief in his pocket, trilby in his hand, a pencil moustache adorning his lip and a spivvy glint in his eye. He knows he looks great. My eight year-old-son Alfie enquired recently why they were so dressed up, and his grandma said, 'Because it was a Friday night.'

It was a dressed-up Friday night at the Hammersmith Palais when my sixteen-year-old mother first met my dad. No doubt her mother, a goodly, God-fearing woman, gently, piously spoken, was a bit perturbed at her daughter courting a rumbustious coster-monger's son from the Dale. She once famously said, 'You don't need to go to the pictures round Ladbroke Grove,' an expression of curtain-twitching distaste which became a catch-phrase in our family. But Mum, herself a mongrel mix, with the dark eyes and complexion of her secretly Jewish father, Isaac Zilas, had already fallen for the blond boy she danced with at the Hammersmith Palais. Go to the pictures they did.

This Albert Elms was actually a more serious young man than his platinum shock might suggest and his mother-in-law might have feared. He'd been dubbed 'the professor' by his six elder brothers and sisters, a boy so bright he'd been offered a scholarship at the prestigious, private Westminster School, unheard of for a market trader's son from the Dale. His mum, her gypsy blood riled from some perceived slight at the interview, refused to let him go. So instead he pulled on dun-coloured overalls as he worked on building sites, married his dark-eyed sweetheart, read political tracts, followed the lowly local team, Queens Park Rangers, wore his best at weekends and went about setting up a home.

It was 1946 and housing was in short supply. The Luftwaffe had done their bit to kick off the process of slum clearance, but Notting Dale didn't need too much help to collapse. Jerry-built as much as Jerry-bombed, and shamefully neglected, the area was crumbling and ripe for ruthless landlords who crammed more and more into less and less. Rachman time. Albert and Eileen, still in their teens but in an era before teenagers were invented, were lucky to have a room in the family home but they were eager to try and find a place of their own. Mum, who worked in Lewis's tobacconists on Norland Market, opposite the Elmses' pitch, spoke to one of her regular customers who she knew rented out rooms in his house round the corner. Number Ten Rillington Place.

It's part of our collective family mythology that none of us would be around if she'd taken up his offer of lodgings. 'I don't know why, he was a nice enough chap, quite jolly, but there was something about him that seemed a bit creepy.' Creepy Christie of course, John Reginald Halliday Christie, murdered half a dozen people in Number Ten Rillington Place, his wife among them, gassing his victims then burying them in the back yard or bricking them up in the kitchen. Finally Mum and Dad found a couple of rooms in a safe house, moving around a bit, trying to better themselves, giving homes to three boys, the last of them in the last year of the fifties. But wherever they went, home was still that big old tumbledown terrace in the Dale, which apart from *Steptoe and Son* and Crippen and victims had one other cause of note. Which is where our story really starts.

'They weren't the Notting Hill race riots, they were the Notting Dale race riots. I should know, I was in them.'

It's only very recently that I heard this revelation from one of my cousins. Chances are it was over light ale and sausage rolls at a wedding or a funeral, and almost definitely it was me who instigated the conversation. I harbour an insatiable urge to know more about the old neighbourhood, the old ways, and so whenever the scattered clan gathers, which is pretty rarely, I tend to niggle and pick away at its recollections. This time I opened a sore.

The so-called Notting Hill race riots of 1958 have rightly gone down in infamy as a nadir in race relations in Britain. For four consecutive nights gangs of white youths in drape coats, urged on by Mosley's British Union of Fascists, fought pitched street battles with groups of young West Indians in trilbys, who had recently settled in the area in search of cheap accommodation and been persistently goaded and abused. It was a national scandal, and propelled Notting Hill to dubious prominence. But according to my cousin, the arena where the battles actually occurred was not bohemian, arty Notting Hill, but down in the lowly Dale, with Latimer Road and Lancaster Road the centre of the action. My cousin put me right on this and put me in a right spin. I have an Anglo-Chinese wife and three mixed-race London kids, and I now discovered that I have a close family member who was part of a seething racist mob. I pushed him a bit. 'I was seventeen, I was a Teddy boy, we ran with the pack. There were lots of problems in the area and we picked on the wrong people. We were wrong. Those young West Indian guys were fantastic, and they looked so cool.'

As well as being shocked and appalled, I was excited. I took no pride in the prejudice, but here was proof that I could trace my family shoe-tree back to brothel-creepers and towards the very start of the story. I'd been chased by Neanderthal second-generation Teds plenty of times in the 1970s, and had little time for their arch, Brylcreemed conservatism, or their silly pink socks, but this was different. The rioters on the streets of West London in 1958, on both sides of the divide, were part of the first flowering, the seething outburst of energy and often wayward creativity that is the true current of this story. Too many times throughout this tale sartorial brilliance and brainless violence will coincide; they come from the same entangled stem. Working-class teenage British boys liked to dress up; working-class teenage British boys liked to fight. And those young Londoners, both black and white, tearing it up for all the wrong reasons on the streets of our dilapidated and soon to be demolished homeland back in the late fifties, were kick-starting something extraordinary.

Colin McInnes, always the most eloquent literary chronicler of this strangely affecting in-between time in London's development, neither pre-war, nor truly after it, was speaking specifically of Notting Dale in his novel *City of Spades* when he said, 'The kids live in the streets, I mean they have charge of them.' An even more powerful evocation of this emerging independent republic of Teenlandia is to be found in the photography of Roger Mayne. Obsessed with the street-life of working-class west London, this educated, quiet soul in a duffel coat spent most of 1956–61 snapping feral packs of wild-eyed boys on bombsites and exhausted, monotone terraces, where they frolicked and fought, posed and paraded unchallenged. These are not the cartoon Teds of later incarnations, but diminutive dandies patrolling their shabby domains in the best they could possibly muster.

White shirts with cut-away collars clean and pressed, narrow ties held in place with clips, hair pompadoured, oiled and quiffed, jackets draping down past their knuckles and held apart to display their many-buttoned waistcoats, trousers tapering to a layered break. And the shoes. The shoes positively shining from those grimy gutters like some evangelical song of cobbled-together salvation. These boys had seen the light and it reflected off their uppers. Ironed shirts and polished shoes when they were living four to a room with an outside toilet shared between four families in a condemned building. That is devotion to a cause. Their look, whether they knew it or not, was an act of proud sedition, a cheeky pilfering of an Edwardian revivalist style originally favoured by homosexual Guards officers and louche Mayfair mercenaries. These no-good, know-nothing herberts from a slum dared to look like that. The judge who famously described such oiks as 'Little Caesars'* was right; they'd nicked the emperor's new clothes and were going to revel in them.

The Teds were pointing two ways at once. They were simultaneously harbingers and hold-outs, a glimpse of the future with its increasingly cosmopolitan collection of teen-driven looks and sounds from far and wide, but also aggressively rooted in the age-old monoculture of the white working-class ghettos. But another Roger Mayne shot from the same streets at the same time gives an even better taste of changing times. This one shows a group of black guys sauntering along the middle of the road with

---

* Julius Caesar was himself a noted dandy as a youth. His chin was clean-shaven and the rest of his body carefully plucked and tweezered; he wore long fringed sleeves and wore his belt loosely draped around his waist. His enemy Sulla called him 'that boy with the loose clothes'.

a nonchalance and a sway which sings out from a still photograph, their immaculate shirts buttoned to the wrist, but undone at the neck, their trilbys and derbies tilted at impossibly jaunty angles, their razor-pressed strides stopping half an inch too short, to reveal natty socks above shoes that are just as radiant. Cool and insouciant, casual in a way it would take white Londoners generations to master, they had a flair and a brio which you can see reflected in the eyes of the locals, gawping at them with something between envy and awe. Those English Teddy boys and those Jamaican rude boys promenading and colliding in those streets where my family lived were between them the basis for all that was to come.

They had their music too, of course. In Notting Dale, in 1959, the year the third of Albert Elms's sons emerged, you'd have heard rock'n'roll ripping out of dance-halls and Dansettes, Little Richard leaping from a wireless in a crowded second-floor bed-sit. Mento and ska and calypso and jazz wafting up from the many illicit blues and shebeens which had colonized basements on Lancaster Road, making these dreary blocks shuffle and sway with their exotic vibrations as curls of curious tobacco swirled within them. Changes were afoot and feet were dancing strange new steps.

ROCK MUSIC had been part of the urban soundtrack for some time. Bill Haley's *Rock Around the Clock* had first upset cinema commissioners five years earlier. But six months before Bill Haley or any rock'n'roll reached these shores there was the first Best-dressed Teddy Boy Contest, held in Canvey Island Essex and won by a twenty-year-old greengrocer's assistant. The look predated and perhaps even predetermined the sound. This is always the way; music, for British kids at least, is secondary to fashion. Very few youngsters can pick up instruments; even records and record players were once expensive items beyond the reach of many. But everybody wears clothes. They can all pull on a pair of strides or colour their hair from a bottle purloined from Boots. The way they look is one of the few things teenagers can control, one of the few statements they can make. Today we are told that teenage girls, pushed by peer pressure, driven by the urges of adolescence, suffer from eating disorders in a crazed desire to control their body image. Well, maybe from the fifties onwards many teenage boys suffered from some sort of clothes obsession, some undiagnosed epidemic of sartoria nervosa, for very similar reasons. I should know – I was one.

In his brilliantly clear-headed book *Hooligan – a History of Respectable Fears*, sociologist Geoffrey Pearson dismantles the notion that antisocial, tribal or violent gang behaviour by over-dressed young British males is somehow a phenomena unique to the second half of the twentieth century. He argues that there have been groups of stroppy, disaffected boys, with a uniform to call their own, roaming the ill-lit alleys and cobbled streets of London from time immemorial. The mid-Victorian period in particular, when the term 'hooligan' first emerged, after a notoriously pugilistic and rowdy Irish family, the O'Hoolihans who terrorized the Elephant and Castle area of south London, had a distinctive youth cult to call its own.

This was precisely when the first Elms was likely to be settling in the Dale, perhaps flogging a few apples from a barrow to the pig farmers or clay cutters. Just possibly he was a 'street Arab', the lurid term of the time for an urchin who cared more about his clothes than he should have done and hung around music-halls and boxing-rings, showing off his fancy duds. Likely he'd have been sporting a pair of hobnail boots, the nails in the heel sending out a ringing sound as they scraped along the cobbles, and perched above them a pair of 'narrow-go-wides', a wonderfully literal name for what we would now call flares. In extreme cases street Arabs tied string just below the knee to make the trouser flare out even more. Above that would be a fancy waistcoat and, as a banner of his ne'er-do-well affiliations, a white silk scarf. This was originally a garment worn by West End swells as a totem of toffish superiority, but one purloined by working-class kids to flout their lowly social standing, just like the Teds and their appropriation of upper-class Edwardian motifs. There was even a specific street Arab haircut, where the head was cropped close to baldness but with a distinctive 'donkey-fringe' of longer hair sprouting out over the brow.

Every single aspect of the street Arab's attire, with the possible exception of the string round the knees – though even that found a brief echo in punk days – would reappear in one way or another in the next 150 years, sported by one of the numerous teen tribes that were destined to follow in their wake. And all of these cults, whose sartorial brilliance burned brightly and threateningly, would have bowled their exaggerated walks along Latimer Road. This is an urban story. Cities are places of trade and theft, innovation and agitation; they're restless, insatiable, tawdry places where showing off is part of the daily interaction. Street fashion relies on all of those, and on precisely the kind of proximity between rich and poor that cities in general and Notting Dale in particular – where the sumptuous villas of Holland Park are within spitting distance of the slanted slums – could provide. No wonder it was a place where kids who had nothing wanted to look like they had it all.

But the 1950s Teds of W10 were doomed. As the new decade emerged, so sleeker styles were bubbling under, waiting to make Teddy boys everywhere appear lumpen and stuffily out of date. More specifically, the area was about to be bashed to oblivion. It's too easy to get sentimental about the good old days, and there was little good about the rancid, insanitary conditions most of the people of Notting Dale lived in, but whether it was right to completely demolish what had been a distinctive and cohesive community is another question. The old terraced streets, with their jerry-built, third-rate Georgian terraces, divided and divided again into suffocating bed-sits, the tiny rows of one-up, one-down railway cottages and the ramshackle totters' yards, with their scruffy stables still smelling of horses. These were to be replaced by the new-fangled high-rise blocks which were beginning to pierce the London skyline, Trellick Tower, Erno Goldfinger's emblem of engineering modernity, leading the way. Even more shockingly, a swooping new thoroughfare, a daring motorway on stilts dubbed the Westway, was to be driven right through the neighbourhood.

This super-highway was supposed to symbolize the white heat of Harold Wilson's technological revolution, to make London a city fit for car-owning sophisticates, which in reality meant a few Hillman Imps heading for Perivale. The Westway, later to star in so many fabulous Clash songs, wanted to go exactly where our family home stood. And as I drive along it now, usually to see the poor unfortunate football team my father loved, I tell people we used to live in the fast lane, although more likely it was the hard shoulder.

The Elmses, along with so many of the families who had thought of these streets as their own, were compulsorily purchased and packed off in the deeply unromantic Notting Dale diaspora, which would see our extended family scattered to the corners of London Town and beyond. Some managed to stay in the area, signing up for the boxes in the sky, or edging over towards Shepherd's Bush or North Kensington, scraping together the cash to buy rotten old houses which are now worth not-so-small fortunes and meeting up at football matches and funerals. Another cousin worked for years as the secretary of the new Holland Park Comprehensive – a school which stood for all the radical, egalitarian modernity of the swinging sixties – and became a well-known character in the area, with its ever more cosmopolitan mix. Others, like my mum and dad, found refuge in 'overspill estates', vast corporate housing projects on the periphery of the city which were filled with exiles washed up from slum-clearance schemes throughout old inner London.

I can distinctly recall standing with Aunt Glad, whose eyes shone to the last, while we watched a giant ball swing the old family home to dust. I must have been about four and she seemed about four hundred, a lady who had lived for ever in a land which was about to vanish, but who rarely succumbed to cheap romanticism. With her grandson in all but name holding tight to her bony, brilliant hand, we watched. She had no tears in her eyes as the bricks tumbled and the last traces of flock wallpaper and ancient anaglypta floated in the air. Pulling on an unfiltered, unapologetic cigarette, she said, 'Don't worry, Robert, it's all for the good. We're going modern.' Aunt Glad, you weren't wrong.

2

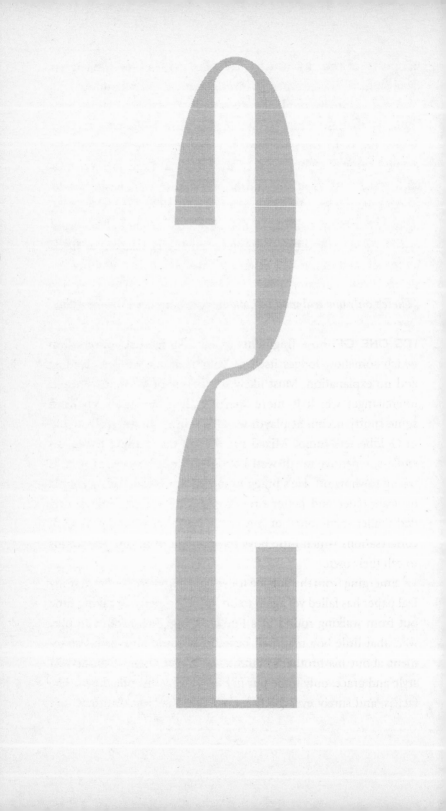

'There's only one real mod in London and that's Lee Davis's brother.'

IT'S ONE OF those fragments of a half-forgotten conversation which somehow lodges itself in your memory with no context and no explanation. Most likely it was one of those playground interchanges which is more sparring than talking, a jab from some snotty urchin at playtime. This skinny, ginger six-year-old in Goldbeaters Junior Mixed Infants, on the Watling Estate, an endless, repetitive north-west London council housing project, is trying to show off. He's bragging perhaps, to some lads a couple of years older and better dressed than he is, one of those 'my dad's taller than yours' or 'my uncle can bash yours up' type of conversations which little boys have in lieu of having any kudos to call their own.

Emerging from the outside toilets maybe, where the hard, shiny Izal paper has failed yet again to do its job properly, or taking time out from walking round in a line chanting, 'Who wants to play war,' that little boy may well have made some outrageous statement about his brother's standing as a paradigm of modernist style and grace, only to be put in his place by this put-down. The fact is, and surely everybody knows this, that *your* brother can't be a real mod, not an ace face, not a top-of-the-range model mod, not an original got-it-all Soho Go Go mod, because 'There's only one real mod in London and that's Lee Davis's brother.' Not yours, and up yours, Elms.

That one sentence encapsulates so much of the eternal appeal of the mod thing, the reason that it is the core aesthetic of this whole caper. Preposterously élitist and exclusive to the point of singularity, yet everyone's included, everyone knows there's only one real mod. It's at the same time passionate but matter-of-fact, precise and completely merciless. Pared down, exact, knowledgeable, sophisticated, cruel – it's very mod. Of all the youth cults which have come and gone and come back again and again, this is the one doomed to repeat itself because it's so damn seductive. It's also just about the only youth cult uniform which doesn't look ridiculous in retrospect.

Mods were modernists. They were the rare ones who opted for the plangent squeal of modern jazz: the stripped-back, black American cool of sharp suits and tart solos as opposed to the baggy bounce of trad, the big craze at the time among podgy students who jived to Kenny Ball and Acker Bilk. These sleek, urban stylists were into hard bop, not college hops, and they forged a look which haunts me to this day.

By day they were casual, continental: slip-on shoes, the leather soft and svelte, trousers narrow, maybe white, shirts cotton, button-down. Miles Davis on the cover of *Milestones*, his pale green shirt an icon, or the soft roll collar Billy Eckstine always wore. Jean-Paul Belmondo in a box jacket, Alain Delon in a crew-neck sweater, Marcello Mastroianni in shades. Maybe a cycling top in Italian blue or a blazer with crested buttons, perhaps an off-white Cecil Gee mac folded over the arm. Hair worn dry and short, a French crew or a college boy, European chic or Ivy League neat. By night, when jazz and soul and r'n'b pinged and popped in cellar clubs like the Scene and the Flamingo, the need was even greater, the stakes stepped up, the style intensified. So it was suits, always suits, made to measure, made to glide, fitted and framed. Mods were smart, mods were clever – clean under pressure.

Mods shopped. It wasn't so much retail therapy with the earnest young modernists of spring 1963 as retail religion, pilgrimages to the sacred altars of Soho. Tailoring by Sam Arkus of Berwick Street, shirts from Austin's on Shaftesbury Avenue, shoes from Stan Georgiou's on Dean Street, and finally the great style seminary that was John Stephen's boutique on Carnaby Street, where every eager little supplicant was baptized into the true faith before donning the vestments. Of course it all went wavy later, went target T-shirts and Union Jack jackets, went overground and over the top as Carnaby Street became a tourist attraction and swinging London became a marketing ploy. The mod thing, the sweet serious liturgical modernist thing, was maybe no more than a moment but it was the moment when working-class kids broke out.

It looked impossibly glamorous at the time to young boys with scarred British Bulldog knees on estates where all the doors were painted the same regulation, corporation colours. Like a series of 1960s advertising slogans, mods were fresh, new, bright. To be a mod was to be on a promise. You may well be a run-of-the-mill also-ran from a crappy suburban secondary modern, but crack the code and you can be the Prince of the city. A sleek fly boy, who has it all: the tailored clothes, the import records, the right drugs in your pocket, the right girl on your arm. The mod knows. And although he's an individualist he also knows he's got a gang to back him up. You can be an arch outsider and a fully paid-up member at the same time. That's why it was so alluring, why scruffy little boys in playgrounds would try to grab some kind of reflected glory by claiming to know one, or even knowing who wasn't one.

Every other youth fashion since has really been an attempt to capture the cachet and the élan of the perfect, probably non-existent mod, in his suede two-eye desert boots, ice-blue jeans, crewneck merino wool jersey and full-length leather coat. Mods would talk of 'colding up', making yourself aloof, untouchable. It's every clumsy, shy, but narcissistic, self-obsessed, eighteen-year-old boy's fantasy. And every six-year-old's idea of what his big brother is like.

And it's no coincidence that the mods, my brother among them, honest, should emerge just as eighteen-year-olds were no longer marched off to do national service in hobnails, but instead found themselves with a degree of independence and affluence that they could spend on Chelsea boots. As the sixties began to solidify, there was a sense that something forward-looking and far-reaching was happening. Most urgent, desirous young males with clipped common voices couldn't be David Bailey or Michael Caine, but they could get a slim-fitting suit made. They had more than before and they were going to prove it by showing less. Teddy boys were baroque and roll, all fancy Dan velvet flourishes and sweaty jumping jive. They were brown ale, sideburns and brothel-creepers, they were Rip It Up, Keep Britain White, Go Johnny Go. But the mods, who followed them, and eventually routed them, were spare, cool bordering on cold. Especially Lee Davis's brother.

Of course the person who tormented the six-year-old me didn't know Lee Davis or his brother. He would simply have known about him, absorbed some folkloric version of the original and ultimate mod myth. Ever since an article appeared in *Town* magazine in 1962 featuring, among others, Mark Feld, soon to be Bolan, a fifteen-year-old boy from Stamford Hill in a bespoke suit, described as a 'face', the search for the first-ever mod has become a Holy Grail of youth culture archaeology. Some will insist he was a Jewish kid from Stoke Newington, whose father was a tailor and who therefore had access to the latest continental cuts. Others say he was a gay art student from St Martin's in Soho, who took his look from the black American modern jazz musicians who had just started to appear in the basement dives. A second-generation

Italian kid from Clerkenwell. A mixed-race boy from Shepherd's Bush. The connected son of a Maltese gangster. Lee Davis's apocryphal brother could, according to various versions of the creation myth of the modernist movement, have been all and any of these.

There's something achingly exotic about these mysterious messianical figures appearing out of nowhere in 1960, fully formed in their skinny suits and shades, as they glide effortlessly down Wardour Street, with Miles Davis ringing in their ears and amphetamines buzzing on their tongues. They're all outsiders, rare beasts compared to the old white bread Teds. Mods didn't want anything to do with anything which had gone before, they were Pol Pot year-zero absolutists. They were the Westway.

But it wasn't quite like that. London in late 1959 wasn't hit by some meteorite which wiped out all the Edwardians, only to see little baby modernists crawling out from the crater. Study the pictures of somewhere like the Two I's , the Old Compton Street coffee bar where the indigenous music scene started to percolate up in the late fifties, and there's a whole rag-bag of looks crammed into that tiny space. It's a primordial soup of all styles and none. Trad jazz fans and skifflers in baggy jumpers and bushy hair-dos, beatniks in polo-necks and pumps, plenty of assorted rockers, in a variety of variants of the old Teddy boy attire. There is, though, the first sign of a schism occurring. Some have started to veer towards American motorcycle chic, jeans and black leather jackets replacing drape coats and drainpipes, the quiff relaxed and tumbling down. The rockers. Others meanwhile have stayed smart, the drape shrinking to a shorter, leaner line which is just starting to come over from the continent, the tie and trousers still skinny, the shirt still pressed and clean, the hair still greased, but a bit neater and slicked back into a Tony Curtis. There, I reckon, is your first modernist. Six months earlier he may well have been a Ted and it will be another six months before the *appellation contrôlée* 'mod' will be formally applied.

The theory of evolution fits like a John Stephen's box jacket, when it comes to street fashion. Things change, that's the essence of it, but they change gradually, tiny adaptations leading eventually to a new species. It will begin with one kid who sports his tie with a different knot, brushes his hair over to the side or tries on a new pair of shoes. He'll wear them out one night, they'll be spotted and noted and next week there'll be half a dozen copyists, each of them with a tiny twist of their own. This little cabal, maybe a group of mates from one area or college, fans of a particular football team or band, denizens of a particular nightclub, will by now have formed a distinct sub-sect. They will then begin to look for a whole raft of cultural supports: music, movies, motors, to fit in with the gear and to distance themselves from what's gone before. Eventually critical mass will be achieved and they'll become a cult and then a mass religion with its own sacred catechisms. If you wear clothes like this, you listen to this, dance like this, drive one of these . . . do like we do. Eventually every two-bit ten-year-old will be wearing the orthodox high street version of the clothes and claiming that his big brother was the John the Baptist of the true faith. Then the process will start all over again.

Look at those early mods circa 1961, say, and they are not really the fully-formed, cosmopolitan sophisticates that they've been painted as, and that they liked to think of themselves as. These are actually the pimply little brothers of the pale-faced bomb-site boys in the Roger Mayne pictures. Maybe they've seen a clip from a *nouvelle vague* movie, shared a frothy coffee in the local milk bar and danced a couple of times to a Georgie Fame disc. Maybe not. London back then was still a stagnant backwater where the wartime taste of powdered egg was far more prevalent than cappucino or Gauloises. Welsh rabbit was still culinary exotica. Things were hard to find and even harder to afford. But what those neat little post-war pioneers did have oozing from every open pore was desire.

Somehow, even if they lived in closed worlds like the Watling Estate, they knew they wanted. The Teds stole the clothes off the backs of their social superiors, but were content to wear them only in their own dilapidated back alleys. They doffed their quiffs and knew their place. The mods started to crave and yearn, to reach out and find out, to go up west and downtown, to look to Italy and France for clothes, to black America for records, to the Caribbean for attitude. They didn't really know what *la dolce vita* looked or tasted like, but they knew they had to get some. So they rode scooters like little Neapolitans, danced from the waist up, like the black GIs they'd seen in jazz clubs, walked with a bowling sway like the West Indian dudes who inhabited the same streets and estates. These jackdaws on speed – following Italian waiters down the street to copy the cut of their strides, making sartorial notes in darkened cinemas showing arty French films, begging their girlfriends to get their hair cut like Jean Seberg in *A bout de souffle*, worshipping Otis Redding – were pretty much the blueprint for all that was to follow. That's why they are so important. That's why I was so anxious to prove that my brother was one. And he was. I'd seen the suit.

The new carpet he shimmied across, in that admirable bit of schmutter, was on the living-room floor of a nice two-bedroomed council house, with an inside toilet and a garden with grass, on a vast, low-rise, low-rent ghetto in Burnt Oak, the penultimate stop on the Northern Line. This was the Watling Estate, a red-brick NW9 NOWETO. By the time Norland Gardens was motorway, our strand of the Elms clan had wound up seven or so miles north up the Edgware Road, and we certainly weren't alone. In the rows of identikit houses that became home for thousands of displaced members of the roistering classes there were at least a dozen people my mum and dad had gone to school with, women called Queenie or Dollie, men called Alf and Wilf.

Kellys and O'Keefes, Murphys and O'Donnells dominated,

sprawling second-generation Irish families who could be seen gathering and fidgeting outside the church and the pub on Sunday mornings in their monotone finery. There was a spot known as Penguin Corner, where the men would gather after Mass, all of them in dark suits and white shirts, like so many waddling Antarctic birds, ready to migrate together *en masse* across to the pub when the signal sounded and the doors opened. Resolutely and noisily working-class, Burnt Oak had a High Street and a street market, a huge branch of the Co-op and a big bingo hall. It also had the Bald Faced Stag, a pub so notoriously rowdy that people still stop me now and ask what it was really like in there. It was the OK Corral with a dartboard. For all sorts of reasons Burnt Oak had a bad name. It was a good place.

One name for the Watling Estate was 'Little Moscow'. This sneering epithet was bestowed upon our community by the many shocked and appalled middle-class souls who surrounded it and hated it. Edgware, Hendon, Mill Hill, Colindale, these were all awfully nice outposts of net-curtain conformity, neat 1930s semis with pantile roofs, drives and standards. And when the Watling Estate was constructed on 500 acres of grassland, with the specific intention of 'relieving the London slums', where these true-blue, blue-rinse suburbanites wanted a golf course, they were outraged, convinced that the dangerous mob who were dumped there would be raving Bolsheviks. There was even a major campaign to erect a wall all the way round the estate, sealing it off, like a grim Soviet enclave, to protect the sensibilities and the property prices of the poor sods who had to live on its periphery.

They never got their wall; they didn't really need it. Burnt Oak was a place where people were put and stayed put. Its boundaries were clear and carefully observed. We were council and they were private. Apart from occasional forays to see family back in the ancestral homelands, and the mass Saturday afternoon migration to the Arsenal, people from the Oak tended to stay on the reservation. It never was a hotbed of political unrest. By the time we'd arrived in 'Little Moscow' the local red cell consisted of our GP, a big-hearted, big-bearded man who wanted to cure the world, another angrier comrade called Frank, who carried a limpy leg, and my dad. He proudly carried the banner for his union every May Day and made sure that the building sites he worked on were properly organized and safety rules obeyed. He took TUC courses to keep his fine mind sharp and took me to QPR, to maintain some links with the old place, even though my two elder brothers had committed an act of gross apostasy and opted to support the Arsenal along with the roaring Burnt Oak herd.

The Watling Estate never was politically active, but it was a seething cauldron of teenage disquiet. At some point in the late fifties there had been a mass brawl of such ferocity, inside and outside the Bald Faced Stag, between two gangs of bike-chain-wielding, leather-jacket-wearing hoodlums, that it had made it to the national papers, and made it into local folklore as 'the big tear-up'. It certainly wasn't the last. There's some unbelievable statistic I can no longer quite recall, which in 1969 or 1970 placed Burnt Oak station third in a league table of London trouble-spots. This was a tiny little tube stop, serving an unsung council estate on the outer fringes of north-west London, and it was the third most troubled spot in the entire metropolis, as judged by the number of arrests. Lads from Burnt Oak would guard their turf, in a ridiculous ritual known locally as 'station duty', standing for hours outside a lowly tube station ready to repel any invaders or get nicked trying.

Years before that, though, before the skinhead sentinels of Burnt Oak station, there were the mods. Huddling together in their gear outside the library or waiting for the 52 to take them into town for a shopping expedition, looking wanly exotic in such a prosaic place, shocking the old dears who trundled their bags on wheels. Nothing about these neat, obsessive cliques would appear particularly startling today – except perhaps their obsessive neatness – but they must have seemed like an apparition in the early sixties. Engerland may have been swinging like a penderlum do, in patronizing American pop songs with sloppy scansion, and London was supposedly the centre of the hip universe, but not in NW9 it wasn't. Austerity and conformity were still the way.

In the High Street was a shop which became a local institution, a shrine to all things cheap and cheerless. Sid the Tricel King was the name of this all-powerful emporium, which specialized in fabrics and bedding and clothes in man-made fibres so inflammable that its customers crackled and sparked as they left the premises. Everything in that place was shoddy and ersatz, a Bri-Nylon wonderland where nothing was natural or nice. And outside it were teenage boys sporting ice-blue seersucker slacks and maroon suede jackets, white lambswool cardigans, slip-on shoes in cream Cordovan leather, for no better reason than that they could. All dressed up with nowhere particular to go, in clothes which were both expensive and smart yet casual and everyday, proudly peacock masculine, yet to many eyes threateningly ambivalent. These clothes, sumptuous and rich, were an affront to the everyday reality of life in a place where Sid was King and Tricel was the peak of most people's material aspirations.

Showing off and showing out was essential to mod, letting it be seen that you had the hot gear. But because you were supposed to be simultaneously cool, you had to strike a balance as you struck a pose. So nothing was drastic, decorum was called for, the early mods at least went about their business, and their primary business was looking just so, in discreet ways in small groups. They were reacting against the mass tribalism of the Teds, and saw themselves as arch individualists navigating their way through a drearily conformist world. That's where the scooters came in, sleek Italian low-riders, made to carry one cool kiddy effortlessly through the morass. Scooters didn't have the oily roar of a motorbike, they were quiet, curvaceous, the perfect dodging machine for a vain lad who wants to get where he's going uncreased.

The first scooter boys used their machines to ferry them to the seaside, so they could stroll along the prom, the perfect way to display your finery on a sunny day. If an English bank holiday proved to be inclement, then they pulled on army surplus parkas to protect their clobber. The irony of course is that this very act of individual freedom became a mass spectacle and, sadly perhaps, the defining image to most people of the mods: thousands of similarly attired scooterists heading for Brighton or Clacton or Hastings to bash it up with a few rockers and terrorize small children on donkey rides. By 1964, when the mods and rockers seaside clashes became national news, and that season's moral panic, mod was no longer the preserve of a small number of elegant élitists. Mod was undoubtedly watered down and beefed up, attracting scores of scallies who donned the basic uniform, a pair of Levi's, a Fred Perry and a parka, and thought they had to fight to prove their mettle. At heart, though, mod was not a violent creed. It was too self-obsessed and narcissistic to puncture its bubble of perfection with fighting. Mods at their best were altar boys, praying at the high church of style.

And despite what they said about Lee Davis's sibling, my brother was one.

I remember walking along with my mum and seeing Barry with his little huddle, hair teased up into a cockatoo bouffant, jacket buttoned just right, leaning on his prop, a perfectly rolled, full-length gentleman's umbrella, its spike wedged in the pavement like some urban shooting stick. Of course he ignored us. The shape he made was all angular and groovy, the nonchalance practised, the effect galvanizing for a boy still latched to his mummy's side. We walked past him in apparent slow-motion, like he was in a film, a movie made in glorious Technicolor, when everything else around us was shot in grainy black and white.

Mod was never to be my thing. I was born too late. Much of what I've learned of the mod ethic and aesthetic has come from meeting people older than myself who were right in there, first time round. People like Jonny Moke, the shoemaker who was a scenemaker at the Scene. Or Peter Smith, now one of our leading session hairdressers, who was among the very first scooter boys, or Sir Paul Smith, now Britain's leading fashion retailer, but originally a clothes- and cycling-obsessed mod in Nottingham. Georgie Fame, who was Barry's hero, is still mod to a T. Always his trousers are in that slim profile, his shoes are dark and Italian, and on his hands are gloves, immaculate thin white cotton gloves. These men are all well into their fifties now, but they were so touched and shaped by mod that it is immediately apparent that it has never left them. They always look good, hold themselves in a marked, understated fashion, stand in a certain distinctive way and stand out in a crowd. They still have the knowledge. Those basic tenets – take care, look sharp, stay ahead – first gleaned as a kid on a council estate in the early 60s have been the code I've gone by ever since.

Mod was on its way out by the time I was aware of it. There was a new look brewing up, the bastard offspring, if ever there were a bastard born. And strangely enough I was inadvertently going to give everyone a glimpse of what was to come and what was to become my entry point into the great gear game.

Kids get nits. Despite the rigorous, almost maniacal cleanliness of the current era, children today, no matter how wealthy or pernickety their parents, are more likely than ever to get headlice; there's an epidemic. But back when I was young, having Nitty Nora, the school hygiene führer, discover creatures crawling around your head was a true blight upon your family, a bell to ring to proclaim your uncleanliness. So on the one occasion Nora found a few eggs on my head, my mother, appalled at the thought of contagion and shame in the house, decided that drastic measures were needed.

If headlice live in hair, my mum had decided, then it was best to get rid of all the hair. I was probably six, certainly less than seven, when my dad walked me on a Saturday morning to the local barber's to receive the ultimate cure for my infestation. Now usually I loved going to the barber's with my dad. I revelled in the astringent maleness of it all. I liked the clinical chemical smell of stinging aftershave and antiseptic, I liked the racing forms strewn around and the Anglo-Italian patter of the worldwise barber. I liked the terminology; styptic pencils and cut-throats and strops, and most of all I liked being close to the man I loved in this deeply male place. But not this time I didn't. This time I hollered and moaned.

I was going to have what my mum, with her odd way with words, called 'a fourpenny all off', a number one crop by any other name, the closest haircut you can have while still retaining a faint semblance of hair. When the time came for the barber to place that wooden board across the arms of the red leather swivel chair and take the clippers to my ginger glory, I protested vigorously. I moaned and I hollered. So my father did something wonderful. Rather than let his son suffer the ignominy of a bald head alone, he volunteered to have exactly the same savage haircut. A man of forty, a man still proudly sporting a full head of brilliant blond hair, sacrificed his abundant locks so that his littlest son would not feel too bad about having his hair cut off. We walked smiling home together hand in hand, the sun bouncing off our minuscule bristles. A big man and a little boy. Unbeknown to either of us, we were fashion forerunners, and a couple of years later, when the skinhead craze was unleashed, I'd be pleading to have exactly this cut.

I have another memory of my father. We went to see *Spartacus*, at the Burnt Oak Odeon – my dad loved history, particularly the epic, dramatic Hollywood version. And at the end, when Kirk Douglas, dimple a-quiver, was dying on the cross, my dad, cradling my hand for his comfort, sobs smothered in his wide chest and tears falling manfully down his face, explained how this was a parable. It was, he said through the muted sobs, a story about the oppression of the downtrodden and dispossessed, the socialist ethic brought to life, a soft old hard-left man teaching his son.

That's it. No more memories of my father. One day during the Easter holidays when I was six, soon to be seven, the phone rang. At that point it was still fairly unusual for a family on the Watling Estate to have a telephone of their own, and it didn't often ring, but Dad had insisted because he was often away working on sites across the country. The phone rang and my mum went quiet. I was sent to stay with Mrs Caffrey on the corner, while Mum took Reggie, who was fourteen now and also off school, with her. By the time I was recalled, members of the family had gathered from corners of London in our little front room with its floral carpet. Aunt Glad was there, looking smaller than ever, the only time I recall seeing her out of her domain, a sign I now know of a world rent. It was Uncle Mac, a stallholder on the Roman Road in East London, who specialized in toilet rolls and kitchen cloths and the like, who took me to one side and said, 'Daddy's gone to heaven.' I was very confused; I knew he was an atheist.

Aged forty-one, younger than I am now, my father died of a heart attack. It was said by his family, who loved him like the earth, to be the result of that bout of rheumatic fever which had gone untreated when he was but a boy. I don't know if that's true. I just know he died on a building site in the pouring rain. He never got to see his beloved Queens Park Rangers get promoted and win things, never got to see his sons become dapper men.

3

BARRY WORE a black armband. It was 1968 when Otis Redding perished in an air crash, and my eldest brother wore a black armband over the left sleeve of a three-button suit to work. This was a mark of moddish respect, a pleasingly in-crowd pose and a genuine way to mourn the passing of a great soul singer and style icon. In the previous two years, we'd got good at mourning.

I've never felt the need to delve too deeply into any great psychological analysis of the effect that losing my father might have had. Because I was still very young, I think I probably got away pretty lightly, although I did develop asthma, which the doctors said was probably caused by the trauma. My two brothers, on the cusp of becoming men, were hit much harder, and my mum still cries every Christmas. But there was one immediate, practical result, which is pertinent to this story. My mother, who up to that point had just been a mother, now had to go out to work to bring up three boys, two of them still at school. She got a job behind the sweet counter in Woolworths on Burnt Oak Broadway, and another one cleaning the houses of the bank managers and dentists and such like who lived beyond the non-existent fence.

As a result, too young to be left alone, I spent many hours waiting in Woolies, with a comic and a bag of pick'n'mix, on a chair at the back of the store by the mops and plastic bowls and buckets. I spent many more sitting stiffly in the neat but joyless homes she cleaned, listening to the patronizing whine of the women who were never pleased, musing on the fussy sterility of it all compared to the ragged tumult of the old Notting Dale den. As a result I developed a sweet tooth and far too many fillings and a lifelong distaste for the English petty middle classes. But I also got to spend a large amount of time in the company of my two elder brothers, especially Reggie, who was often lumbered with the task of dragging along his skinny, clumsy, wheezy, embarrassingly ginger-haired little brother. If I was going to hang out with Reggie, I had to look the part.

Reggie Elms was a tasty geezer. He had the olive skin, dark hair and piercing eyes of the Jewish side of our family, and the swaggering street smarts of the Notting Dale clan. He was fourteen when the phone rang that fateful Easter, and a pupil at Orange Hill Grammar School for boys. He'd ambled through the eleven plus, and arrived at the exalted school in his barathea blazer, the only kid from the council estate, the hopes of his father, who'd been denied an education of his own and craved one for his sons, riding on his still slim shoulders. He could hold his own academically with the boys in his class, but by the time he became a fatherless child, he was leagues ahead of them in the things that really matter to most fourteen-year-olds. Good at football, confident with girls, a clinical playground scrapper and the owner of a pair of proper red-tag American Levi's. Despite his intellectual prowess, Reggie was very much a Burnt Oak boy. And by the time Otis Redding and our dad had both passed away, Burnt Oak boys were skinheads in all but name.

Unlike the genesis of mod, the start of the skinhead era is little documented or debated. The whole look is so tarnished by its reputation for rowdiness, racism and violence and so ill-served by its numbskull tattooed revivalists that it's somehow buried away, a stylistic skeleton locked in the darkened far reaches of the closet where married men keep stained dirty books. But the reality is that if you were aged between say ten and twenty-two and you lived in a working-class area in any of our major cities from about 1968 to 1971, that is what you wore and what you were. The other fact is that it was one of the most precise, rigorous and potent images ever to be conjured up by a group of supposedly brainless yobs.

For the first time in this tale I was actually around when a new look emerged. Reggie, came home one day, a short while after the supposed summer of love, with his hair shorn to within a quarter of an inch of his scalp. And he didn't even have nits. Reggie and his gang of mates – who played football together in the car park by the station and hung out outside Tonibells, the first Italian ice-cream parlour in all London with its own van, replete with bell – weren't the first skinheads. But they weren't far off. What little digging has been done suggests that the original skinheads were out of east London, possibly the Mile End gang, who followed West Ham. Reggie, like all true Burnt Oak boys, was an Arsenal fanatic, and chances are, when Arsenal played West Ham that season, a clique of shaven-headed Hammers chanting on the Clock End or stomping into the North Bank would have been noted, abused and admired on one Saturday and emulated by the next. That's how it happens. Certainly when it happened to Reggie they weren't even called skins. When my mother shook her head and asked what this new stylistic abomination was known as, Reggie said that he was a 'peanut', the first label applied to this look. Really, he was a pared-down, proletarian mod.

If you were so inclined you could see the switch from the sleek, almost feminine image of the individualist modernist, with his fancy clobber and up-town aspirations, to the tough, regimented fashion fundamentalism of the skinhead as a textbook story of action and reaction, schism, revision and socio-semiotics. As a nine-year-old whose main desire in life up to that point had been to acquire a Johnny Seven, multi-function rifle, like Eamon over the road, I saw it as a chance to get into the game and get some gear.

Actually I had already succumbed to one clothes craze. Tuff Wayfinders were the shoe every kid in England craved, and I'd secured and seen off at least two pairs. These were essentially standard cheap black school shoes, but with the oddest gimmick imaginable. On the rubber sole they had moulded facsimiles of ten wild animal tracks: otter, fox, rabbit, beaver, deer, etc., so that you could recognize the real thing when you saw it imprinted in the earth. And in order to help you in your search for these creatures, there was a compass secreted in the heel of the right shoe. Who thought of those? And who would have thought that they would catch on with hundreds of thousands of urban kids? But they did. I recall taking off my shoe to make sure I was pointed north as I tried in vain to spot otter tracks on the pavement in Watling Avenue, Burnt Oak's main shopping street. I desperately wanted to match up the tracks on my shoe with at least one real-life animal and never did. What a cruel trick to play on a city kid.*

Tuff Wayfinders apart, I hadn't yet been tempted by any particular fashion fad. Barry's mods had been too far away from me, too remote and untouchable. I was too young. But when Reggie walked in with this striking new image, bristling with pride and bald-headed bravado, well, I figured that I could do that. The trendy new thing seemed to consist largely of a bizarre haircut, which had already been foisted upon me once, so why couldn't I get it again and play too? OK, at nine I was still too young, but this time that wasn't going to stop me.

---

* Wayfinders, which sold in their millions, were followed by Grand Prix shoes. These came in a box adorned with a chequered flag and boasted different tyre tracks on the bottom, but sold badly. Even I knew you were less likely to see Ferrari tracks in Burnt Oak than you were otters'.

From the moment that I first saw Reggie's barnet, I started a pleading and cajoling campaign with my mum to let me have a crop. For a while she resisted, weeks, maybe even months, of her little boy bugging her rotten as she sank down in the evening after taking care of two jobs and three kids. She realized I'd look ridiculous. She hated the stark severity of it. But I had to have that haircut, I just knew that my whole future happiness and rank depended upon that haircut. My mum has never been good at saying no and eventually she gave in. This time Reggie took me to the barber's and there was no moaning and hollering. At the end, when the floor was scattered with little ginger wisps and my head was almost entirely bereft, the barber took a cut-throat razor and incised a parting about three inches into what little hair remained. That was it.

I paid the man myself, felt like a man myself as I handed over seven and six, or eight bob including a tip. Aged nine, I felt like I was making my entry. As I walked alongside Reggie Elms, two skinheads together, bowling past Sid the Tricel King and other local luminaries, there was a swollen pride playing in my little clogged-up, malfunctioning chest which has rarely been as prominent since. My brother has a rolling, slightly splay-footed gait that involves an exaggerated sway of the shoulders, and as we strolled through Burnt Oak together I tried to emulate that too. We stopped at the station, as was Reggie's way, to survey and be surveyed, put in a little station duty. Maybe he eyed up and even talked to some girls, perhaps he bought 'a single', one lone cigarette from Tonibells for sixpence, telling me sternly not to tell Mum. Certainly at some point we were joined by some other members of his crew, with their regimented coiffures, and as they towered above me one of them ran his hand across my head, smiling, and said, 'You look good, but you've got to get the proper gear.'

From now on if I wanted kudos and acclaim from male elders and betters, if I wanted someone to ruffle my minuscule hair and smile, it was going to come from teenage boys with button-down shirts and big boots. Wanting, no, that's not the right word, it's *needing*, to wear the right clothes was the norm in places like Burnt Oak. Great store was set by how you looked and what you had on. Isn't that always the way in ghettos? Perhaps it was the paucity of any other kind of material possessions. My kids today can boast about Gameboys and PlayStations and cupboards full of crap, but back then we only really had clothes and bikes to flaunt with pride. Chopper bikes would rival clothes for a while as objects of youth pride and opprobrium, but to have status you had to have style. I wasn't especially unusual in needing to have the right clobber, but perhaps because of being the youngest of three boys with no father to mediate, I was younger and more obsessed than most.

The basic gear that an aspiring skinhead needed had all been part of the well-dressed mod's stylistic vocabulary: Levi's, jeans and more particularly Sta-Prest, usually in off-white, always worn without a belt, a Ben Sherman button-down shirt, boots and brogues, a windcheater and maybe a pork pie hat. (Barry, for instance, managed to move smoothly from mod to skin with only minor modifications, although he only ever opted for the slightly less savage number two crop, a sign perhaps that he was not as much of a zealot as his younger, balder, brother.) Only now these one-time mod garments were put together in a short sharp sentence which shouted, 'We're hard.' Because in truth, that's what skinheads were, hard-core, working-class, no-surrender mods.

By the late sixties, the mod movement was moving in two very polarized directions. The arty, psychedelic end of the scene had gone hippy-trippy. Combine paisley prints with cheap acid and guitar solos, and you end up with Afghan coats and bells on your bell-bottoms. Look at the sartorial journey that the likes of the Who and the Rolling Stones had made from the early sixties, in their neat sweaters and desert boots, to the elaborate, decadent way they dressed by the end of it. Flower power was blooming on the

King's Road. Mark Bolan, 'the first face' when he was Mark Feld, was about to be launched as a Byronic troubadour in a cloak, riding a white swan. The zippy, edgy energy of swinging London had turned into something altogether more hazy and darkly, dreamily hedonistic. Boys from places like Mile End and Burnt Oak don't do dreamily hedonistic.

So in a fantastically blunt riposte to the excesses of the hated 'hairies', with their airy-fairy peace and love, beads and beards pretensions, the younger hard nuts from the council estates, a million miles from the Chelsea flower-power show and arty happenings, shaved their nuts and sharpened their wardrobes. Like the predominant architectural style of the time, when unadorned, strictly functional blocks were springing up everywhere to house the lumpen masses, we were about to witness the age of sartorial brutalism. And all too often there was the behaviour to go with it.

When the late sixties are universally portrayed as a time of love-ins and freak-outs, when space cadets in crushed velvet changed the world by smoking dope and wearing loon pants, I am forced to giggle. Not round our way they weren't. It was fighting and football, not peace and love. The story of the sixties has been hijacked by middle-class kids, who grew their hair while listening to Cream albums in the sixth-form common room. I guess they're the ones who went on to tell the tale. But at the height of the supposed hippy era, I don't recall seeing a single person who could even vaguely be described as a hippy on the Watling Estate, whereas there were hundreds of little cropped haired, hard-nut herberts in the correct skinhead attire. And I suspect that was true all over Britain. For every long-haired, spaced-out sixth-form 'grebo' in a greatcoat, there were a dozen razor-cut fourth-form diehards stomping down the corridor in Levi Sta-Prest with sparks flying from the Blakeys in the heels of their highly polished brogues.

If you'll let me indulge in a pseudo-historical analogue, I would like to draw a link between 1969 and 1642. All things considered, the English civil war is basically a battle between two types of haircut. The Cavaliers of course have long hair, a style favoured by aristocratic fops who have been fighting as mercenaries on the continent with various Catholic royal armies and who come back to stand by the King's banner with their flowing locks and twirly facial adornments, à la Prince Rupert. Lined up on the other side of the affray, meanwhile, are the Roundheads, thus called because the first group to rush to the parliamentarian rallying cry were the London apprentice boys, a fearsome mob of inner city thugs, who were notable for their close-cropped hair (to avoid lice) and therefore sneeringly dubbed 'round heads' by their aristo enemies. On one side upper-class high-church dilettantes with flowing locks, incense and incantations. On the other puritanical, shaven headed, no-nonsense urban ragamuffins. The skinheads of 1969 were the New Model Army, Levellers in Dr Martens.

PUTTING ASIDE the skinhead propensity for a punch-up, there was something undeniably militaristic and regimented about their get-up. This was a generation of working-class kids without a war to fight or an army to belong to, so they created their own, including their own distinctive regimental colours. And now as a nine-year-old with a shaved head and little else, I had to get them. Perhaps because it was a reaction against the free-flowing, anything-goes sartorial licentiousness of the hippies, the skinhead wardrobe was the most precisely prescribed ever. Every label, every detail, pretty much dictated to those who wished to look the part, by those who already did, with just a fraction of room for individual invention. I now had to plague my poor, in every sense of the word, mother to make sure that I could acquire the attire. It wasn't going to be easy.

The true, high-born skin would have two different uniforms. There was the dress one for night-time, discos, weddings and court appearances, the other for football matches, station duty or hanging outside Tonibells smoking Players Number Six while watching blotchy-legged girls in mohair skirt-suits and flat shoes go by.*

The dapper, dressed-up version of the skinhead apparel was indeed one of the very smartest assemblages ever put together. One day I recall opening the door of our house and three guys were standing there, asking for my brother Reggie. These were not the usual, local suspects, and I didn't recognize any of them, but I think I'd still recognize them now. These three chaps were almost identically attired, each in a three-button, two-piece suit, all of them in the latest two-tone tonic mohair, a special weave which gave off contrasting sheens of different hues as the cloth moved: navy and rust, petrol blue and bottle green, airforce grey and silver. (You know that dreadful Jonathan King exploitation record of the time, 'Johnny Reggae', which described tasty geezers in tonic strides. These were three extremely tasty geezers indeed waiting on our doorstep.)

The jackets were a little longer than a mod would have worn them, fitted and waisted, flaring slightly from a tight middle, split by a single, eighteenth-inch vent. All were adorned with silk hankies shaped to a point. The trousers were single-pleat, but cut narrow in the leg, ending perhaps an inch higher than Savile Row would suggest, to reveal socks which were either red or white, depending on local custom and possibly football affiliation. Their shirts were all crisp cotton poplin, with button-down collars, the neat Ivy League style, probably bought at the famed Ivy Shop in Richmond. Button-downs were absolutely mandatory throughout

---

* Skinhead girls, or 'sorts', were much rarer than the boys. This kind of fanatical adherence to a teen uniform seems to be primarily a male trait, but there were girls who went the whole way. They too got number one crops, but with a longer spray of hair at the front and back. This was precisely the donkey fringe which had been worn by male Victorian street Arabs a century before.

this era, and two of the boys on our doorstep were in pastels, pink and yellow probably. The third was a gingham check. I know this because it was the first time I'd ever seen gingham check, and within weeks gingham check would be all the rage and all over the place, as thousands of kids dressed like tablecloths. All were undone, just the one button at the neck. I stared at them with a mix of trepidation and admiration, feebly calling my brother's name.

Their footwear was of course immaculate. Either brogues, the classic heavy lace-up leather walking shoes, with a wide mudguard sole and a punched, filigree pattern on the upper, or Royals, which were also known as smooths, essentially the same shoe but without the patterning. Truth be told I can't recall what colour, but you can bet they were either black, brown or ox-blood, no other colours were acceptable; all were buffed to a brilliance. Two of them had on Crombies (from the upper-class Scottish manufacturer Crombie and Sons of Aberdeen), woollen navy gentleman's topcoats with a fly-front and possibly a black velvet collar. One of them, maybe the dude in the prescient gingham shirt, even sported a full-length, below-the-knee, dark tan sheepskin coat, trimmed with dark wool collar and cuffs, which took my breath away. A coat like that would cost sums that were, to me, unimaginable back then. All three had hair which looked like it had been cropped that day and every day.

These guys were a warped cross between two sets of fraternal sixties style icons, the Krays and the Kennedys. But without hair. So neat and correct was this trio of young men standing on our doorstep, politely asking for my brother, that they could almost have been a troupe of particularly devout Jehovah's Witnesses eager to sell him a copy of the *Watchtower*. I suspect they weren't.

Reggie wasn't in.

And I was never in that sort of gear. The remarkable level of sartorial exactitude which some, admittedly few, top-ranking skinheads displayed was relatively rare, although any self-respecting skin would have a whistle, a pair of brogues and a mock Crombie.

The basic starter kit was still difficult enough for a nine-year-old to acquire. But acquire it I did.

Levi's jeans, as yet, were out of the question, as they simply didn't make proper red-tag, dark denim, shrink-to-fit Levi's, which were only ever available as expensive imports from America, in such little sizes.* I could, though, get hold of some Levi Sta-Prest. These were essentially slacks, in some kind of mixed fabric, cotton and man-made stuff, which kept their shape and their crease at a time when sharp creases were very important; a little like chinos perhaps, but much slimmer and sleeker, and very much part of the look. Anyway I managed to get some Sta-Prest in off-white, a size or so too big, but taken up by my mum and held up by a pair of narrow clip braces. Braces were one of the most totemic accessories of the whole skinhead era, a kind of celebration of old-school English working-class iconography, which was handy, as they stopped my over-large strides from falling down below my non-existent hips.

The shirt was not a problem, but it was a great joy. I would still wear it now. It was a Ben Sherman, bought with saved-up birthday money or some such stash on a trip to Selfridges on Oxford Street. It's the first time I ever recall going 'up west' and it was to get the shirt of my dreams, every young skinhead's dreams. You had to have a proper button-down Ben Sherman, with a pocket on the breast, a pleated back, a button on the back of the collar and a hook of fabric on the top of the pleat, finished with a straight rather a than shirt-tail bottom. My first one was in a very pale blue, with a fine burgundy stripe. I wore it home from the shop and

---

* For years I'd assumed that correct Levi's were always button-fly, 501s, the James Dean, Elvis Presley jean. But I now know that almost nobody back in, say, 1970 had button-fly 501s, they wore a zip-fly version, called the 505. If that sounds insanely pedantic, well, as Mies Van der Rohe said, 'God is in the details.' Mies would have made a good skinhead.

wore it every day without fail. My mum had to wash it overnight so that I could wear it again. This was not a second-rate Brutus, this was not a snide copy, this was a bona fide. This was my shirt.

Knitted cardigans and V-neck jumpers were always part of the look, but the 'must have' jacket of the time was a Harrington. Named after Rodney Harrington, a minor hoodlum character played by a young Ryan O'Neal in a tawdry American soap opera, *Peyton Place*, which was watched by everybody's mum, including ours. I think the Harrington character wore a beige jacket on TV every week, although I never actually saw it, as it was on after my bedtime. Basically a Harrington was a weatherproof windcheater, with shirt-cuff sleeves, an overlapping storm back, a stand-up, button-through collar, an elasticated bottom and a tartan lining, a bit like a classic golfing jacket only shorter. God knows why, but this became the essential casual jacket of an entire generation. People still wear Harringtons today with no knowledge of the etymology of its name, nor the trouble I went through to get one. I recently bought a very nice, preposterously expensive, chocolate brown Prada version of a Harrington in Milan, just to remind myself of the sense of triumph when we finally tracked one down. It wasn't that Harringtons *per se* were difficult to get, but they weren't made for midgets. Eventually, after trying everywhere, my mum had to order one for me. It was a black one, so oversized that I wore it for maybe five years, until it was literally 'taxed'* off my back by a bunch of Liverpool supporters on a tube train on the way to a match at QPR. Thanks, chaps.

Shoes were difficult, not impossible, but difficult and potentially dangerous. My mum had decreed that I couldn't have a pair

---

* Taxing was the name for taking a desirable piece of clothing from a kid by force. Mugging for gear. There was a huge taxing scandal that hit the national headlines in the 1980s about designer trainers, but it had begun many years earlier.

of boots. She would occasionally hold the line, and although I did later acquire a pair of monkey boots, Eastern European, soft-soled boots that were the kind of skinhead-lite option, I never really fancied a proper pair of bovver boots, Dr Martens or Cherry Reds. They were too much of an invitation and I was never into fighting, always a coward, never a true Burnt Oak boy. What I wanted was a pair of brogues. I knew where to get them. A shop a couple of miles away in Kilburn, called Factory Footwear, specialized in all the right stuff, a mecca for the trendy shoe fetishist, but something of a problem for Burnt Oak lads. You see Kilburn and Burnt Oak didn't get on.

This was an era of insane territorial rivalries, and the gangs from Burnt Oak and just about everywhere else didn't get on. The Burnt Oak mob, who were highly respected in low places for their near-insane fighting prowess, had many local enemies: the Hendon Mafia, the Camden Town Tongs, the Willesden Whites, the Maida Vale Mob, and most especially the Kilburn whatever they were calleds. Now my brothers would dutifully stand outside Burnt Oak station with their crew for many pointless hours, just in case any marauding Kilburnites would dare to come to Burnt Oak and invade their patch. They didn't try very often. But it also meant that kids from the Oak couldn't go anywhere else. Especially Kilburn. To confuse matters, Barry actually had a long-term girlfriend from Kilburn, with long straight hair parted like a pair of curtains over her deathly pale face, and this caused terrible trouble. Like a character from a particularly cheap production of *West Side Story*, he literally had to fight and run his way home after taking her back to her manor one night, and eventually could not venture to within a mile of her house. Barry and Reggie Elms, as recognized members of the Burnt Oak mob, were *persona non grata* in that part of the world. And I was asking them to take me there to get a pair of shoes. No wonder they pulled faces. No wonder they had to say yes, they were Burnt Oak boys.

With trepidation disguised as bravado, the three of us boarded a 32 bus south, then strolled along Kilburn High Road one Saturday afternoon, with the theme music from *The Magnificent Seven* playing in our ears. I don't suppose too many of the old biddies nattering on corners or the be-suited Paddies migrating from boozer to boozer were aware of our presence, but my brothers were undeniably edgy as we approached Factory Footwear. There was a queue stretching outside the door and along Kilburn High Road, as there often was, and rather than stand in it and chance being spotted, we sashayed to the front, making a risk analysis that this was a safer option than standing in the street to be seen. Once inside the shop my brothers stood around me twitchily, looking out for any known faces who might spot theirs, while I bought a pair of black brogues in the smallest size available, in the quickest time possible.

Now I have a real thing about the smell of new shoes, especially well-made leather shoes like these with that layer of tan leather lining, which gives off the most perfect aroma. It's like coffee and brandy, dense, rich, addictive. I have to sniff new shoes, place them over my face and inhale deeply. I'm aware that it makes me look like a mad person or a pervert, but it's worth it for the rush of hide. But my brothers were more than a little anxious to get out of there, so we ran up the street, me desperately trying to smell my new shoes as I tried to keep up. Eventually, me still with my new shoes clamped over my face, we jumped on a bus heading towards the safety of our turf, exhaling wildly. These were paranoid and violent times. Peace and love indeed. The outfit was almost complete.

I never got a Crombie, not even a snide one off a market stall. Most kids did that, accepted second best. Some rascals even pulled the red lining up from inside the breast pocket, pretending that it was a silk hankie. But I never did that. I never got a Crombie until twenty-four years later. Twenty-four years I harboured and nurtured the desire for that coat. It never left me, though it would be a lie to suggest that it worried away, ruining whole years of my life. It didn't do that. But I never let go of the idea that there was only one pukka overcoat. Then one day, when I was in my mid-thirties, strolling along Savile Row, planning suits which would never get made, I saw that a certain Crombie and Sons of Aberdeen, Scotland, had opened a new shop of their own, and there in the window was the coat. Navy blue, heavy felt wool, fly-fronted, square shoulders, black velvet collar. I was nervous when I walked in. After twenty-four long years a tiny dream was about to be realized. I was enthralled when I walked out, wearing the coat of course. I still have my Crombie, occasionally study the label to see that it still spells out the correct, all-important word. I wear it to football sometimes when it's cold, which makes me smile. It's an excellent coat.

BACK THEN instead of a Crombie I got a hat. Chances are my mum was convinced that I'd catch a cold through having such short hair. To this day my mum is convinced that I'll catch a cold in most circumstances. So I got a hat. It was a pork pie, I guess, although I don't recall anybody calling it that at the time. It was a trilby, a snap-brim trilby with a double band, very acceptable in skinhead circles, so I wore it incessantly, including to school. I was still in the final year at Goldbeaters JMI, and there was no uniform, so the hat was fine. One day Georgie Relf turned up with the self-same hat and I felt a little confused. Georgie Relf wasn't a skinhead. The only other kid in school who was a skin was Jean Reddy, a girl whose mother, Dolly, had gone to school with mine in East Acton. Anyway, Georgie Relf had the hat, but none of the other gear to go with it, and for ages I didn't understand this. It troubled me. It has taken me a very long time to comprehend that some people, most people, sane people, don't feel the need to go all the way with clothes. Funny that.

So here I am aged ten, as the 1970s are about to emerge. A wheezy little boy with a second-hand gait and one outfit, which he wears almost continually: chunky brogues with a pair of insoles to keep them on his feet, a pair of red football socks, off-white Sta-Prest, hiked up by skinny clip braces, over a striped Ben Sherman, with a black Harrington at least two sizes too big, topped off by a pork pie hat, lifted occasionally to reveal a number one crop incised with a razor parting. I must have looked absolutely ridiculous. But at least I *looked*.

That was undoubtedly what I was wearing when I went and bought my first ever record. It seems odd now, when almost all music is easily available, but even the act of buying a tune back in those days was a major investment of money, time and effort. You had to have the know-how as well as the wherewithal. If I had wanted an ordinary chart record, my mum could get those cheap from Woolworths, but of course I didn't want an ordinary record, that would have been far too simple. I'd set my heart on an import ska record. Not some particular ska record I'd heard and fallen in love with, I just wanted whatever was the latest, coolest plate to be shipped over from Jamaica; music was a style accessory. And to get it entailed a trip back to the ancestral homeland.

There was a shop in Shepherd's Bush which was rated as a purveyor of the very best ska and rock-steady discs, hot off the boat from Kingston, Jamaica. Of course it wasn't a record shop. This place was some kind of general store, which sold Daz and vacuum cleaners and copies of the *Gleaner* and yams and salt fish and tunes by the likes of Prince Buster and Slim Smith and the Trojans, from a little DIY sound booth in the back. The records, all 45s with the centres punched out and home-made labels, were kept in a big cardboard box. And I was going to get one.

I'm sure we combined the trip with a visit to Aunt Glad, who was now in a nicely ramshackle house up the road, but that Saturday I was absolutely focused on getting a record. So I made a pilgrimage to this store, where a bizarre congregation had gathered. There were the local Jamaicans, who used the place as a kind of hang-out and information centre, gossiping and laughing loudly. Then there was a small group of skins, who, with an exaggerated, almost silent reverence to the clipped rhythms which constantly rebounded around the room, also used the place as a kind of hang-out and information centre. I waited in line with the skins, and when my turn came, the wise old Jamaican guy who looked after the music side asked me what I wanted. Of course I had no idea, so with a gentleness which was rather moving, this man played me a few of the latest rock-steady sides, until finally we agreed that I should purchase a chugging ditty, just in from the island, called 'Mr Popcorn', by Laurel Aitken. I still have it now, scratched beyond playing, but still here, in my hands in fact. It's a beautiful thing. Although I now know it's a little saucy for a small boy.

The relationship between skinheads and West Indians was bizarre and complex. On the one hand there's no doubt that some skinheads were racist. All right, let's be horribly honest, almost all skinheads were racist, in the way that sadly most British people were racist at the time, when the putrid language of 'paki' and 'wog' was commonplace amid the supremacist verbiage of a dying empire. And skinheads, being a particularly aggressive embodiment of old white working-class values, were aggressively racist. Yet to kids in places like Shepherd's Bush and Notting Dale, the next generation on from the rioting Teddy boys, West Indians were no longer outsiders. These cropped-haired, working-class teenagers were actually the first generation of British people anywhere to grow up in a multicultural environment, going to schools where maybe a third or more of the kids were black, and absorbing so many of the aspects of their lives. The music, and the skanking, rolling dances which went with it, were the most obvious example, but if you could read the clothes it was there too.

The classic skinhead look was derived from three sources. The boots and braces were white working-class stuff, the sartorial polemic. Then there was the Americana, all Ivy League button-down shirts, penny loafers, blue jeans and Harrington jackets, which had come directly from mod. Finally, though, the stylistic antecedents of the skinhead package, the narrow trousers hitched up, the suits and the overcoats, above all perhaps the hats, like the one I wore to the record shop, were nicked from those swaggering rude boys in the Roger Mayne picture. They were West Indian style for white boys.

The import ska record completed the picture for me, and I really felt like I'd arrived. We had an end-of-term party at Goldbeaters JMI, and they said you could bring along a record or two to play. I presented my copy of 'Mr Popcorn' by Laurel Aitken to the teacher, who warily put it on for the delectation of a class of nine- and ten-year-olds. Up to that point the music had been the Beatles and the Hollies and the like, and the class had jumped about happily. Suddenly this strange, staccato rhythm with a West Indian voice chanting above it came out and the kids didn't know what to do. But Jean Reddy and I did. We stepped forward and did a little Moonstomp together, showing off our stolen steps for all our worth, which wasn't very much, to a room full of our classmates, who just looked at us as if we'd suddenly started speaking Amharic. After a minute or so of this bizarre spectacle the teacher took off this odd, foreign-sounding tune, which was undoubtedly unsuitable, with a harumph. Triumph. Jean Reddy and I would dance together again later, much later.

I felt special then, as if I knew more, had an edge, and it was clothes and music that had done it. Clothes and music, in that order. It was a feeling I was going to try to replicate time and again throughout my life. It was pride before a fall. Literally. Within a short while of the junior school disco ska record sensation, I was doing more conventional boyhood stuff. I was playing football, which to my eternal shame I could never accomplish with any élan, when I fell and scraped my elbow on the street. Now scraped elbows are hardly the stuff of lasting childhood trauma, but the elbow wound was not what made me cry. It was my shirt; I'd ripped my beloved Ben Sherman with the pale blue cloth and the stripe. I knew we couldn't afford another shirt and the tears were unstoppable. I was inconsolable. I hurt my shirt.

At about the same time as the great Ben Sherman disaster, there was another knock on our front door. Again there were some well-dressed chaps standing there asking for my brother Reggie. Only this time their outfits were all blue. Serge. Reggie was in this time. He was in deep. He didn't cry though.

4

DID DOVER come before Minehead, or was it the other way round? For Minehead which was the holiday camp, I'm sure it was Levi's jeans, Gola pumps and a Fred Perry, with a grown out suedehead. Whereas for the trip to Kent and the Borstal visit, I was still attired in Sta-Prest, braces and a Harrington. That would suggest that the holiday camp definitely came later. Which means that Reggie never came on the holiday, as he was still pleasuring Her Majesty in some decrepitly gaunt Victorian institution. I have real trouble recalling the chronology of those two trips. But then there's something almost comically logical about confusing these particular seaside excursions. One was to a regimented, grim ex-army barracks where the inmates lived in Nissen huts, ate stolid canteen food, worked hard to earn cigarettes and played countless games of ping-pong in the company of a load of tough-nut, miscreant males. The other one was a Borstal.

The time when my brother went down – and we went down to Dover to see him – is still shrouded in a swirling, scalding family fog. But the bare facts, as I understand them, are these. Reggie and Barry and all the other Burnt Oak mob were embroiled in yet another pointlessly bitter tribal dispute, with another set of identically attired working-class north-west London boys, and it all went off. I may, in fact, be confusing and conflating a few fights, because there were certainly a few, but I think this particularly fateful tear-up took place on the Tottenham Court Road in London's glamorous West End. Burnt Oak had gone mob-handed to some club or other to skank to ska and smooch to soul, and had bumped into their sworn enemies, whoever they may have been that week, and of course it ended in a mass brawl. That would all have been pretty par for the course, a typical Friday night out. Had it occurred, as they usually did, in some two-bit suburban disco on a forgotten council estate, nobody in authority would have bothered unduly and the repercussions would have been measured solely in black eyes and swollen reputations.

But this particular dust up was up west, and when it spilled out of the club, it went straight on to one of London's main thoroughfares. I can envisage the scene, scores of enraged tasty geezers in two-tone tonic strides, kicking and punching and running and jumping and shouting and nutting and swearing and bleeding their way up and down the Tottenham Court Road and loving it no doubt. These Crombie-clad berserkers must have terrified the bemused tourists and traders and good folk trying to go about their pleasures. For once the police had to do something about it. In this era, when white on white working-class violence was absolutely commonplace, consenting juveniles were usually free to kick lumps out of each other to their hearts' content in their ghettos. But this time the constabulary felt the need to actually investigate. They asked a few questions, came up with a couple of names, and came round our house to ask if Reggie Elms was in. Reggie, aged just seventeen, walked manfully out of the house and into a police car. My mum crumpled. It was a bad time.

I suppose I could just ask Reggie exactly what happened, but understandably perhaps this whole sorry episode is not one that crops up all that often in conversation when we meet back at home on a Sunday afternoon with our kids. Reggie is now a hugely respectable and indeed admirable father of five, a big man with a marriage more solid than any I've ever seen, a prominent position in his chosen business and a massive gleam which gives only the merest hint of his former tearaway ways. If you're reading this you can assume he said it's OK for me to tell the tale.

My mum had lost the husband she adored while still a young woman working ferociously hard to keep the family afloat. Although I'd seen her cry many times – tears staining her dark Hebraic skin at the end of a long day when she was exhausted and lonely – I had never once seen her weaken. But when her beloved boy, truth be told, hers and everybody's favourite, the clever, charming, handsome apple of many an eye, stood in court charged with causing an affray and was sentenced to a period of penal servitude, she slipped for a short while. Maybe my chronology went with her.

I understand now that the reason my brother received such a sentence for a first offence was because he refused to give anybody away. His was the name the police had, so they put him down as the ringleader of the Burnt Oak mob, even though this fatherless lad, just out of school, still traumatized by the death of his dad, was one of the youngest involved. A clever lawyer would have milked all that, but of course working-class widows don't run to clever lawyers. Had he grassed up his mates he would have faced less of a term, but he didn't, and although his crime was banal and ugly and deeply silly, you can only respect him for that. As a ten-year-old I certainly did, I idolized and idealized him, and I wasn't alone. Growing up on the Watling Estate was made easy for me. I was an asthmatic, under-sized, red-haired and by local standards rather bookish kid (which meant I'd read one), with none of the skills which gave you standing in such a place. I was rubbish at football, and I couldn't fight to save my life. Thankfully I never really had to. Because Reggie Elms was such a respected figure that his little brother was untouchable, free to dress up and swan about. I was the lucky one.

Reggie was less so. He spent the first part of his time in Wormwood Scrubs, a truly scary Victorian Bridewell, rammed with scarred old lags. Mum went to see him there, of course, and came back reduced and resigned. By the time he was finally sent to Dover Borstal to serve out his time amid bracing sea breezes among boys of his own age, I could use one of the two monthly passes to go with my mother to see him. This is where the confusion with the holiday begins. You see we only ever got on trains, proper, overground trains where you shut the doors yourself and showed your tickets to an inspector, when we went on holiday. We hadn't had a holiday since Dad died, but there was definitely one to Pontin's holiday camp in Minehead around this time.

That holiday has its own sartorial tales to tell, but before that, and it must have been before that, the trip to Dover presented problems. This was still in the time of the torn shirt, and I suffered sleepless nights worrying about what to wear to go and see Reggie. I didn't have a proper shirt. It seems shameful now that I should have been so self-obsessed as to be bothered by what I was going to wear to go and see my brother who'd been banged up, but I was desperate to look right for him. I don't suppose I really understood the severity of the situation he'd got himself into, didn't really grasp what had been going on. I just knew it mattered to look right. But I didn't have a Ben Sherman, or at least not one in serviceable condition. This is where mothers come in very useful.

The torn sleeve was beyond repair, but somebody had a brainwave. Ben Sherman also made a short-sleeved, summer version of the classic button-down, and we were going to convert the shirt. This was a more complex operation than you might imagine, though, as Ben Sherman short-sleeves had a trademark inverted V shape cut into the sleeve and two tiny buttons, one on either side. Without those nobody would be fooled. So my mother, always prepared to do anything for her boys, hunted down just the right buttons and laboriously cut the correct shape into the shortened sleeve, hand-sewing the edging. Providing I didn't let anybody get too close to my non-existent biceps I'd just about get away with it.

Somehow I'd built some kind of perverse, anticipatory glamour into the trip to Dover. Maybe I even thought there was glory in it. But the reality was chastening. I guess rightly so. A special bus took visitors from the station to the Borstal, siphoning us away from the decent people as we huddled together waiting to board. A muffled collection of marked mothers and brothers and watery-eyed girlfriends and even a few tiny sprogs, all of them frayed in some way, clutching plastic carrier bags of sweets and meagre treats from poor people's shops. Dover is a pretty grim frontier anyway, but I began to realize that this place where they'd placed my brother, Reggie Elms, with all his swagger and swank, was ugly. In its way, this whole business about clothes, this passion for style, was a search for something beautiful. Getting searched by a fat guard outside a gaunt house of correction in a ragged line of shuffling, blotchy souls on a grey day by the white cliffs is not beautiful. I fretted now, cared not about my appearance, cared suddenly about my brother.

We waited in a hall that smelt like a school only bad, a bad school, while my mum, her countenance shot, tried to be strong. We both looked out of the window quietly worrying. I recall being scared now to see Reggie, in case he'd changed. The inmates began to emerge from a block somewhere and walk across a parade ground towards us. They filed over in twos and threes, hurrying, eager for a visit, but my brother was not among them. Still they came and still no Reggie, then finally he appeared, last out, paired up with a boy who carried a pronounced limp, slowly making their way across the yard. My big fear was that he would walk differently, that the bowling, defiant gait would be gone. It was slowed certainly, taken down to accommodate the fact that his friend could barely drag himself across the space to get to the visiting hall. But as I stared intently out of the window looking for signs, it was there, the shoulders were rolling, dignity was intact. Then we met and his eyes still shone. They were older though. They've been older ever since.

Inevitably and thankfully, the skinhead look was changing. I say thankfully because although it was a truly potent display of clothing as social statement, a manifesto of hard-line working-class power, it had gone wrong, ethically, socially wrong. Here was a style which was intent on keeping kids in their place, its rules so rigid, its pride so insular, that it became yet another fence forcing you back in. I think seeing my brother fenced in gave me a notion that I didn't ever want to be in such a situation, didn't want to pay that kind of price for being a true Burnt Oak boy. I wanted to get out.

And by that time every other schoolboy in England was reading scabby little exploitation paperback novels called *Skinhead* and *Skinhead Escapes*, following the tawdry exploits of Joe Hawkins, tooled-up, blood-splattered thug in a Harrington, under the desk, the whole thing was well on the way to parody. Later on it would reappear in two very different contexts.

The first was a nasty stain. In the late 1970s gangs of dim-wit neo-Nazis reduced the skinhead look to a snarling, tattooed cartoon of its former self, missing out all the precision and stern élan of its early days. I recall being on Anti Nazi League demonstrations, squaring up to seething little squadrons of cropped-haired, big-booted fascist thugs, where I felt as much aggrieved by what they had done to the memory of my first youth cult as by their abhorrent politics.

Later the shaven-headed skin style was colonized by gay men who proudly disported themselves in this apparently ultra-macho uniform. Whenever I saw a couple of cropped queens trolling along Old Compton Street in tight Levi's and braces I thought of all the hard-nut, undoubtedly homophobic Burnt Oak boys, and what they'd make of it. Thankfully by the beginning of 1971 the skinhead look was changing, even in Burnt Oak. But I can't say I was happy about it at the time.

It seemed to me then that no sooner had I managed to acquire all the accoutrements than I had to get new ones. I was reluctant to give up my first uniform, undoing, with a heavy heart, the button-down collar of my beloved shirt so that it looked more like the new longer collars, which were all the rage. I felt almost treacherous. It took me a while to understand the mechanics of youth fashion, that it is a perpetual-motion machine powered by some collective psychological engine, which runs off vast reserves of pure, high-grade adolescent desire. There is always a kid somewhere who's not content with the current dress code, who wants to play the game, but by his own rules, wants to fit in and yet shine out. Even during the original skinhead era, a time of almost Stalinist subservience to the party clothes-line, there must have been secret sartorial Trots in the ranks, plotters who knew that this fashion caper is more perpetual revolution than five-year plan. For suddenly, unorthodox items began to appear.

Golfing jumpers, for example. Watch the James Bond film *Goldfinger*, the famous scene where Sean Connery is playing a round with Goldfinger and Oddjob, and you'll see that the ever immaculate British agent – a style icon if ever there was one – is sporting a black V-neck Slazenger jumper with the symbol of a sleek, outstretched jaguar on the breast. A few years after the movie, towards the end of the skinhead epoch, this early form of designer branding became the focus of a major little craze for sportswear. Fred Perry shirts, Adidas or Gola trainers, Slazenger jumpers and even golfing jackets predated and presaged the whole label-obsessed clothes culture we now live in.

I can distinctly recall furtively walking to Colindale, the next stop on the Northern Line and a half-hour hike, way beyond where I was officially allowed to wander, all because they actually had a sports shop which stocked golfing stuff for the executive classes.

I couldn't buy a Slazenger jumper, they were far too expensive, but I could and did gaze longingly into the window at the serried ranks of sweaters with that all-important logo. It's a very strange thought, an eleven-year-old desperate to don the attire of paunchy Rotarians and smarmy all-round entertainers. But I even remember thinking that golfing shoes looked pretty smart too, though the spikes would perhaps present a problem on the lino in the kitchen.

By now my hair, along with everybody else's, was being buzzed less regularly and less savagely, a sign that the party clothes-line was crumbling. This new, smoother, less abrasive look would later be described as suedehead, although I don't remember anybody actually using that term at the time. Rupert trousers were another indicator of strange stirrings. It seems truly bizarre, writing this now, to think that a tough lads' fashion craze could be provoked by a cuddly cartoon bear from the *Daily Express.* But suddenly there were herberts swanking along Burnt Oak High Road, and I'm sure every other High Road, in loud, check trousers inspired by a truly irritating little fellow from Nutwood. Some even got the scarf. Others, including me, got channel seams; trousers with a tiny French pleat, folded in on itself, along the outside seam, a look which has, as far as I know, never reappeared in any form anywhere else. Perhaps because they were such a bugger to iron. Shoes too were undergoing a transformation.

Loafers, the slip-on moccasin style, a collegiate American classic which had always been the standard-issue casual footwear from mod onward, started to sprout unnatural mutations. Instead of the standard penny loafer, so-called because you could place a shiny penny under the leather cross strap, there was a barrage of variations which were almost impossible to keep up with. First came tassel loafers, with two little leather tassels dangling down from the tongue. Then buckle loafers, obviously with a cross buckle on the side. Then fringe loafers, where the top had some kind of Davy Crockett buckskin business tacked on. Eventually, just when you thought you were on top of all this loafer lark, combinations started to appear. Fringe and buckle, fringe and tassel, even a truly horrendous all three at once, fringe, tassel and buckle affair, which made your feet look like they had construction work on top of them.

The out-of-control loafer craze culminated in a mysterious shoe which, as yet, has never been properly explained. The shoe which my Liverpudlian mate at the party pulled out to produce his winning shot. The legendary Salatio box-top loafer. I can describe one. They were a wide, thick-soled, square-toed slip-on, with an interwoven lattice of leather on the top, which we called basket weave, and a heavy welt or mudguard round the edge. And they blazed and roared their way through the collective teenage psyche of 1971. Nobody knew where this shoe came from, even fewer knew how to pronounce them. Were they 'Salaytio' or was it 'Salattio', or maybe even 'Salayshio'? It's a word I've never seen written down myself, so even now I don't actually know how to write it or say it correctly. Nobody knew how to say it yet everybody was talking about them. From talking to friends now, it seems that there were regional variations on the pronunciation and some, rather than attempt such a markedly foreign word, took to calling them pork pies, due to a faint resemblance to Melton Mowbray's finest. The big question that remains, though, is who or what was Salatio? For about six months, there was absolutely no question about it, you had to have a pair. I never got them.

SIX OR SO years after my father died, my mother remarried, to a kindly, quiet, Fulham-supporting man called Ken, actually the brother of her brother-in-law, who gently courted her after a seemly amount of time. That meant a little more cash coming into the house, but for the years she struggled on her own, money was tighter than a Ted's drainpipes, and although it hurt her like new shoes to say we couldn't have what we wanted, sometimes we couldn't. One time I couldn't accept this. That was the time we went to Minehead.

My mum had saved and saved for this holiday, a week at Pontin's, a kind of downbeat half-brother to Butlin's, and I was to get a new pair of jeans for the trip. A boy has to have jeans if he's going to fully partake of the myriad pleasures of a holiday camp, and my mum vowed that she would buy me a pair. I'd never had a pair of Levi's to call my own, and I remember being terribly excited by the prospect, more than I was by the idea of the holiday itself. Mum came home from the shops and announced with a smile that she'd got my jeans. But when they were ceremoniously pulled from the bag and presented to me I was absolutely crest-fallen. They weren't Levi's. They weren't Levi's, but some no-name, no-prestige pair of dodgy denims, 'Tesco bombers' as I knew they would be scornfully dubbed by my pitiless peers.

I couldn't wear those, couldn't possibly go on holiday in such shameful apparel. I threw the mother of all tantrums at my mother, threw the third-rate jeans into the bin, threw the poor woman into a dreadful dilemma. So she did what working-class mothers have done for years in such extremes, she went out and got a Provident cheque. This was a form of legalized loan-sharking. You bought a cheque from the Provident Finance Company, a pauper's coupon which was accepted at most shops in places like Burnt Oak. You then paid the Provident man back over a matter of months, when he knocked at your door on Friday afternoons, at hugely inflated interest rates. It was an extremely improvident thing to do.

I can't remember too much about the holiday, bar the fact that the chalets looked distinctly like they were army surplus, and the place had a bizarre system of houses into which all the happy campers were divided. The houses, though clearly based on the old public school system, were named after makes of cigarette, so that we were in Embassy house and had sworn enemies in say

Rothmans or Players. I can only assume it was an early form of sponsorship. You gained house points by winning knobbly knees or glamorous granny competitions, or simply by singing loudest in the nightly proto-karaoke sessions. And if you did really well you won prizes of cigarettes. Even then, as an eleven-year-old, this struck me as morally dubious and downright sad. I was mortified when my mum entered a talent contest and then proceeded to warble some melancholy old pub ballad, way out of tune. I hid in the toilets shaking with shame, appalled that she could do this to the son she claimed to love. She came last. But the real competition took place in the games room.

A large, neon-lit hall full of snooker tables, table tennis tables, games of various kinds, this was where boys who were too young to go to the bar hung out when it was raining, which it seemed to be most of the time. I was about as adept at parlour games as I was at football, no hand–eye co-ordination. But it was clothes co-ordination that really mattered here. Looking cool was the real sport, and it was played with a ruthless will to win. Gangs of pubescent, pigeon-chested boys strutted pointlessly about in the clothes they'd acquired specially for the occasion, trying to cut the next group with their up-front, up to the minuteness. I did my best with my new, not-yet-paid-for Levi's and a rather natty Fred Perry, the latest model, with a loose-knit weave and the essential laurel leaf crest on the chest, which drew the attention and maybe even admiration of a couple of lads from East London, who thrashed me at snooker while simultaneously sporting huge tulip lapels. They were pretty tasty, but it was a gang of older lads who really did it.

There were four or five in this crew, and they were maybe sixteen or seventeen. I had no idea where they were from, as I never drummed up the courage to talk to them, but these lads had girls trailing in their wake and boys like us drooling into their Coca-Colas. They were way ahead. The first shock was that they had long hair – long hair, can you believe it? But this was not a greasy hippy mess, oh no, this was some kind of tousled, chopped-about look that looked both wild yet carefully contrived. It was a feather cut. This was paired with loud stripey tank tops, sleeveless jumpers with low scooped necks, and, most shockingly of all, wide, baggy trousers, not flares, but Oxford bags, as I soon discovered they were called, which were wantonly wide all the way down. From Ted, through mod to skinhead, trousers had always been narrow and fitted, but these could not have been baggier and broader. And to top it all, at the bottom of the trousers they had shoes that made Salatio box-top loafers look normal. These were some kind of duck-billed platypus of a shoe, Toppers they called them, with a splayed, spoon-shaped toe with a red star or a blue circle on the toecap. They were mad. They were brilliant. I was scared. These boys with their skin-tight tops and voluminous baggy bottoms looked like they were upside down. This was a *volte face*.

After about nine months out of circulation Reggie returned, chastened, wiser, but still the lovable rapscallion, glad to be home, but perhaps a little less sure of where home was. He had a problem. If you've seen *The Italian Job*, you'll know the scene where Michael Caine's character, Charlie, the super suave head of the self-preservation society, comes out of prison and utters the immortal lines, 'Take me to my tailor.' The tailor in question is bizarrely played by the swinging TV presenter Simon Dee. Tailor Dee looks at Charlie's clothes and says scathingly, 'Did you do life, darling?' – so out of date are his duds. Well, Reggie went inside when skinhead was still the rage and came out to find that his mates had performed a sartorial somersault. So it was straight down to the shops to get a pair of big wide Oxford bags.

As a little addendum to this story, maybe fifteen years later I was getting a suit made by a tailor called Brian who had a place behind Oxford Street. I wanted a whistle just like the one Michael

Caine had made in that scene in *The Italian Job*, double-breasted, very fitted, high-breaking, long jacket, etc. In order to achieve this I took along the video of the movie to show Brian, so that he knew exactly what I was after. We put the tape in, scrolled through to the bit where Michael, alias Charlie, gets measured up by Mr Dee, and Brian freeze-framed it, staring intently at the whistle. 'My father made that suit,' he said, 'those are his sleeves.' His father had been a tailor on the film.

5

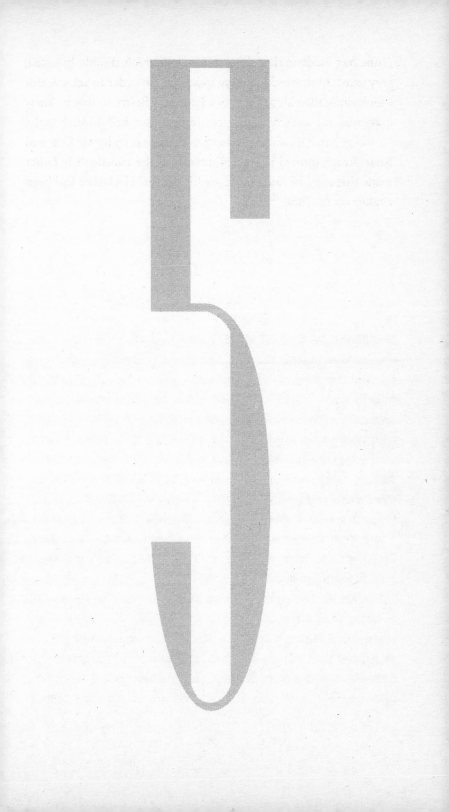

Cry havoc and let slip the dogs of fashion.

SHAKESPEARE MUST HAVE been into clothes. He penned the line 'apparel maketh the man', and the early seventies – the rigid stasis of the skinhead era shattered – was a time when sartorial tragedy and comedy combined to reach almost Shakespearian levels of theatricality. A flamboyant anarchy prevailed and a truly feral pack of fashion bitches was unleashed, marauding all over the place, with no order or pattern, but lots of clashing checks. Mangy, rabid items would leap out at you every other week, trenchcoats and tank tops, platform shoes and cheesecloth shirts, satin jackets and velvet trousers, tulip lapels and scoop necks. These were 'interesting times' in the Chinese sense of the term. I'm so glad to have lived through them. Gladder still that there are few photographs.

By late 1971 when the world suddenly went weird, I was a pupil at Orange Hill Grammar School for boys. This was Reggie's alma mater, and I'm sure they were a little nervous about another Elms arriving at their slightly pompous educational establishment. My feelings were more mixed. I was made up to have passed the eleven-plus, part of the last year of kids to do so before comprehensive education kicked in. When Mum walked me to school in my new uniform on the first day, saying goodbye out of sight round the corner, so as not to embarrass her son, already self-conscious at being trussed up in cap and tie, she said that my dad would have been proud and that I had to make him prouder still over the coming years. But over the coming weeks the pride I felt at making it to the exalted school would compete with a bubbling resentment against the place, which never entirely went away.

Although it always claimed to be in Edgware, Orange Hill Grammar School was actually right in the middle of Burnt Oak. Of the ninety-three boys in my year, I was the only one who actually hailed from the Watling Estate. The rest were all from beyond the wall. Lots of garrulous Jewish kids from Edgware and Golders Green, many more ever-so-ordinary middle-management scions from Mill Hill and Colindale, even a few Hampstead arty archetypes, whose parents opted for state education out of a handy mix of political conviction and financial expediency. But of the scores of eleven-year-old boys who lived in the regimented, ramshackle rows of the Watling, only one was deemed bright enough to grace the school right in their midst. Can that be right? was a question I asked myself more and more.

Right or wrong, being so selected made me feel like a proper little chosen one. It filled my chest and swelled my head, perhaps partly accounting for the confidence bordering on (and often ambling firmly into) arrogance which has always been part of my personality. But it also made me angry, or maybe it was sad.

Many of the boys I'd grown up with, wiry angular things, all whippet synapses and switchblade wits, were brighter and better than half the stolid students in my school. Burnt Oak lads were crisp and quick, they were dodgers, not always artful and rarely intellectual. You'd have been hard pushed to find a book in a house anywhere on the Watling, where there were four bookmakers and no bookshops, but many were fantastically capable and terrifyingly funny. I wasn't the only one who would have benefited from pushing and showing.

This was the class divide, and I felt at times like I had betrayed my people by being siphoned off to the other side. The early seventies was a time of friction and action, trade-union militancy, political agitation, wildcat strikes and Angry Brigades. Reggie had been in a cell in the Scrubs briefly with one of the young anarchists from the Angry Brigade. You had to decide which side you were on, and I grabbed hold of my father's left-wing views, perhaps in the same way as I cherished and clung to his football team, as a keepsake of the man himself. I had real qualms about being in a class with exclusively middle-class kids. I also loved it. I was an Orange Hill pupil by day and a Burnt Oak boy in the evenings and at weekends, but as a result you're never quite either. Reggie must have felt the same nagging pulls, but arrived at a different response. He opted to stay firmly, perhaps perversely, in the Watling, proving tenaciously that he belonged by overplaying the Burnt Oak boy role, and paying the price.

Something I soon cottoned on to was that my background gave me an edge. I was an exotic species to some at Orange Hill. A few of the older boys (and lots of the teachers) remembered Reggie, most of them fondly. When I'd only been at the school a few weeks, a couple of the more cool-looking fifth-formers, lads four or five years older than myself, with nascent feather cuts and possibly girls outside the gate, took me to one side during break. I was walking down the corridor with a couple of first-form chums when these two big kids stopped us, pulled me over and in serious tones said, 'You're Reggie Elms's brother, right?' I nodded, scared in case they were intending to exact retribution, for something my brother had done years before. I looked at my mates to see if I could rely on them for help, but they were already edging nervously away. I was preparing to leg it myself when one of the fifth-formers said, 'Could you help us settle an argument, is it 54 46 or 44 56?'

I didn't have a clue what they were talking about and it showed on my face. 'Toots and the Maytals, does he sing 54 46 or 44 56?' Then I got it. Toots Hibbert was a reggae singer, his band the Maytals, one of the best, and this tune – '54 46 Was My Number', – referring to his prison number – was a massive club cut at the time. Thankfully we had a copy in the pile of reggae platters which sat by the Dansette in the living-room, and I knew it. 'It's 54 46,' I pronounced sagely and these two chaps, who had some status in the school, thanked me, a pesky first-former, most graciously. I swanned over to my classmates, who were amazed.

I began the age-old process of whittling away at the rigours of school uniform. The cap, one of the long list of essential items Mum had scrimped for, was dispensed with by the end of the first day, and shortly afterwards flung over a garden fence. Within a month or so, lots of little modish modifications were manoeuvred in. Those channel seams, which were 'all the go', were purchased in charcoal grey, on the basis that no teacher was going to be savvy enough to spot such a subtle but essential detail as a pleat on the seam. Sensible shoes were replaced by whatever was that week's loafer in regulation black of course, but with Blakeys added. These were small crescent-shaped metal plates with protruding nails, designed to protect the heel of your shoe. They were popular among noisy oiks because they made a wondrous ringing sound as you stalked the corridor, and even produced sparks if you caught them just right in the playground. The tie was reduced to parody by giving it a huge, bulbous treble Windsor, which meant it was all knot and no tie. I even placed a metal QPR badge under my lapel, to be flashed at strategic times, a trick I learnt in history, as Napoleon's followers had done just that with their tricolour cockades during his exile on Elba. Finally, with winter approaching it was time to make a truly revolutionary statement.

I had to get a trenchcoat. An entire generation had to get a trenchcoat. Basically this was a mac, in the grand Humphrey

Bogart private dick tradition: black, double-breasted, tie-through belt, overlapping storm back. The trenchcoat is one of those items which burned brightly for one season, then slipped back into the fashion margins. It's like some lumpen centre-forward who can't stop scoring for a few games, fills every back page, gets talked of in exalted circles, before he gets sussed out, dries up and returns to his rightful place in the stiffs. This was a time for flash-in-the-pan gear, and all the Flash Harries had a trenchcoat. And what's more, you could actually wear it to school.

Ever since the record-buying expedition to Shepherd's Bush, I'd built up the idea in my head that the more effort you put into buying something the better it was. So instead of getting a Burnt Oak or maybe a Wembley Market trenchcoat, which I could have done with some ease, and that I'm sure would have been exactly the same, I had to travel, via about eight forms of public transport, to an emporium in Bethnal Green, into the deepest East End. Most probably it was because my cousin Ian, best friend and son of Uncle Mac, bearer of bad tidings and keeper of stalls, lived in Old Ford, just up the road from Kray country, and had raved about the trenchcoats from this specific shop. I liked very much to be specific.

I also loved the feel of the East End. Back then this was a crumbling warren still replete with bombsites and bad teeth. It reminded me of the Dale, a proper old London neighbourhood, with murky alleys and bird-shit railway arches, street cries and drinking men. Burnt Oak, despite the urban antecedents of its population and the shabbiness of its fabric, could only ever be suburban. I'd already shopped once in the far east, securing myself a pair of those strange duck-billed shoes with comedy toe-caps which were procured at Levitts, or Blackmans. These were a not-quite-matching pair of noted Dickensian shoe shops, little more than hollowed out, dimly lit retail caves, bulging with boxes, yards from each other on Brick Lane. This skanky thoroughfare with its bagel shops and whelk stalls, string suppliers and synagogues soon to be mosques, was the very epicentre of London's brooding far east, mysterious and Oriential, where side-locked Hassidim mingled with floating Lascars and old lags with young hipsters in search of footwear heaven. The trip to Blackmans, and/or Levitts had whetted my appetite for a spot of exotic shopping, and now the time came for a coat.

I have no idea of the name of the shop, but it was hard by the dripping darkness of Bethnal Green station and seemed like proper trenchcoat territory. I wore my best gear to go there; polo-neck sweater, which made me look even more like a dwarf, and a new pair of 'parallels', wide, straight trousers, which fell over the stellar spoon-shaped shoes. In that get-up they would surely know that I was worthy. This place was staffed by real arch lads; dismissive, arrogant, vain, fantastic. Of course they ignored me for ages, but finally, once I'd established some kind of bona fide, they deigned to flog me a coat, and actually showed me how to do it up in the correct manner, which entailed fastening the belt around itself at the back. It's important to know these things.

I wasted the rest of the day cheerily walking round E1 looking in shop windows, not so much at the gear they had to sell, but at my own groovy attire, basking and brazen, just like those preening ones in the shop. I wasted the rest of the winter walking round in this bloody coat, always pulling it on over my uniform for school, only taking it off, grudgingly, if specifically ordered to do so. I would have slept in it if I could. I was the only kid at Orange Hill with a trenchcoat, therefore the only kid sitting sweltering next to a radiator with a coat on during double French. But I certainly wasn't the only Burnt Oaker embroiled in the current fashion turmoil.

A ritual developed, Catholic in its devotion and Mediterranean in its flamboyance, whereby every Saturday morning, every Saturday morning for most of my youth, before the faithful traipsed off to their respective football grounds to pay devotion and shout obscenities, the peacocks would parade in their finery. 'Doing the rounds', we called it. This was a languorous circuit of the high-lights of the High Street, a prosaic *paseo* that took in the station, Tonibells, Soundrax, the record shop, where you might stop to listen to the latest Tamla Motown or glam rock tune, Pete's Café for a tea or a Tizer, the Co-op, the clothes shop on the Broadway which occasionally had some pieces worth ogling. Finally, those old enough to lie about their age would sneak into the Stag, where Reggie and his raucous mates would be holding court in the Dancing Bar. This was the ironically titled home of the young ruffians, an insanely laddish redoubt which reached a peak of hedonistic intensity as football approached and the assembled hoods cracked wise and roared on, in inimitable, indefensible Burnt Oak fashion. This was the bar where more than once they kidnapped the governor, locking him up and distributing free beer. This was the bar where the big boys would gather Saturday lunchtime, all dressed-up, pissed-up bravado, Arsenal parapher-nalia dragging from their duds.

For the rest of us, me especially, at just twelve, the youngest of a group of half a dozen early teenage clothes-obsessed kids, the climax of the parade was a pocketful of Nick'n'Mix from Woolworths. Then swing back round the Oak again, in case there were any people who hadn't noticed what we were wearing first time round.

After the regimented uniformity of the skinhead days, there was no telling what tawdry horrors might be unleashed of a Sat-urday morning during the rounds in 1971–2. Hair got longer by the week, so that former skins were soon sporting a look which made the estate look even more like a reservation. There was an American Indian thing going on, Cochise on a council estate, with long straight centre-parted locks tumbling proudly if greasily down their backs, like their hero Charlie George. Shirt collars too started to sprout. First it was spear points, long arrow-shaped shafts of fabric, which were followed by penny rounds, longer still, but curved at the ends, which were in turn superseded by jumbo collars, which as the name suggests were positively, preposterously elephantine, huge pachyderm appendages dripping pendulously down from your throat. Floral prints, then contrasting yokes, paisley, gingham again, random, abstract patterns, any old rubbish plastered all over these overstated, over-designed shirts.

The jacket would have one big button, possibly in a silly colour, and tumescent tulip lapels, exaggerated, elongated roundels which engulfed our under-developed chests in cloth which might be houndstooth or Prince of Wales or some other lurid, clashing check. Trousers too continued to swell, and shock. I remember sporting one pair which were brown on the leg, but with a contrasting saddle of beige around the bum, a truly horrendous sight, which did provoke a fair ribbing as we began the rounds. But not as much as my tank top.

Of all the clothing crimes committed in the name of fashion in the early seventies, the tank top was arguably the most heinous. I'd first seen one at the holiday camp and thought it looked droolingly cool. They were basically knitted vests in loud, primary coloured stripes, high ribbing on the waist, with low scoop necks, low-scooped armholes and no sleeves. Of course I wanted one, of course I'd already spent far too much money on clothes, and so my mum suggested that she would show her prowess with a pair of needles and knit me one. I rather liked the idea of a bespoke garment, so went along with this plan. I think the colours we chose were yellow and blue, or maybe it was orange and blue. Certainly it was a mistake. Maybe my mum is not such a great knitter after all. Hand-knitted jumpers, I've since learnt, are of a much looser weave, and we obviously chose the wrong sort of wool, because this thing just sagged disastrously in all directions. I looked like a wasp who'd lost a lot of weight.

I've since learnt that deep down, in your heart of hearts, you always know when you look a twit. It's just that sometimes you want to be told otherwise. I allowed myself to be convinced that this saggy, baggy travesty of a jumper was all right, so I wore it one Saturday morning to do the rounds, half expecting a few admiring comments. Instead I was met with a withering tirade of abuse, from falling-about friends, and spent the whole morning cowering, trying to decide whether to give in and take it off or brazen it out. One by one, though, my mates all got tank tops knitted by their mothers. They all looked at least as bad as mine.

It was an era of bad taste, or more accurately of no taste, no standards, no real way of judging what was good or bad. The overriding look was bulbous and overblown, more is more, an over-reaction to the pared-down rigours of what had gone before. The overriding aim was to be the first one in that particularly dreadful garment. It was also resolutely cheap: most of this stuff was market-stall wear, designed to be worn for a few weeks then discarded as the next bad idea was unleashed. Cheesecloth shirts were a prime example of this. I've got no idea what cheesecloth really is, but this thin, crinkly cotton certainly looked rank enough to have been wrapped round old rinds of smelly cheese in a former existence. Yet it became a true craze. I recall seeing Reggie, who had been most admirably correct as a skinhead, in a threadbare cheesecloth shirt from a souk somewhere, undone to the waist, over a preposterously wide pair of bags, with his long dark hair tumbling and knotting like rats' tails. He looked like a hippy. A street-fighting, Arsenal-supporting hippy.

Some of the garish bits which flashed momentarily before our eyes exist in my memory as merely shards of cloth, nightmarish split-second glimpses of clothing travesties: a skinny, long-sleeved, stars-and-striped T-shirt with a low neck; split-knee jeans, with a contrasting colour from the V-shaped knee seam down; ice-blue satin jackets, bottle-green velvet suits, turquoise piping on seams, crimson heels on shoes. Perhaps most unsettling of the lot is a terrible reminder of once wearing a white plastic belt plastered with the logo of Wrigleys chewing-gum. Why? Then suddenly, in the midst of all this unseemly, unsightly chaos, a kind of orthodoxy, albeit a mad one, emerged from the most unlikely source.

It's hard now to recall the impact that *Budgie* had at the time. It only ran for two series, twenty-six episodes in all of an LWT comedy drama, about an irresponsible but irrepressible little toerag on the make in the strip-clubs, gambling dens and dirty bookshops of Soho in the early seventies. Budgie Bird was a loser with a winning smile, a bird called Hazel, an ex-wife called Jean, both of them deeply sexy in a downmarket way, and a big bruiser of a boss, Charlie Endell Esquire. It was funny and sharp and occasionally shocking, but what made it so special was that Budgie, alias Adam Faith, alias Terry Nelhams, played a cheeky, money-hungry, street-savvy young working-class guy obsessed by wearing the right schmutter, and got it absolutely 100 per cent right. He was every would-be urban wide-boy you've ever met. He walked and talked just like you and you wanted to be just like him.

It was Budgie's gear which really got you. It was Budgie's gear you had to get. Although Harrington jackets had come from *Peyton Place*, never before or since has a television programme started an entire fashion craze. *Budgie* did. Here was this lovable Jack the Lad on tele with long feather-cut hair, big tulip lapels on his shirt, an extraordinary suede jacket made of lurid patches of bright contrasting colours, flared satin strides and a pair of white clogs, always white clogs. He was a guttersnipe peacock, and within a couple of episodes playgrounds across the country had completely changed as boys everywhere clamoured to look like Budgie. As for that jacket, you had to have a Budgie jacket; your entire status and standing relied upon having a proper, zip-up, suede, multi-coloured bomber jacket, with massive rounded lapels just like Budgie.

The top bods rushed out to Mr Freedom, the ultra-trendy West End boutique which actually kitted Budgie out, and bought themselves the real thing. Being a bit young for such up-town extravagance, I bought mine at Wembley market. This was a ramshackle weekly affair, held in a cratered car park in the shadow of the old twin towers, where you waded through puddles of mud and piss from the previous day's game to buy your gear from stall after stall of tacky but up-to-the-minute tat. Although I couldn't stretch to Mr Freedom, I did make sure that I bought a piece of the very first consignment to make it as far as Wembley market. Royal blue suede, with a maroon yoke, perfect. I left early for school that Monday morning so that I could wear it in the playground and piss off every other kid in the place. But there were already three or four others lounging around in their Budgies, milking the glory. Within weeks half the school had one. Some lunatics even mangled their ankles trying to play playground football in clogs.

Years later I interviewed Adam Faith for the *Face* magazine. He was still something of a hero of mine, a wide-boy made good, from the same dreary bit of West London as my mum. He was a very short man in his fifties, but with incredibly radiant eyes. The eyes belonged to the swaggering kid who first became a teen sensation and national heart-throb with the aptly titled 'What Do You Want (if you don't want money)' back in 1959. At the point when I talked to him, Adam Faith had considerable amounts of money and wanted some more. He wore a camel-coloured cashmere coat and owned a mustard-yellow Roller. We drove together to Fortnum & Mason in St James's, where he held court every afternoon in the Fountain Rooms, their lavish tea-shop. As we arrived, he stopped outside, on ultra-posh Jermyn Street, and just left the car there with the engine running, knowing that one of Fortnum's staff would come and park it for him. I jokingly asked why he didn't have personalized number-plates: AFA ITH or BUD GIE or some such. He looked at me askance and said with some seriousness, 'Robert, it doesn't pay to be *too* flash.'

When I asked him about Budgie's gear, Adam Faith's already luminous eyes lit up. 'I picked the clothes for Budgie and I knew I had to get it right to get the character. He was flash and he thought he was a dandy, he had that street thing of spending all his dough on clothes, so we got the very latest look and then went just a touch over the top. That jacket was a masterstroke, and clogs, I mean clogs. What is the most stupid thing you can wear if you have to run away a lot, which poor Budge did? It's clogs of course, you can't run in clogs, but Budgie was such a fashion victim that he had to have clogs.' Budgie was the fashion victim who became a fashion icon.

The Budgie craze only lasted for a few months, but it pointed the way to an era when street fashion, instead of fermenting up from below, obeying its own highly combustible chemistry, would start to follow the trot of a few famous clothes-horses. David Bowie and his boys were waiting, all made up and ready to go.

I HAD TO GO to hospital. It was the summer of 1972. Certainly Arsenal had already done the double, Burnt Oak had never been so happy, Reggie had rarely been so drunk and my hair had never been so long. There was a battle going on between just about every kid in the country and their school about the length to which their hair would be allowed to grow. It was a sign of the times that the unisex salon, where camp men and common girls fussed around blow-dryers, had replaced the traditional barbers with some Italian bloke in red nylon. I'd tried telling the camp hairdresser to cut it so that it still looked long. I'd tried tucking the back under my collar to make it appear short. But the only thing which achieved the required effect was not cutting it during the long summer holiday. Maybe it was the stressful prospect of having to get my rampant mane shorn for the new term which led to the sharp pains in my stomach as the end of the holiday approached. Whatever the cause, after an educational internal examination by our GP (I never knew that was a two-way valve), I was immediately dispatched to hospital to have my appendix whipped out. I had to run to Woolworths to get my mum and then get to Edgware General.

In hospital my precious clothes were taken away and I was given a nylon robe to wait in. I stood shivering, a skinny, pallid, long, flame-haired thing in a waiting-room, until a nurse came and told me I had to go to the loo before being examined. She showed me into a cubicle which had a picture of a girl on the door. I remember thinking that maybe the gents was out of order. Then I was taken to a ward and given a bed to climb into. I looked around and saw that everybody else there was female, but said nothing. Eventually, a kindly woman came round with a trolley full of books, to see if I would like something to read while we waited for the doctor. I nodded and she proffered a copy of *Black Beauty*. I was appalled, being rather proud of the fact that I read proper books. I'd even taken the Communist Manifesto out of the local library (though admittedly I hadn't actually read it), and would certainly not stoop to such trite girly nonsense as a book about bloody ponies. I said as much and the poor woman was mortified. 'But all girls like *Black Beauty*,' she said, taken aback.

It was then I realized what had happened. I could have been horrified by the fact that without my clothes on I was mistaken for a pre-teenage girl, but instead I saw it as something to be proud of. My hair was obviously long enough to fool everybody, and I got a buzz from the idea that my appearance could shock and confuse, a feeling I was to revel in many times later in life. Now, though, I was offered numerous unnecessary apologies and led off to a male ward where I was probed and prodded and starved for a few days, as my operation was imminent. My mum reminds me regularly that I actually wrote out a will, as I was convinced they were starving me to death. I probably left my Budgie jacket to the nation. Throughout this process, I didn't have the heart to tell anybody that my stomach pains had stopped, but eventually a bearded doctor of some stature pronounced that there was little wrong with me and sent me home. Unfortunately the first stop was the hairdresser's to get my feminine tresses shorn before returning to school.

6

ONE THURSDAY EVENING [illegible]

ONE THURSDAY EVENING in July 1972, a month or so after my thirteenth birthday, our world stopped in its tracks and was nearly derailed. I was now a teenager, spurting volcanic hormonal lava and deeply curious about what came next. I'd tried alcohol, masturbation, snogging (well, sort of) and platform shoes. But I wasn't prepared for this. Like most of my generation I'd finished tea, which probably involved Cadbury's Smash and Angel Delight, or some other powdered 1970s culinary futurism, and raced through my homework, spurred on by all those e-numbers, in order to be good and ready for the holy show. At a time when there were only three channels, one of which was too posh to watch, this was just about the only programme aimed at teenagers and everybody, but everybody, scrutinized it. Parents sat and pontificated on a world gone noisily to ruin, while kids prayed that their particular favourites would be paraded so that they could lord it in the playground the next day.

As an apprentice skinhead, *Top of the Pops* had been particularly frustrating, because they so rarely showed ska and reggae acts, or even very much soul. I do recall my brothers being rather excited when Desmond Decker contorted his way through 'The Israelites' one week, but usually the main reason for watching

TOTP was to moan and adopt a superior pose. I'd already developed that protective snobbery which says only mainstream pap goes on *TOTP*, the same very British form of élitism which kept the likes of Led Zeppelin and later the Clash off the show. I still had to watch it religiously, though, to be fully armed for the inevitable playground arguments. But by 1972 I had a pop idol of my own to root for.

Rod Stewart, an Arsenal-supporting north London boy who looked like he could swagger into the dancing bar of the Stag and hold his own (he'd have got a terrible coating over that hooter of his, though), had charmed the nation with his gravelly voice and groovy barnet. Somewhere between Budgie Bird and Otis Redding, when Rod appeared on *Top of the Pops*, performing 'Maggie May', with his band of unrepentant bar-room revellers, larking around and kicking footballs about on stage, well, that was it. Love. His group were even called the Faces, harking back to the old mod heritage. He was surely one of us, therefore he was mine. I already had a football team and political affiliations; I now had a band to go with them.

To go with my Rod Stewart fixation I tried to tease and tousle my hair into the requisite spiky mop, getting it layered and lacquered, but having to plaster it down during the week to avoid getting sent home from school. I searched high and low, without real success, for a skinny long-sleeved T-shirt like the one Rod wore on the back of *Every Picture Tells a Story*. (It seems incredible now that you couldn't just go out and buy something as simple as a plain, close-fitting casual shirt, but you couldn't.) I did, though, secure myself a grandad vest with three buttons, which Ronnie Lane, Rod's bass player, always wore. A pair of low-waisted, semi-flared cotton pants and a pair of stack-heeled boots, where the heel was built up of layers of 'wood-look' veneer, completed the outfit. Well, almost. Because Rod liked to flaunt his Scottish ancestry with a touch of tartan, I bought a number of clan scarves.

My favourite was a white Royal Stewart dress plaid, very Rob Roy. I liked Rod.

It was his fault that my first proper suit was such a stonker. The first time I remember choosing a suit myself was for a family wedding in 1972, and I opted for bottle-green velvet, with one button, big wide, curved lapels and flared strides. I'd seen Rod in just such a suit in a photo. Unfortunately I twinned it with a pair of coffee and cream platforms, which I'd got from a stall in Shepherd's Bush market, the same market where until recently my family had flogged fruit and veg. Platforms were the new big thing, the bigger the better. These stilt-built contraptions, which were a startling throwback to Restoration foppery, saw hefty builders and plumbers tottering giddily about after work, as they tried to get used to balancing on five-inch podiums. They were the talk of the time, with heady articles in newspapers and magazines charting every precipitous excess as the nation's feet became increasingly preposterous. Platform shoes with goldfish swimming in the clear perspex heels were the ones even I thought were ridiculous, when they appeared on television. Platforms, in all their giddying glory, were the crowning extravagance of a time of deep sartorial silliness. Yet we all shelled out and laced them up. I firmly believe that if periwigs had reappeared in 1972, guys on the Watling Estate would have dutifully pulled them on and reached for the powder.

The particularly gaudy style of platform I chose, coffee and cream, had dark brown and beige uppers, with a brown heel about three inches high and a built-up beige sole, a tacky homage to classic correspondent shoes and hinting at a 1920s influence. This was when I first saw a girl hobbling along in a pencil skirt, and guys with boxy, double-breasted jackets, like little Chicago mobsters who'd got terribly lost. Not too many animals had been sacrificed to make these new two-tone shoes I'd purchased, and they weren't worth sniffing, so of course I wore them straight away, in the sticky detritus of a street market. They were ruined.

I've always had a thing about wearing clothes the minute I buy them. I often wear things out of the shop, or walk around the house as if going to a wedding or a trial. I have even been known to organize special social events just so that I have somewhere to go to display my natty new gear. Apparently my dad was exactly the same – he once wore a pair of pyjamas in the house all day because my mum had given them to him as a present and he couldn't wait until bedtime. It's a sign of an excitable soul, one who gets real joy out of a bit of schmutter. It's instant gratification.

Then I read an interview somewhere with Rod, in which he said that he hated platform shoes. This complicated matters enormously. I'd just invested in an expensive new pair from a remarkable shop which had opened in Burnt Oak called Ravel Chaussures. This was a sensation, a French name selling fancy footwear to the masses, where once we'd only had Sid's poxy Tricel. The natives seemed to see this as a sign that we were coming up in the world, and so made a great effort to buy overpriced shoes. I chose 'rocking-horse basket-weaves'. I am proud to say that I made the name up myself. Shoes had to have a name. From Smooths, though Toppers, to Salatio box-top loafers, all types of footwear came with a name, how else could you talk about them?

These rocking-horse shoes of mine, as my mother gleefully pointed out, were disturbingly akin to the kind of built-up orthopaedic shoe worn by shuffling souls with club feet. Instead of a separate sole and heel, they had a single, very high platform, running the length of the upper, with just a slight indent and curvature to echo the arch of your feet. Later on I learned that these are termed wedges, and they hark back to the 1920s, when girls wore a similar but smaller wedge sole on their slingbacks. Mine, though, were entirely covered with a sort of rope affair, akin to espadrille material, which started to fray the minute you walked out of the shop with them on. Despite this I loved them, and named them, so that I could talk about them on the rare occasions when they weren't on my feet. And then Rod Stewart goes and says that he doesn't like platform shoes. Well obviously nor do I, so it's a good job these fantastic, and possibly French, creations are not platforms but rocking-horse basket-weaves. And then David Bowie appears on *Top of the Pops*, performing 'Star Man'.

It's hard to recapture the intensity of feeling on that Friday morning at school. This was different from the ebullient rush of Budgie-mania, far darker and more divisive. People talked in hushed tones, not so much reverential as scared shitless. Such was the trauma induced by that one three-minute appearance that in fact most didn't talk at all. It was as if we were all too frightened of having our private fears confirmed. Eventually, maybe not until lunch break, someone sheepishly said, 'Did you see *Top of the Pops* last night?' Of course they knew you had seen it, but what they meant was, did you see that David Bowie, and what do we do now? Then everybody started nervously debating the ramifications of a bloke with dyed scarlet hair and make-up in a skin-tight jumpsuit and knee-length boots, singing louchely with a guitar slung across his back and his arm lovingly, perhaps sexually, draped across the shoulder of another slapped-up, jumpsuited chap from Hull. Now there was nothing else you could possibly talk about, and the few poor unfortunates who hadn't seen it had the scene recounted to them again and again. This was it, this was one of those moments when the curtains are pulled back and you get a glimpse, albeit momentarily, of the future, and it fills you with dread and awe and excitement and absolutely, no doubt about it, fear. It was the fear.

It wasn't that we were naïve. We knew what glam rock was. We'd seen Bacofoil billies and space cadet hippies and just about every kind of spangly pop ploy. We'd seen men on the tele in make-up, and we knew that was just a game. But what Bowie had done in the nation's living-rooms on that Thursday evening was different again. Bowie, unlike Sweet or Gary Glitter or any of those lardy buffoons, was stick-thin cool. Unlike Mark Bolan, the old mod face turned corkscrew troubadour, who made groovy tunes but looked like a wobbly slab of psychedelia gone silly, Bowie appeared genuine, as if he were born to this radiant half-light. He was somewhere arch and vain and glorious, somewhere neither gay nor straight, stoned nor straight. He was decadent and deeply attractive. Bowie managed to show us all that there was another world, a parallel universe perhaps, which we could potentially inhabit if only we had the right gear. And the bottle to wear it.

In 'Star Man', the song he performed in his best Anthony Newley drawl, Bowie says that Ziggy Stardust, his theatrical creation who is of course himself, 'Would like to come and meet us, but thinks he'd blow our minds.' Well, he did on that Thursday evening. And believe me he did. And when your mum said with a sneer, 'He's on drugs, he's a queer, he's a weirdo,' well, you knew for once she was right. But you didn't know what to do about it.

Somehow, even as thirteen-year-olds, we understood that we would have to decide which side we were on. Here was an invitation you could choose to accept, but at a terrible price. Up until now every trend and scene I'd witnessed had been a clarion call to come and join us, they were proselytizing religions. Even mod, with its élitism and its pills and its import records, had quickly become a mass cult, with thousands of its followers descending on bank holiday beaches on holy days, to don the vestments and follow the sacraments. Its ace faces were merely charismatic lay preachers, with humdrum jobs and normal lives. This was different. This was a chance to step over the line. Bowie didn't call you to come and join him, he dared you to be different.

One of my closest friends, Gary Kemp, says of that Thursday night, 'I watched it at a friend's council flat. My reality was so far removed from where Bowie was that my journey from that moment on was to get there, and I think the same applies to the rest of my generation.' I wouldn't be so sure, Gary. At school the next day I said something slightly different. I said, 'He wears platform boots, he's crap.'

I like to think that it was my ardent Rod Stewart affiliations which meant I didn't rush out to get my hair Ziggy'd up and start borrowing the eyeliner from my mum's drawer. I've always been a Manichean, and because I loved Rod it seemed inevitable that I would hate Bowie. But it wasn't just that, I had the fear. I was excited by what David Bowie did, titillated, touched, turned on, terrified. Going Bowie, which was obviously and immediately an option, meant going to the back of the bus to sit on your own, it meant skulking in the shadows, it very probably meant getting a hiding from some neanderthal. Of course it also meant the promise of places and pleasures we never previously knew existed: New York, gay clubs, art schools, arts labs, Berlin, mime troupes, hairdressers, oral sex, Anthony Price, Kansai Yamamoto, clothes designers for God's sake. Who before Bowie had any idea that clothes were actually designed by somebody?

I was having none of it, Rod Stewart was good enough for me. But others answered the siren call. You started to see them blurring in and out of the margins, blurring all your carefully constructed prejudices as 1972 shaded into '73 and *Cabaret* and *A Clockwork Orange* filled the screens with cinematic decadence. Bowie boys we called them, proud and precious, cool as fuck and brave too, as they followed the master's lead, then started to run with it. Eyeliner and shoulder-pads, bolero jackets and boxing boots, sequins and earrings – this was when I first saw a lad with an earring, a simple sleeper in his left lug, and it upset my equilibrium for quite some time. Things have been upset ever since.

I live in Camden Town now, and whenever I walk down the high street towards the market, which is pretty much every day, I brush past a lurid Technicolor cast list of goths and punks and new romantics and old rockers and Japanese electro-b boy hip-hop glam trash, past a dazzling array of libertine looks, all made-up and dyed-up and pierced and preened, and none of them would exist, none of them, but for the first few pioneer Bowie boys who slithered into the leaden grey of early seventies England.

Do you remember Jean Reddy? The other baby skinhead in my class at junior school? Well, I hadn't seen Jean for some time, even though she lived just round the corner on the Watling Estate, and then one day I spotted her and another girl proudly strutting in all their gear. Arm in arm they were, Jean sporting pale blue high-waisted hugely flared trousers with turn-ups, matched with the tiniest lemon satin bomber jacket cut half-way up her back, and her friend in a leopardskin-print jumpsuit, both of them with hair dyed flagrantly unnatural hues and make-up that made them look like boys made-up like girls, pale yet prominent, like Bowie and like nothing you'd ever seen, ambling along the Oak. 'Poor Dolly's having a lot of trouble with Jean,' said my mum. I said nothing, but I thought she looked incredible. I was intensely jealous.

Perhaps because Jean was a girl she could get away with it, but Burnt Oak never really took to the Bowie look. It's impossible to imagine Reggie and his mates playing with designer androgyny, and the Watling Estate at this time was still a bastion of beer-drinking, football fighting and facial hair. Sideburns were large, hair was long, denim was ubiquitous. South Sea Island Bubble Company jeans, a pale, lightweight brushed cotton denim, very wide, with designs of palm trees on the back pocket, were one of those crazes which crash out of nowhere, get everybody excited, then float away with the tide. This was also a time for sewing stickers on to your jeans, butterflies and lips and stars and any old rubbish bought from Wembley market for five bob. While you were there seeking out patches you could also get the latest show-off shirt: thin artificial fibres with a cartoonish photoprint repeatedly plastered all over it of a man walking his dog, or riding his bike, or Charlie Chaplin or Mickey Mouse. It wasn't a glorious time.

1973–4 was a cultural black hole, into which many strange and terrible things were drawn. One of the bizarre trends which came and went was what I can only call gypsy chic. David Essex was the most famed proponent of this style, and with genuine Romany blood flowing through his veins he had more of an excuse than most. An earring in one ear, almost concealed by hair tumbling down, a collarless shirt, invariably worn with a neckerchief roughly tied beneath it, a waistcoat over a pair of corduroy trousers and stout shoes. Maybe even a poacher's cap. It was a look which sang of a despairing desire to return to a better, pre-urban, pre-power-cut England. And plenty of singers wore it in an effort to become pikey icons. Ronnie Lane left the Faces and formed his own band, Slim Chance, whose biggest hit was actually called 'The Poacher' and who toured in gypsy caravans. Bands like Steelers Wheel, McGuinness Flint, Sutherland Brothers and Quiver all made pastoral, melodic rural rock while dressing like they were at a horse fair.

THE EARLY 1970s was a dire time for fashion, and also a truly extraordinary era in British history. From the perspective of a kid entering teenage it was like careening through tumult after turmoil after strike after shortage after stoppage after dispute. Then came the bombs. All the optimism and forward thrust of the sixties had ground to a halt like some badly made British car conking out as it tried to swoop up the Westway. Unemployed and under-employed, militant and malcontented, we were mired in angry class friction and complacent corporatism. Beer and sandwiches were served at Number Ten, and tins of pilchards and boxes of toilet rolls were stored in every larder for the next time the country shut down.

Edward Heath and the Tory government confronted by the British trade-union movement, stolid paternalistic conservatism versus grim, block-vote socialism, in what felt like it might actually be the regional final of the big one. The TUC conference and the CBI conference were major television events, just about the only things regularly broadcast live, and I would watch them assiduously on afternoons when I was off school, to see where the next round of mayhem might come from. As with Rod Stewart versus David Bowie, I had picked my side and was enthusiastically rooting for them: Arthur Scargill and Joe Gormley, Mick McGahey and Vic Feather, Red Robbo, the feral leader of wildcat strikes at Midlands car plants. These balding, sour-dour men might seem like odd idols for a clothes-obsessed fourteen-year-old; the British left has never exactly had the existential élan of their continental counterparts, but it didn't matter. It was all kicking off and I was standing at the back shoving.

Shortages were good. Petrol rationing was the big one, the world oil crises resulting in extremely grumpy company car owners queuing up at service stations in the Home Counties with dun-coloured vouchers to get their allotted dribble of fuel. This too seemed to me to be an excellent thing. We never had a car, so it was only the hated middle classes who suffered. Sugar shortages, coffee shortages, even toilet-roll shortages, were a different matter, though. Rumours that some new product was about to be in short supply would fly around and people would rush out to bulk-buy, thereby turning the rumours into self-fulfilling prophecies and their kitchens into stockpiles. Our house became like a minor field dump in a shabby little war, as we grabbed what we could and stacked it up. Uncle Mac, with his stall in the Roman Road, did very well out of all this, as he seemed to have a direct link to the great toilet-roll stash. Knowing that we always had access to extra supplies gave my mum a certain calm through the storm, as the country crashed and staggered into a quasi-apocalyptic chaos, desperately clutching at rolls of contraband bog paper.

The miners' strike of '72 was the great push, and we cheered and we cheered as Scargill and his pickets flew around the land, storming down country lanes and closing down depots. I even gave them a mental dispensation for wearing such dodgy old gear; after all, everybody would be able to afford designer clothes come the glorious day, which didn't seem all that far away. Especially once the power cuts started. You imagine the joy when you're a teenager and you know that there are going to be long hours of evening darkness, barely enlightened by flickering candles, which of course were in short supply unless you knew my Uncle Mac. The potential for mischief was unlimited and fully exploited. Especially when there was a game on.

One of the consequences of the power cuts occasioned by the miners' strike was that midweek football matches had to be played in the afternoon, as there could be no floodlights. This meant that every time there was a half-decent match played at, say, one o'clock on a Wednesday afternoon anywhere in north or west London, almost every kid from our area would bunk off school and go to the game. I recall a QPR versus Chelsea derby one weekday when seemingly every fourth-former in the city went awol to go to Loftus Road. Schoolteachers set up road-blocks with the police to try to trap their errant flocks, but failed miserably as thousands of kids scaled walls and drainpipes and stormed turnstiles to swamp our ground in a heaving mass of naughtiness. Even more of us went to Highbury for a game against Derby, doctored school uniforms competing with the ranks of older Gooners, including Reggie and the fearsome Burnt Oak contingent, who stood at the back of the North Bank in their polo-necks and baggies, beneath ominous white butchers' coats. Such was the crush that smaller kids were being passed over the heads of the crowd as they passed out and were laid out on the periphery of the pitch.

It was at that Arsenal game that I saw a gang of guys from Camden Town, a couple of years older than my cheerfully miscreant mob, who really stood out among the scruffy toughness of the terraces. They were not exactly Bowie Boys, but there was definitely something odd going on. There was a touch of skinhead revival involved, as they wore Dr Martens boots and tight trousers rather than the mandatory baggies, but their boots were painted in numerous Day-Glo colours, as was their hair, which while long was more mannered than most. Some even had a hint of make-up. There was definitely an element of *A Clockwork Orange* about it all; maybe one sported a bowler hat. Put together it was both threatening and alluring. Years later I learnt that some of these Day-Glo skins had gone on to become the basis of the crew which would spawn Madness. It was yet another odd element gestating in the seething darkness.

After the shortages, inflation and power-cuts came the best bit of the lot, the three-day week. This has gone down in history as a nadir in British life, when we couldn't even get it together to get the economy functioning for more than half the allotted time. This proud nation had been reduced to a shabby shambles, somewhere between a strife-torn South American dictatorship and a gloomy Soviet satellite, Bolivia meets Bulgaria, a banana republic with a banana shortage. The reality, of course, is that almost everybody absolutely loved it. They took to the three-day week with glee. They took terrible liberties.

The three-day week of late 1972 was an extraordinary measure ordered by Prime Minister Heath in an attempt to conserve dwindling coal stocks during the miners' strike, whereby offices and factories were only allowed to function on three allotted days. For many this was a grown-up version of that school-kid's heaven when you're sent home because the boilers have broken down or flu has decimated the teaching staff. It was an opportunity to doss and drink and watch another exciting TUC conference, or *Indoor League*, presented by Fred Truman, while gorging on tinned pilchards from your stash. It was perfect for a malfunctioning, bureaucratic, deeply divided, horridly backward, randomly violent Britain, riddled with inertia, indolence, envy and snobbery.

This was a grim, colourless land, a place where you had to put your name on a waiting-list to get a telephone and had to declare the amount of money you were taking with you on holiday; a land where pubs shut at lunchtime, shops shut on Thursday afternoon and television shut down at midnight with the national anthem. Patriotism meant slagging off Europe, yearning for a return to pounds, shillings and pence and cheering when we took on mighty Iceland in a pathetic fishing dispute known as the cod war. It was into this lost and sorry England that the Bowie boys poked their pale faces and lit it up. Not that I was one of them.

Instead I was flapping about in baggies and being active in something called the National Union of School Students, who added to the merry mayhem by organizing school strikes and walk-outs and waging noisy, disruptive campaigns on everything from uniforms to gender equality. I was part of a cabal at school which was intent on disruption in the name of direct political action, and undermining the uniform at all times. Meanwhile back in Burnt Oak at weekends, a group of like-minded herberts had taken to spraying BOUG, Burnt Oak Urban Guerillas, on walls. Should your life ever take you to Burnt Oak, you can still see this risible acronym on the bridge just by the station. Yet despite all this I was doing pretty well at my studies and keeping firm friendships with the firm who did the rounds and sprayed the walls. It was a balancing act that I enjoyed, as I learned to subtly alter my accent and my cultural identity as required, rather as you dress differently for different occasions.

The big occasions for me at this time of my life were Faces concerts. My best mate at school was Danny Stern, one of the roaring Stern gang, a trio of Jewish north London brothers who all went to Orange Hill, all espoused radical left-wing politics, all supported Spurs, all had that knowing, street-smart, cosmopolitan way which made them a charismatic, creative clan. Their Dad, Dov, with his foul mouth, fine mind and piratical grin, encouraged his kids and their mates to jump into everything from picket lines to reggae clubs. Danny's elder brother, Peter, was a musician who seemed to spend his life hanging out at gigs and rehearsal studios, and who offered to take Danny and me, still only fourteen-year-olds, to concerts. The first band we saw together was the Jackson Five at Wembley, supported by Junior Walker and the All Stars, featuring Michael Jackson when he was black and brilliant. Over a three- or four-year spell we went to see everything from dodgy pub rock bands in dodgy pubs to Bob Marley and the Wailers at the Lyceum. But the highlights were always Faces concerts.

Danny Stern was also a Faces fanatic and we took to going together to all their London gigs. They were always wonderfully shambolic affairs, with much of the communal, knees-up boisterousness of the terraces about them, but with none of the fighting which made going to football such an edgy business at the time. They were a great live band. The gigs I remember most, though, were a series of concerts at the State, a bizarrely elaborate old art deco cinema in Kilburn which normally hosted bingo, but for three consecutive nights put on north London's favourite son. The old skinhead war between Burnt Oak and Kilburn had long since died down, so we were free to go there, and indeed spent all night there, queueing up in the street when tickets were put on sale, so we could be right down the front. But Kilburn was at the centre of another ongoing conflict.

It was the home of the largest Irish population in Britain, and therefore deeply connected to the troubles. The barn-like old boozers of Kilburn and Cricklewood, with their stained carpets and veined barmen, were a law unto themselves, liberties seemingly outside the jurisdiction of the authorities who rarely ventured into such smoky Fenian dens. Which meant that as under-age drinkers we would regularly travel up the Edgware Road for surreptitious supping, and hear the defiant rebel songs of the boys from Cork and Kerry, and witness the ritual of the Irish national anthem played at the end of the night. Those who could make it to their feet would stand and sing along, and those who wanted to keep their knees intact would place a couple of bob in the collection box for Irish orphans. I was never sure whether it was helping them or creating them.

At the time all this seems normal. There's even bread rationing, because of a strike by bakery workers which results in guards on bread shops and the dramatic hijacking of a van-load of split tins in east London. It's like an Ealing comedy gone wrong, the place is falling apart, it's teetering on a precipice. I'm getting dressed up. A boy of fourteen, I am carefully preparing to go and see Rod and the Faces. My only desire is to look right, to lord it along the Kilburn High Road. In the past, dressing up has been for myself; now, though, I want to stand out among the massed ranks of Faces fans. Secretly I am even toying with the ludicrous idea that some female will take a shine to such a dashingly dressed young man.

I sift through my collection of tartan scarves and drapes, and raid my mum's scant jewellery box to borrow a couple of brooches and pins to keep them in place. I even take a book out of the local library which has some pictures of clan chiefs, to see how most effectively to wrap myself in plaid in order to resemble a dashing laird. To top off the look I buy an army surplus beret from a shop in Euston called Lawrence Corner. Hours are spent in front of mirrors fiddling with yarn and pins and hats. I've never worn a beret before and trying to get the requisite heroic angle isn't easy. Finally, satisfied that I have arrived at the nines, I get the 32 bus to Kilburn and our allotted meeting-point, Biddy Mulligan's, a famous old spit-and-sawdust Irish house right by the State.

Kilburn High Road is in its usual state of disrepair and dishevelment when I get off the bus. I am wrapped up like a box of shortbread, trying desperately to walk the walk among the good citizens scurrying home to nibble on their one allotted loaf as they wait for the news of the next disaster. And there it is.

Biddy Mulligan's huge old gin palace, site of many a shebeen, has a dirty great hole blown into its side. I absolutely stop dead. Our rendezvous is surrounded by Old Bill and stripy tape and confused-looking Faces fans, and I am furious. I have gone to all this trouble to look just so, and the bloody IRA have blown up the one pub that is likely to let me in. For a few moments I take it personally. Then I realize there's something truly surreal about this. Here am I theatrically swathed, prancing melodramatically about, in a war zone. My city under siege, and my response is to seek out the nearest unshattered shop window, to make sure my brooch is correctly fastened. Little am I to know that this is a portent of things to come.

Rumour has it that Biddy Mulligan's was given a gentle little explosive charge by the IRA because the governor refused to contribute to the orphans. I've no idea if that's true. What's undeniable is that at about the same time, Danny Stern's brother managed to get tickets for the hottest show in town in a generation. David Bowie had decided to kill off Ziggy Stardust, and was playing his final concert as Ziggy and the Spiders from Mars, one last appearance in front of the faithful at Hammersmith Odeon. This was going to be a rally of every precious Bowie boy and girl, every cool outsider and in-crowd character in town. Ziggy's last stand has gone down as one of those epochal concerts, one of those mythical nights which everybody claims to have been at, except me. When Danny asked if I wanted to go, I said, 'No thanks, he wears platforms.'

7

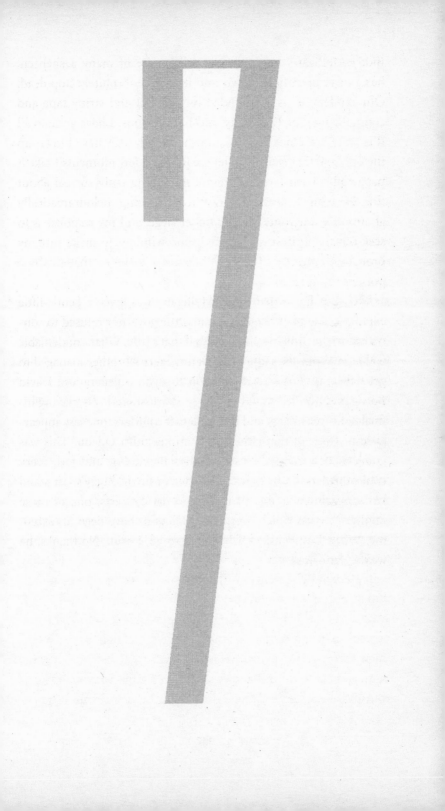

EVERY MONDAY MORNING, regular as clockwork, Reggie would sub some money from Barry to get to work for the week. Come Wednesday he'd also be tapping Mum for a pint and maybe a night at the pictures with a girl. Then every Thursday, pay-day, he'd pay Barry back, pay Mum her housekeeping, plus what he owed her, and have enough over for a new bit of schmutter to wear for a weekend of carousing and footie. Come Monday the cycle started again.

I lived in a place where people lived hand to mouth. For those in full-time work, the money they earned on a Thursday, in cash, was invariably gone by the end of the weekend and there was a constant process of borrowing and subbing, taking with one hand and giving with another. This juggling act was supplemented by things like Christmas clubs and holiday clubs, organized at the workplace or by a group of neighbours, where you paid an amount into a collective kitty to provide a stash for the festive season and a seaside jaunt. There was also the ubiquitous biscuit tin, with the occasional fiver tucked away where the Peek Freans had once been. Then there were Provident cheques, with their hideous interest rates, and rumours of shadowy shark-like figures who would help you out of a crisis and then plunge you head first into a much worse one if you couldn't keep up the payments. But most of the time, people just spent what they had coming in and worried about next week next week.

So on a Friday afternoon or Saturday morning, if you had a few quid in your trousers, buying another pair of trousers or a jumper or a pair of shoes was both an appealing and a feasible prospect. We aren't talking expensive designer gear here. Apart from the big set-pieces like suits or coats, most of the clothes were affordable, at a stretch. It probably meant that you wouldn't have the fare to work come Monday, but clothes matter. And besides, there's no other stuff to spend your hard-earned on. In these profoundly materialistic times, it's difficult to imagine just how few things people like us had. I can consciously remember wincing with anger and shame when I first heard John Lennon, who at the time lived in an apartment block in Manhattan with a temperature-controlled room just for his fur coats, mawkishly singing 'Imagine' in that smugly sentimental voice. Imagine no bloody possessions, we just had to look round the living-room. Apart from a small collection of knick-knacks, including a wooden deer with a broken antler which sat on the mantelpiece for at least a decade in its malformed condition, there wasn't much. The same record player which had hosted Otis half a dozen years before, and a rented tele which only worked if you fed ten-pence pieces into a meter on the side, so that Mum wouldn't have another bill to meet each month.

None of this was unusual; we didn't feel, and indeed weren't, particularly poor, we never went without, it was how everybody we knew lived. Ordinary people didn't have the money to buy possessions. They spent their income on living rather than acquiring, getting by rather than buying things. That old adage about being able to leave your door open was only true because there was nothing to nick. But there had always been an exaggerated pride in appearance. Spending money on clothes was never seen as wasting it; they were a priority. I was shocked when I first went round the houses of kids from school. I'd expected their rambling Hampstead homes to be swish and their posh parents to be clad in swanky gear. I was simultaneously disappointed and yet chuffed when I saw that their houses were invariably scruffy jumbles of books and scrubbed wood, while their mums and dads would shuffle around in some no-mark jeans and open-toed sandals. That was unlikely in Burnt Oak, unthinkable in Notting Dale. 'Smart' is still my mum's ultimate term of approval.

IN ORDER TO look smart, you always had jobs. Saturday jobs (when they didn't conflict with football), evening jobs, morning jobs, holiday jobs. From about the age of twelve there was some way of bringing money in. Before that, even, we'd collected beer bottles or washed cars or cut hedges or whatever would secure us a few pennies for two ounces of sweets. By the time I was established at senior school, though, and buying my own gear, I was also working. Filling shelves in shops was first I think, then it was into the family tradition of fruit and veg. Barry was in offices in the city, swinging his umbrella and courting a girl with a soft-top car and no glottal stops, looking for his own way out. Reggie had joined him for a while, but you couldn't keep Reggie still. He worked on building sites as a labourer, but, almost inevitably, was now a greengrocer, managing a shop rather than a stall, but with a proper set-up, a trestle table outside, covered in fake grass, stacked with ripe fruit. I used to work for him at weekends, after school and through the holidays. Sorting onions with seeping eyes, coughing as I swept the floor, then after a while stocking the front, weighing, bagging up and serving customers. Reggie was brilliant at this, flirting with all the old girls, shouting his wares, pulling a crowd, bashing out bananas and aubergines at an alarming rate. Then he fancied a change and started a milk round.

During termtime Mum wasn't too keen on me working with Reggie on the milk. She figured that getting up at four in the morning wasn't the best preparation for a day's schooling, and I was her last chance of getting one of her kids through to higher education, fulfilling a vow she'd made to my father. But on Saturdays and during the long school holidays I would go out with my brother at dawn to fill up at the depot and then on to drop off two bottles of gold top and a carton of yoghurt at number 37. I loved it. I loved the clean silence of it and the rhythm you build up as the round progresses, skipping with bottles between your fingers, hearing them clank against doorsteps in the bright air. I loved the banter with my brother and the way you could watch the world drowsily wake up and feel superior because you've already been on the go for hours. I also liked the float. I could drive that float. Sort of.

Near the end of the round one morning, Reggie was collecting money and the float was at the end of a cul-de-sac, so I said I'd turn it round to join him. Now I've never been good at machinery, but a milk float is not the most difficult craft to manoeuvre: there's only two pedals, stop and go, and go only gives you about ten miles an hour after a long run-up. So how I managed to hit a lamppost, and then in slow motion continue to nudge it over until it was virtually bent double and the light was almost touching the pavement, I'll never know. My poor brother watched all this in horror, realizing that because I shouldn't have been driving the thing, he would have to tell his bosses that he'd somehow contrived to knock a lamppost over. I understood immediately that it was time for me to get a new job. This new position would also eventually lead to an embarrassing incident. But it also led me on to the first real youth cult I could call my own.

Clothes and records. From the time I stopped playing with toy soldiers aged about nine or ten, those were the two things I wanted, they were the things everybody wanted. Clothes and records, in that order. That's what you worked for. Burnt Oak never had a particularly good clothes shop; if you wanted good gear, especially if you wanted to beat the herd, you had to travel. Records, though, were different – we were quite well served for records. I was about to start serving records.

There'd always been a record shop on the Watling. I have the vaguest recall of standing listening to Tamla Motown singles with my brothers in one of those booths where the sound came out of the side of the walls, which had the appearance of perforated egg-boxes. For some reason I also remember a window display of a row of Jethro Tull LPs which I used to look at scornfully as we walked past. I knew that Burnt Oak at the time was a skinhead bastion, and it seemed disturbing, disloyal even, that our local shop should put hippy records in the window. But then we didn't often buy records there. They weren't up on ska and rock steady, they didn't do Jamaican imports, so you had to seek out specialist stores like that yam shop in Shepherd's Bush, or a newsagent's in West Hendon that kept all the latest sides from the island in a glass case above the cigarettes. But by the time I was wearing flares, jumping about to Rod Stewart and slagging off David Bowie, Soundrax, the local purveyor of vinyl, was a real centre of activity.

Increasingly this shop, with its cool manager, a slick Oriental guy called Phil, himself something of a rarity in strictly white-bread Burnt Oak, became a focus for the rounds. We'd stand in there in our schmutter, me and a selection of Kellys, O'Keefes and Mulcahys, discussing football, leafing through big, thick cardboard album sleeves and waiting to see if any girls came in looking for David Cassidy or whoever was that week's heart-throb. One week I remember Gerard Mulcahy, one of the boys who was perhaps a little older, a little more advanced, raving about the Isley Brothers new album *3+3*, saying that it was really funky and he'd danced to it at a club. This was the very first time I was aware of anyone using the term funky or any of my mates talking about going to 'a club'.

We all went to Watling Boys' Club, a classic bit of breeze-block and pinboard social engineering designed to keep us suffering estate boys off the streets by providing wonky table-football tables and cups of Tizer. There was even an annual subsidized holiday when we were bundled into a coach and plonked on poor unsuspecting horses in a field somewhere in Devon. This rapidly turned into a scene from a comedy cowboy film, with whooping slum types and baffled nags scattered in all directions. We did, though, have an exalted reputation for football and boxing, producing a few pros at both sports. There was a monthly disco when local girls in far too much make-up were wheeled in to watch the boys show off, and Mr Hedges, who ran the place, had to work even harder than usual to stop the members taking lumps out of each other as the hormones Krakatoa'd. But Watling Boys' wasn't a club in the way that Gerard meant. Gerard had been to a *night*-club.

My brothers had always gone on about clubs. I can still reel off a list of names of places I heard them talking about: Tiles, the Cavalier, the Water Wheel, Scamps, the Birds' Nest, the Tottenham Royal. I never knew these clubs, had no real idea of what happened in them. The only reason those names should have stayed with me is that the very sounds seemed full of shimmering nocturnal portent. My brothers and their mates never went to see bands, though. By the time I was hanging out with the Stern gang from school and regularly going to gigs, I was aware of a strange social divide. When I told my mates from the estate I was off to see a band they'd ask why. They were deeply into music, but music meant records, and soon their lives would be driven by the beat of the right records, in the right clubs, where you wore the right stuff.

The only explanation I can come up with for this marked class difference is that the estate kids had no real concept of passive appreciation. They hadn't grown up being entertained by books or trips to the theatre, museum or gallery, they enjoyed events in which they were involved, where they were participating. Even football was not strictly a spectator sport for them; they stood on teeming ends as part of crews, their chanting and singing, even their taunting and fighting, an integral part of the event. The terraces of the early seventies were far from passive. Music for Burnt Oak boys was not an end in itself either, not an art form to sit back and enjoy, or analyse and discuss; it provided the back-beat for their own show – they dressed the part, they danced, they pulled, they fought. Clubs could provide the perfect arena for all of that.

And the music they played in the kind of clubs that Burnt Oak went to was soul music. The Bowie boys had shimmered and shocked their way into the shadows, illuminating the edges of the early seventies with their lustrous androgyny. The mid-seventies was the era of the soul boy, and soul-boy gear was to become my other uniform. One afternoon, though, while I was still sporting a semblance of proper fourth-form attire, Dr Wheaton, my history teacher, and a truly inspirational man who liked the fact that I liked his subject, asked me which university I wanted to go to. This stopped me in my tracks for a few seconds. I honestly hadn't even considered the prospect. When I did, it put a big grin on my face and even more of a spring in my already ebullient gait. But it did make it more and more clear that I was on a divergent path. My mates from the Watling were already looking beyond school to building sites and pay-packets, or just as likely dole offices. We were moving apart, but for the next couple of years we had something to bind us together. Soul was definitely a working-class thing. When I ran beyond the gates of school I was definitely soul.

It's summertime 1974 and the trousers are high. High-waisted strides, cut in what I now recognize as a classic Spanish style – with a waistband rising up towards your rib cage like a cummerbund, cut revealingly tight around the bottom, but flaring out gradually over your shoe so that footwear is almost concealed. High-waisters we called them, and they were the first really distinctive soul-boy totems to swing their way on to the British high street. Technically they came via black America: think Shaft, John Shaft, and that fly New York *On the Corner* look, all elongated legs, short fitted waist-coats, figure-hugging shirts with long thin collars. They came via black America, but they came from Latin America. The Hispanic community who shared the east and west coast ghettos in turn inherited this dandy, sexy, preening style back through Cuba and Puerto Rico to Spain, where bullfighters and flamenco dancers still wear a version of those trousers to this day.

Fifteen-year-old London lads don't usually have quite the panache of the average ghetto dude or Latino groover, but boy, did we go high-waisted. First they had one button, then two, three, four and five. There was talk of mythical, hopefully apocryphal, ten-button monstrosities, the waistbands climbing higher and higher, hitting our chests and clinging to our skinny boy bottoms. First they were worn with a belt, then two belts, then three belts, stacked up one over the other, sometimes in matching colours, sometimes garishly contrasting. And what colours these strides were. Lemon, salmon and mint were particularly tasty, but they came in every lurid shade imaginable and some you couldn't possibly dream up. Cheap cotton lime-green trousers worn with three flaming orange belts. These duds were slick, and they were made for dancing. In a pair of lime-green high-waisters with a satin-backed waistcoat over the top, you just have to hustle.

It would certainly have been at a Watling Boys' disco, probably some time early in the summer of '74, that I first saw a boy dressed to dance. It was Pat Kamara – Patrick and his elder brother Francis were half Irish, half Jamaican kids, the perfect soul-boy combination. Good footballers, good dancers, excellent balance, very natty. Afro hair with a long blade comb sticking out of it, high-waisters fitting tight on his slim hips, flaring out over a pair of Dunlop Green Flash plimsolls on his darting feet. Pat Kamara: swaying from the upper body as if throwing a dummy, short hustling steps, serious face, perspiration building up under the tight-fitting, short-sleeved Adidas top with three black stripes down the arm, an Adidas bag standing on the floor of the gym where he stepped and spun. We stopped playing ping-pong or gawping at the imported girls and stared. Silent. Admiring. No mere girl looked as good as this. Here was a whole new dimension to dressing up, a whole new way opening up.

But the new soul scene, as personified by Patrick in his pomp, was also redolent with memories pouring back. His soundtrack may have been Juggy Jones, 'Inside America', or the Fatback Band, 'Yum Yum' or 'Wicky Wacky', but this soaring American ghetto music with solar plexus rhythms was essentially Otis again. Patrick, with his clothes just right and his steps just so, was my brother Barry, was nothing more than a mod. There's always been this extraordinary bond between the music of black America and the lifestyles of working-class British kids; it's the beat that drives this whole teen caper. After a few years in the stylistic wilderness, that searing mod aesthetic was back. Different clobber, different beat, but back.

Soul boys like Patrick were actually called soul boys because they weren't reggae boys. It was a term of mild rebuke specifically aimed at the relatively small number of black kids who chose soul and its attendant fashions over the indigenous reggae scene. Back-street blues, pay-in house parties with their booming sound systems, and small high-street reggae clubs were an integral part of London life by now in all those areas that had a sizeable Caribbean population. The music at these raves was strictly reggae, the crowd almost exclusively West Indian, the vibe and the patois and the air thick with Trenchtown. The reggae scene was locks and ganja and red, gold and green. By contrast, the black Londoners who frequented the soul clubs were seen by their peers as a bit too slick, too ready to mix and mingle with the thousands of white youths who instinctively flocked to the numerous sweaty rooms which sprang up across London and the south-east, specializing in American soul and funk. For this cultural apostasy they were sneeringly dubbed soul boys.

What they really were – black and white, male and, female, and, remarkably for the time, gay and straight, all these chic, 'Good Times' kids – was yet another sign of the cosmopolitan, mongrel culture which was developing in our urban centres. 'England half English', Nick Cohn,* the greatest chronicler of early British pop culture, had dubbed it so presciently back in the late fifties when the Teds had co-opted American rock'n'roll. Then the mods had mixed hip Americana with chic continental threads, the skinheads had added in a large dollop of Jamaican flavouring to their Ivy League duds and John Bull fundamentalism. After that there'd been a hiatus. The Bowie boys had been too far out to be a mass tribe. As a fourteen-year-old swathed in biscuit-tin tartan I'd been desperate for a cult to call my own. And as soon as the soul scene surfaced, with its hybrid of council estate and ghetto culture, I realized straight away that it was deep in the tradition. It was mod made modern.

From the first night I graduated from the Watling Boys' Club to a night-club, this was it. I loved everything about it, even though these places were far from glamorous. These weren't swish and swanky seventies discotheques into which Bianca Jagger or Joan Collins might sashay, and they certainly weren't purpose-built designer haunts with massive sound systems and numerous, glamorous rooms. It was usually just a big old tatty hall in the back of a boozer with a sticky carpet, a scuffed dance floor and a disco ball.

---

* Cohn also wrote the piece of journalism for the *New Yorker* from which *Saturday Night Fever* came. Entitled 'Tribal rites of the new Saturday night', supposedly about a club in Brooklyn, where blue-collar boys in white suits danced, and containing the epochal line 'he hurt my hair', it became the ultimate disco movie. Years later, though, Cohn admitted he'd made most of it up, basing it all on mods he knew from the Goldhawk Road in Shepherd's Bush in the early sixties.

Getting in would cost a few bob, and you might have enough money left to buy one drink. The important thing was to be there and to be seen to be there.

The local hotspot for kids from our bit of suburban north-west London was a place called the Bandwagon in Kingsbury. It was a Burnt Oak ritual to head off there mob-handed for the Friday night funk sessions, and I would wind myself up all week in preparation. It was your duty to look as good as possible, because you were being judged collectively as well as individually; synchronized dressing was a team sport and Burnt Oak had an Olympic-standard squad. We'd meet up at the bus stop at about seven, maybe fifteen or twenty kids, mostly boys, but with a good smattering of girls hovering, all dressed, all excited, some carrying the sports bags which were part of the ritual.

This excitable gang would get the bus a few stops to Queensbury, then change on to the tube for the one stop to Kingsbury, leaping the new electric barriers which had just been put in place, using force of numbers and Friday night energy to swindle London Transport. Once at the Bandwagon, though, we had to suddenly curb the enthusiasm and noise and queue quietly in the long line of adolescents snaking across the car park, waiting to be let in. Probably half our gang were under-age, and I was always one of the youngest. The trick was for the 'baby squad', the fifteen- and sixteen-year-olds, to mingle with the legals, to avoid detection and slip quietly in.

It was out in the line in the car park that you could clock the details, check the trends, before shuffling into the spinning darkness of the club. If it was really cold some might be sporting a topcoat, perhaps a short leather blouson jacket – mine was nut brown with a stripy elasticated back. Cardigans were a big thing, because they were small enough to fit into that bag, which was handy to avoid the queue for the cloakroom. Most, though, braved the cold as only the young and wilfully underdressed can, displaying their wares and their goose-bumps in the ritual car park parade.

At some point, provoked in part by the movie of *The Great Gatsby*, starring Robert Redford, there was a brief diversion into thirties preppy attire. I bought a cream double-breasted blazer with wide lapels and a pair of worsted parallel trousers with two-inch turn-ups. I sought high and low for a pair of brown leather sandals of the kind only posh young children and very old men wear, with the perforated toe and the cross strap. In the queue outside the Bandwagon for a couple of months in late '74, there were boys with cravats and co-respondent shoes, white cotton shirts worn with the sleeves rolled high to the forearm or with elasticated metal armbands. It was smart to be smart again. Any illusion of which would be shattered the minute you got inside and started doing the Bus Stop or the Latin hustle and the sweat started sluicing down the walls and on to the floor, making it sticky even to the slickest leather soles.

Those tunes, blazing out of New York, Philadelphia, Detroit and Chicago, blending the gospel vocalizing of soul with the African rhythmic punch of funk and the improvisatory zeal of jazz, were not the kind you'd hear on mainstream radio in England or see on *Top of the Pops*. They certainly weren't the kind of thing cerebral middle-class kids with their ELP and Yes albums wanted anything to do with. As with all decent youth cults, you had to have an element of élitism, and these records, seven-inch singles on import, were the core of it. I of course got bang into buying obscure tunes and talking about them to Phil, the boss of Soundrax, who was very much a jazz funk man himself and had turned the shop into something of a local Mecca. In the end I hung around his increasingly hip emporium so much and bored him so often, with talk of Lonnie Liston Smith and Brass Construction, that he offered me a job.

By the time I was spending Friday afternoons, all day alternate

Saturdays and half days when QPR were at home behind the counter in Soundrax, the classic soul-boy uniform had solidified. I saw it at the Bandwagon, I saw it on the punters who came in the shop searching for tunes, I wore it every day I was in civvies. From the feet up it went like this: flat shoes were essential for dancing, so plimsolls and trainers were in, but strictly old school: Green Flash, Converse baseball boots, Adidas Samba and Mamba and Stan Smiths. Most importantly, though, the loafer had returned, including fringes and tassels, but I opted for the simplest black leather beef-roll loafer, the one closest to the American Indian moccasin on which it's based, with two scrolls of leather, one either side of the low cut tongue. Loafers were perfect because they displayed a large chunk of white sock. The great and most derided soul-boy trademark was a pair of springy towelling Marks and Sparks white cotton socks. These were vital because they showed you were clean. Like their mod forebears, soul boys were eager to be clean, and you can only wear white socks once.

Above the socks inevitably sat a pair of pegs. Pegged trousers, full at the top, but with two or three pleats just below the waistband on either side of the fly, so they billowed out, baggy to the knee, but then sharply tapering in, narrow at the bottom, breaking high over the socks. I favoured baby blue, but pastel pink was also popular. They were hard to get, though, and I secured mine mail order from an advert in the back of *Blues and Soul* magazine, which was the flimsy monthly bible of all true believers.

Atop all this, tight T-shirts were still in vogue, Adidas stripes or just plain cotton crewnecks. Then, about this time, 1975, baggy shirts came billowing in. Bowling shirts, classic fifties Americana, with the name of a garage or a construction company on the back, a curly signature above the breast pocket, white pleats of extra material under the arm to allow you bowling or dancing room, always worn outside the trousers. The real up-town top-rankers sought out original, one-off, second-hand bowling shirts from shops in the King's Road, which imported them in sacks from Baltimore or somewhere. They also sold proper American Hawaiian shirts with garish palm-swaying prints on silky fabric. Most of us, though, bought snides, copies which were mass-produced for the growing soul boy market.

When it came to a haircut, though, I made sure I got the real thing. Smile, a hairdresser's in Knightsbridge, way up west, was *the* and I mean *the* place to get your hair cut, and the only haircut to have was a wedge. Smile was where Bryan Ferry got his hair cut; he even gave them a credit on Roxy album sleeves. Smile was where the hippest older kids who you saw at the clubs in little cliques, or occasionally browsing through the imports in Soundrax, were rumoured to get their hair cut. And the haircut they all had was a wedge. The wedge was more than a haircut, the wedge was a tonsorial banner, a statement of intent, a manifesto of hedonistic desire, the wedge was a heraldic symbol, the wedge was . . . Oh, for God's sake, it was a chunky, lopsided, exaggerated pudding-basin, originally invented for a female fashion-spread by Trevor Sorbie at Vidal Sassoon in 1974, but soon adopted by hard-core soul boys everywhere.

The first time I saw a guy with a wedge, a guy called Micky Asset, a boy who wasn't strictly from Burnt Oak but hung around with the older, tastier members of our crew, I stopped dead, nearly dropped dead. Fit and tanned and smooth, Micky Asset, whose name still produces deep respect among the old soul fraternity, looked like a surfer, looked like he moved through this world with ease, and he had this hair. At the same time long yet short, masculine yet feminine, rebellious yet smart, clean-cut yet daring. The wedge was all the things the soul scene was about. The wedge bounced as you danced.

Peter York, style analyst and inventor of the Sloane Ranger, said, 'The wedge was the uniform of the southern English club-going working-class soul stylist.' And it was. It spoke of trendy salons and Californian suntans, it was aspirational and exceptional, it marked you out. I had to get one and I had to get one at the top place. I dreamed of that haircut. I planned that haircut. I worked out that you could get free haircuts at Smile if you acted as a model for their juniors. The kid cutting my hair wasn't much older than me, but he clearly knew his way around a wedge and my straight thick ginger mane was perfectly suited to this chunky style. Loafers, white socks, pegs, bowling shirt and now a wedge. I thought I had it all.

At the start of this chapter I said that working in the record shop led to an embarrassing incident, far worse than crashing my brother's milk float. It was actually a couple of years later, by which time I wasn't wearing pegs and loafers, wasn't paying as much attention to the soul scene as I should have done. It was a Saturday afternoon, the shop was full and buzzing, a few of the local tasty geezers were in, there was a girl I fancied, looking through the racks, just possibly looking at yours truly. A guy came in and said to me, 'Have you got Quincy Jones, stuff like that?'

I didn't know. I wasn't aware that Quincy Jones, classic jazz and now trendy jazz funk musician, had a new single just out called 'Stuff Like That', a record which was hot in the clubs and would go on to be a real classic. I rather dismissed this kid who didn't even seem to know exactly what he wanted and so, lazily and loudly shouted out to my boss, 'Phil, have we got any stuff like Quincy Jones?' The whole place went quiet, then it burst into uproarious laughter at my inexcusable *faux pas.* 'Have we got any stuff like Quincy Jones?'

I was teased for weeks about that, still get ribbed about it occasionally if I venture back to the Oak. But you see, I did have an excuse. By the time Quincy Jones had made 'Stuff Like That' and I'd made a fool of myself in Soundrax a whole new scene had exploded, born out of soul but very different from it. By that time my mind was elsewhere.

8

IT'S LUNCHTIME in the sixth-form common-room and the divide is clear for all to see. It's their turn to take command of the record player, so Van der Graaf Generator has just segued into Camel, filling the scruffy room with a dense prog rock fog. There's a few exploding horsehair sofas, but they would rather sit on the floor, cross-legged, constructing roll-ups they know they can't smoke until after school, discussing the yin and yang of their greatcoats. A few have even mastered facial hair, wispy 'taches and would-be beards, and they stare across at us with a lazy, proudly hirsute disdain. In our cleanshaven, neat and tidy, white-sock-wearing way, we glare back, Danny Stern and Andy Scar, Graham Smith and I, waiting for the moment we can put on a Roxy Music record, or maybe really wind them up by playing Brass Construction and shadowing a few moves.

That is how it manifests itself at school. Out in the real world, though, by 1975, proper hairies are an endangered species, and the enemy is much less obvious, even more ugly. A few superannuated grammar school hippies apart, the average lad ambling his way along the high road of a British town looks roughly like this: a pair of unpolished, flat, rubber-soled, dark shoes. Then, almost inevitably, comes a pair of shapeless baggy denims, which haven't been washed for quite some time. If he has a belt on, it will be a thin plastic one, possibly white, but most likely these old jeans just hang around his crotch, creased up from weeks of continual wear and discoloured around his private parts. A bobbly V-neck jumper one size too small is pulled over a tight T-shirt or a brightly patterned, ill-fitting, open-neck shirt made of no known fibre. This fetching ensemble is topped off by a bomber jacket or a jean jacket, which also hasn't been cleaned for the couple of years he's worn it.

This paragon of 1970s normality could well be sporting a heavy, patterned, zip-up acrylic cardigan with collars. One Christmas he got one of those *Starsky and Hutch* jumpers, a long great thick thing like Starsky wore in the first four episodes, like a dressing gown only bulkier, white with geometric patterns all over it, tied with a belt. Another little mini-craze involves this lad of ours wearing a shiny polo-neck jumper with an open-necked shirt over the top, all tucked into his jeans, so that his nascent beer belly pokes out even more. Hair is mid-length, centre parted, untended. He's seventeen or eighteen, say, and although dole queues are rising rapidly, chances are he's working. Perhaps he's a delivery boy leaping in and out of a van all day, unless they can pull a fast one, dump the gear and sneak into the pub for a couple of hours for a pint and a game of pool, which is the new craze. Or he could well be in the employ of the local council, maintenance, or the parks department, which is a particularly good job because you don't actually work much, especially if it rains. And what's more they give you a donkey jacket.

This kiddy is not into ducking and diving as much as dossing and skiving. He doesn't need much dough because he doesn't do too much and doesn't want to. Musically he has no great affiliations, but he did buy that double live album by Peter Frampton, although he's not sure why, because there's only one good track on it. Politically he supports Labour because his dad does, and he's in a union. The National Front does have a certain appeal because he doesn't agree with bringing in the darkies. It's not that he's against all black people, there's that kid who drinks in his local who's all right, he's a good laugh, puts up with a lot of stick. And then there's that little firm of black lads at football. They are very handy, good fighters and staunch, which means they aren't really black, not in his eyes.

For entertainment our boy likes a drink. Lager is the latest thing, Skol and Harp, but actually he drinks light and lager, because you get more for your money that way. Sometimes of a Friday night he'll do a bit of speed maybe or some Tuinal, which makes you talk soppy and fall about, a right laugh but a bad idea if there's a fight. He likes a fight. Not that he's one of the lunatics who's always at it, but they all like a scrap now and then. Certainly it is not a good idea to look too polished in his presence when he's drunk, he can easily take umbrage at anything fancy. But if he really wants a good ruck, then that's what football is for. At football he looks a tad different.

There's always been a close relationship between football and fashion. The terraces, when there were terraces, were the perfect theatre of display, and the most immediate means of communicating new trends. The skinhead look, for example, emerged from mod via the West Ham mob, and in the one season, 1968–9, spread around the country. I can still vividly recall being taken to Chelsea as a ten- or eleven-year-old and seeing a guy standing at their end in a canary-yellow Harrington, and being told that he was the leader of the Shed. I have no recollection whatsoever of the game, but that vivid bit of gear, shining out from the thousands of people on that heaving terrace, has stayed with me ever since.

And ever since skinhead days, lads have adopted slightly different attire to go to games. Back in the late sixties it was a near-paramilitary rigour, but by the crumbling mid-seventies the football look reflected the dishevelled despair of the times. This was still a wantonly violent era, and although the petty turf wars of the skinhead era had died down a touch, football grounds, those decaying Edwardian arenas, had become even more routinely and savagely embroiled in what seemed to be a perpetual punch-up.

If you went to football in, say, 1974–5, especially if you stood on one of the ends and chanted and shouted, and, even more specifically, if you travelled to away games, chances are you would see, and be at least indirectly involved in, a fight or a mêlée of some kind. It was part of the point of going. The apologists and the authorities always insisted that it was a tiny minority of football fans who were involved in trouble. They were wrong. There was a hardcore of serious fighters, and everybody knew who they were and pretty much acknowledged and even respected them for it. I recall a lad in Burnt Oak who could recite the names of the 'leaders' of every London firm from Watford to Crystal Palace. He was clearly obsessed, but a very high percentage of young male football fans were running with the pack, shoving from the back and cheering on the nutters. I know I was one. But thankfully I wasn't dressed like one.

My natty new soul-boy gear coupled with my natural cowardice meant that I never really got to sport the garb of the hardcore, hard-nut, mid-seventies football thug. Lucky really. Boots were back, but not the highly polished, highly visible DMs of the skins, these were any old building-site kickers and the more scuffed and dusty the better, as they told people you were indeed a proper manual labourer. You could only really see the boots, though, if the wearer was trying to boot somebody, because his trousers were so baggy. Mostly it was just big, wide flappy old jeans, worn and faded and creased and possibly held up by a plastic belt emblazoned with the club logo, or perhaps with an old silk scarf tied around them.

One variant on saggy denims were what we called Millwall bags, even wider white cotton baggies, first and most memorably worn by the rightly feared Millwall firm. See a pair of those walking up the terracing towards you and you knew trouble was imminent. If the wearer also had on a white butcher's coat, possibly scrawled in biro or felt-tip pen with the symbols and slogans of his team, you were in the company of a true berserker. There were a lot of them about. I once saw a chap thus attired on the Loft, QPR's cramped little home end, pull out a sabre from beneath his butcher's coat and with a rallying cry of CBL (Cold Blow Lane, Millwall's firm) pull scores of similarly clad south-east London lunatics around him. I had legged it through the crowd, under the crash barriers and away from the trouble by the time he'd got to stand B.

The real symbolic terrace garment of the era, though, the one which said everything about the grim, ugly, yet somehow perversely celebratory terrace clothes culture of the time, was the donkey jacket. A dark navy or black, thick woollen, mid-length single-breasted coat, with a yoke of shiny black protective leather-look material across the shoulders. Donkey jackets were traditionally worn by navvies and dustmen and the like. They were handed out by local councils to their manual labourers, usually emblazoned with the initials of the council on the back, so that it was obvious that they were actually the property of the employer, not the wearer. Like prison uniforms. If you were a Tottenham fan, for example, there was no more exalted garment in 1975 than an old donkey jacket with HBC, Haringey Borough Council, stencilled on the back.* It said: I'm the real thing, I'm local, I'm working-class, I'm here straight off a tough old building

---

* There's an amazing book called *Tottenham Boys We Are Here*, self-published in 1978 by Spurs fan and photographer Paul Wombell, which chronicles their mob and this donkey jacket look in all its striking anti-glamour. Originals, which were banned at the time, change hands for a fortune, but reprints are occasionally available. It is perhaps the only real document of an otherwise entirely uncharted style.

site and you don't want me to mess with you. Some even twinned them with an old-style flat cap to double the desired proletarian effect. A donkey jacket, with or without the borough logo, but usually emblazoned with a small metal club badge on the lapel, was the surest sign that you were in the company of a serious chap. On Saturday afternoons they were everywhere. These were serious times and I was swanning around in pink trousers and white socks. No wonder my abiding memory of the mid-seventies is of running away.

One time, though, I didn't run fast enough. I think the guy who hit me round the ear with a half-brick in a street of decaying old terraced houses outside Sheffield United's ground after a tense 0–0 draw was wearing a donkey jacket. Truth be told, I didn't look at him too closely from the moment he pointed out that he didn't much like me. His antipathy was not just because I was a QPR supporter and therefore a soft southern bastard, but because I was dressed as 'a pouf'. I had on a pair of narrow navy straight-legged cords, pointy black winklepicker shoes and a light blue (some might say baby blue) mohair jumper, with my wedge bouncing wildly as he chased me up the street. By the standards of the time he had a point. I was a soul boy for God's sake, this was the radical new look. I had to look like that. The ironic thing, though, is that my assailant was perhaps a soul boy too. Northern soul that is.

Whenever you talk about the mid-seventies soul scene you have to be geographically specific. There's a line which runs through Bedfordshire, roughly through the centre of Leighton Buzzard, dividing Essex from East Anglia, Bristol from Birmingham, South Wales from Liverpool, and most importantly London from Wigan. This stylistic Mason–Dixon split the land in two. Below it London was the centre of the southern soul scene, based on new funk and jazz-funk tunes, with their own swaying dances and a very distinctive style of dress, which soon came to be boiled down to pegs and wedges. Above the line came northern soul, with its alternative capital in the unlikely spot of Wigan, with its massive club the Casino. They had their own whirling dances and a very distinctive style of dress, which soon came to be boiled down to huge baggies and vests. And the two sides, divided by a common love of dressing up and dancing to black American music, did not get on.

The northern scene, with its sew-on patches proclaiming 'Keep the Faith', had actually done just that. The original sixties mods had danced to American soul records in clubs, entire weekends high on uppers, stepping out to stomping tunes on Stax and Sue. By the end of the decade in the south things had mutated and moved on. In the north, though, and specifically in the north-west, from Nottingham up through Stoke to Wigan, in clubs like the Torch, the Twisted Wheel and most notoriously the Casino, a hardcore, up-tempo sixties soul scene had survived. This was very much the mod faith maintained, same drugs, same music, and at first the same clothes, as second-generation modernists in blazers and Sta-Prest provided the original audience for these massive all-day and all-night sessions. Clean clothes, talcum powder and a towel in a bag, a bag of dexys in your pocket. The music was exclusively fast and furious, the more obscure the better. The dances which went with these tunes were incredibly athletic, with their amazing spins and splits and flips and kicks, as kids turned into flailing dervishes and dance floors turned into showdowns. Once Oxford bags had replaced Sta-Prest throughout the land, the northern lads realized that having wide trousers made your spins look even more dramatic as the material ballooned out from centrifugal forces. After that their strides just got wider and wider.

Down in Burnt Oak, Pat Kamara in his lime-green high-waisters was wide, but at some point the insane inflation in trouser width stopped in the south as we turned to pegs instead. In the north country, though, they just kept on going. Skinner jeans, that started big and just got wider and wider, but ended high on the ankle, so you could see socks below, and had side pockets way down low, so you had to stoop to put your hands in them. Even more preposterous were Spencers, a uniquely northern brand sold on market stalls in places like Bradford and Halifax, which had up to twenty buttons on their waistband and flared out in a vast triangle of material, like sails on a wayward ship. Singlets, usually with some sort of piping around the armholes and neck, were all that was needed on top to display spare but athletic frames. If warmth was required, on the journey between clubs perhaps, then out of the everpresent holdalls came skinny ribbed V-neck jumpers, with cropped, truncated bodies due to the height of the strides, and adorned, for some reason, with star motifs.

A pair of voluminous Spencers, a tight star jumper and a thin moustache. These were the signs that you were in the presence of a northern soul boy. Except we never were. We only heard rumours about this very different scene and style they had up there, until poppy, sanitized versions of northern soul records started appearing on *Top of the Pops*, when acts called Wigans Chosen Few and Wigans Ovation leapt about on our screens to their bouncy bouncy tunes. We thought they looked so pikey with their flappy threads, and their corny old records. By contrast me and my coterie of wedge-head mates, just about enough of us to fill a second-hand Cortina, considered ourselves to be the height of metropolitan sophistication.

That must be why that Sheffield United supporter walloped me.

9

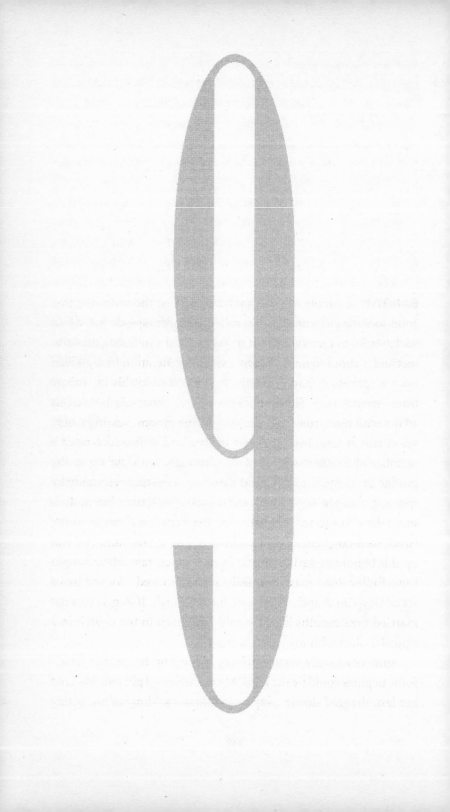

BARRY IS a couple of years married, not for the last time, to a good-looking girl who suits his milieu, using the speedy wits of his background to race away from it. Reggie, still a milkman, has also met and is about to marry Mary, a second-generation Irish colleen from a sprawling family and the one true love of his life (apart from Arsenal FC). The wedding is one of those big boisterous affairs with tears, rows and sing-songs, the groom wearing a blue velvet suit at least two years out of date and sadly redolent of a member of Brotherhood of Man. I, though, am right up to the minute for the year of 1975 and therefore upsetting everybody by sporting a baggy, big-shouldered, shocking electric-blue mohair suit I have borrowed specially for the occasion from a young Greek soul-boy mate of mine, Christos Tolera. His mum had run up this blindingly garish whistle from vivid curtain fabric bought from Ridley Road market in Dalston, and indeed I looked like a set of Day-Glo drapes. They were lucky though. If Reggie had got married nine months later I would have been in the church in a ripped T-shirt with my legs tied together.

Aunt Glad sadly wasn't present, departing before her handsome nephew could tie the knot. My favourite old girl had wheezed her last, dragged slowly away by emphysema, clinging on, sitting in a wheelchair, an oxygen tank and mask by her side, still grasping my hand when she could barely make a sound. She'd been reduced and reduced, and finally she just wasn't there any more. With her went the last real link to the old Elms world. Notting Dale now just a yellowing memory.

Even Burnt Oak was ebbing away for me. With the discovery of up-town clubs and clothes shops, and a whole new gang of similarly style-obsessed mates from all over town, the Oak increasingly became little more than a dormitory. Thankfully school got a little more interesting. In one of the most benign and timely decisions ever taken by the ill-fitting suits who sit in local government, they decided to deliver some girls to Orange Hill and deliver us all from our frustrations. Just as sex was raising its engorged head, my school combined with its sister school, the girls' grammar, and plunged us into a spot of incestuous co-education. The next year's intake would be both mixed and comprehensive, and so full of females of all kinds. We took all kinds of advantage.

My first real girlfriend was a sassy fourth-former called Julie Beresford, who swaggered and swanked her way into my attention, precisely the kind of bird who would never have made it into the old Orange Hill. She came from a council estate, but a different one from mine, which produced problems of its own. One night we were snogging and probing in a back room at a party near her home, when a group of local lads, fired up on a snakebite of cider and testosterone, decided that we both had to pay for this act of fraternization. I was about to be beaten up and Julie tarred and feathered, or whatever was the Edgwareberry equivalent. We had to climb out of a window and leg it, hand in hand, across the estate in the dark and the drizzle with a pack of enraged spotty people chasing us screaming threats.

What burned this particular chase scene on my mind was the fact that we were both improperly attired for such an endeavour. Julie was wearing a big full skirt, all hoopla fifties style; layers of it there were, not an easy obstacle for a fifteen-year-old boy in lust, but even less appropriate for the hundred-yard slippery dash. I was also sporting a hint of fifties, a Hawaiian shirt with parrots and palms. But what really sticks in my mind, and what really slipped on the mud, was my footwear. Plastic sandals. Hoofing it for my life across a sodden council estate with the girl of my wet dreams, a slowly deflating erection still impeding my progress, and I had on a pair of clear, see-through plastic beach sandals over my white socks. Do you have any idea how difficult that is? Do you have any idea how important plastic sandals were?

The pursuing posse can't have tried too hard because we lived to tell the tale and explore our tonsils and tunnels further. I guess it's a sad reflection on me that what I recall most about this whole episode is not really the girl but the gear. But then this gear, and that unlikely footwear in particular, is among the most pivotal of this whole narrative. Plastic sandals marked a major turning-point.

Friday nights at clubs like the Bandwagon got even sweatier as the soul crowd swelled from its original adherents and everybody wanted to be in on the party. The music was pushing deeper and harder, War and Kool and the Gang, Headhunters and Blackbyrds, and the clothes were edging further out. The new focus for this scene was a club way out amid the coastal detritus of Canvey Island in industrial Essex, famously called the Goldmine, where DJ Chris Hill had indeed uncovered a Klondike. He rammed this place on the outer fringes of nowhere, three or four nights a week, with hoards of eager funkateers, bussed in from all over southern England on coaches. The Goldmine, captured in an ebullient TV documentary by Janet Street-Porter, herself an ex Fulham mod, became a shorthand for soul-boy ways.

What they portrayed was a vast heaving crowd of Club 18–30 suburban ravers, almost exclusively white, many wearing specially prepared T-shirts with the names of their particular group or posse emblazoned on the back, some building human pyramids or doing formation dances, most blowing whistles. Others turned up at the Goldmine in fancy dress, done up as Chicago gangsters and their molls or GIs and their brides. Hill, a good DJ and a terrific showman, inserted a little section of swing music, Glenn Miller and Benny Goodman, where these young soul revels suddenly became jump and jive sessions, just like my mum and dad back in the Palais. The Goldmine, which I dutifully went to just the once, with a group of sceptical north London boys, was great fun and a great shame. Its success solidified the idea that the soul scene was all froth and frolics.

But just as this shiny new estuarine orthodoxy emerged, so did a hardcore, out there; an urban reaction to that uniform and that club was already under way. This scene was smaller and darker, more intense, more élitist, focused on clubs and clothes and record shops in central London, where the tunes were tougher, the dancing was harder and the gear was suddenly much odder, daring and difficult. The faces were pulling away, upping the stakes, and the first real sign of that was plastic sandals. I'm fairly certain it was Gerard Mulcahy again. I have a mental image of Gerard standing in the Oak, his feet planted, somehow pulling you down to stare at them. And what they were encased in was a pair of cheap Woolworths Jellies. These were rubberized, moulded plastic sandals, in a not quite translucent material, with a flimsy little plastic strap and buckle. Blimey. It took a little while to get used to that idea, I'll tell you.

Up to that point the prevailing look was slick, up-market, up-town; it was the suave-Marve, Take Six take on fashion. By the standards of this shabby, careworn era, the soul boys were beacons of sartorial grace. But plastic sandals weren't smart, and the clothes which went with them weren't particularly sharp or neat. This new look, which revealed itself over a matter of months, was truly radical and it took me some time to adjust. As a sixteen-year-old, I was a typically conservative teenager, holding zealously on to the style tenets of the moment. I had genuine doubts about this odd new direction, resisting for a few febrile weeks while the sartorial experimentation went further and further out. This soul train was pulling out of the station and I only decided to jump on at the last carriage. I got the gear.

By spring 1976, that legendary summer just heating up, we were on our way to small, hardcore clubs in Soho and Covent Garden. Two or three times a week heading into town, unknowingly beginning the process of trendification which would alter the fortunes of inner London. Dedicated groups of young, overdressed soul-searchers headed through the often deserted streets of an unloved and unlovely city as the daytime temperatures kept climbing and the air became dense with heat and expectation. The Lyceum on a Monday night, Sombreros in Kensington on Thursdays,* the Global Village, where Heaven now is, on Fridays, the 100 Club on Oxford Street on Saturdays. Most notable and most potent of them all was Crackers on Dean Street, on the edge of Soho itself and at the very centre of a world.

Crackers, little more than another dodgy disco to look at, was one of the most influential venues of any year, and by late 1975, into the fabled summer of '76, it was at the core of this still largely secretive inner London scene. We, for me, meant two or three of the boys from Burnt Oak, who had really got into it and wanted to push on. And as soon as you got to places like Crackers, where the best dancers were, the most righteous young black kiddies from Tottenham and Brixton, the best-looking girls, the most knowledgeable music buffs, the most daring dressers, you just knew you were in the inner sanctum.

---

* The licensing laws at the time were so puritanical and arcane that this small gay club had to provide food. So all punters were handed a slice of Mother's Pride and spam as they entered and you could see these sandwiches littered round the dance floor at the end of the night.

Amazingly the hottest session at Crackers was on Friday afternoon, twelve until two-thirty. This was a direct revival of an old sixties tradition, when Friday lunch-hour had been a prime-time slot at Tiles, a late mod club. The idea was that nobody does too much work on Friday afternoons anyway, so who's going to notice if somebody is not at their desk or behind the counter for a couple of hours, and they're dancing or preening instead. Indeed half the crowd at Crackers on Friday were in their work-wear, office suits with the ties tucked in the pocket, hairdressers' smocks or even schoolboy blazers abandoned at the door. Others who somehow had avoided the pressure to work or study, and could make a performance of it, were attired to the nines. A young crowd, predominantly aged from sixteen to twenty-one, gathered from all corners of London to duck into this doorway amid the tacky shops and kiosks of the wrong end of Oxford Street, down the stairs and into a packed, darkened room, pounding with tough, black American tunes and throbbing with that almost tangible confidence which says this is the place to be.

The dance floor itself, a small sprung wooden square, was strictly for dancers, and by that I mean *dancers*. Anyone who ventured on to the square at Crackers had to have steps, and the bottle to produce them under the gaze of the unforgiving throng. Some of the top guys at Crackers are legendary still: Horace, Tommy Mac, Jaba, and the daddy of them all, Clive Clark, a charming black guy who went on to become a professional choreographer, but started out scorching the opposition on Friday afternoons in Dean Street. When these boys were on the floor, a circle would form to give them an amphitheatre in which to perform. They would then pull out moves and steps with a wickedly competitive edge, legs flying like lasers, some new twist or turn eliciting spontaneous applause from the closely watching circle. Unlike northern soul, with its dervish spins and flailing kicks, its wild amphetamine abandon, the southern style was tight and precise: feet made rapid tap movements, knees were bent, hips sashayed, shoulders rolled, heads bobbed. The whole effect was somewhere between boxing and bopping. And if you couldn't cut it, you didn't go anywhere near the floor. Around the square stood contenders and pretenders, who rated their chances but hadn't yet stepped into the ring. Some enrolled themselves at Pineapple, the dance studio which had recently opened up round the corner in Covent Garden. They pulled on sweat-tops and legwarmers to learn moves from ballet, jazz and tap, provoking the craze for dancewear which would result in dodgy thick socks around ankles a few years later. Others simply spent hours on council estate carpets, honing their footwork, their dips and turns while avoiding the furniture.

Behind the dancers, at the bar, at the back, the rest of the club grooved and swayed, perpetual motion. My place, as a young suburban boy, was way at the back, bobbing and watching and noting and loving every super-saturated, hyped-up little minute of it. And then, come half two, the last strains of Dexter Wansel or Charles Earland still swirling round your brain, it was out. Blinking against the light, the sweat freezing on your face as you hit cool air, into the rushing maelstrom of Oxford Street. Leg it over the road to Hanway Street, a charismatic, piss-smelling dogleg alley, where up the stairs of an unmarked doorway was Contempo.

Contempo Records was the epicentre of the London black music world in 1976, entirely contained in a room about eight feet square above a Spanish bar with an Irish name, in a forgotten street. On Friday afternoons it was the only place to buy the records the DJs had been spinning over the road at Crackers. So punters literally queued up the stairs, shouting out names of songs and artists, or listening intently to the sides which had arrived in crates from the States that day, deciding whether that was the one to invest in. Contempo was staffed by two of the coolest black guys in the metropolis, who had mastered an almost Zen-like level of arrogance. They'd spin just thirty seconds of a tune, flipping them on to the decks with an unfailing nonchalance born of repetition and high bred élan, just thirty seconds of a jazz funk intro, for the poor, unwashed (and after a session over the road you could smell the funk), to make their minds up. I worked in a pretty savvy record shop, but that meant nothing in Contempo. It was nothing like Contempo.

One of my most cherished memories is of being first in the queue one Friday afternoon to buy one of only two copies of a new import album, for some horrendous sum. It was *Pressure Sensitive* by Ronnie Laws on Blue Note, the title track going on to become an absolute standard. That night I went to the Bandwagon, proudly cradling that album under my arm at all times, for all to see. Next day I spun it again and again in Soundrax, winding up punters who would have to wait weeks before they could secure a copy. Buying yourself a few weeks' grace was what it was all about.

New sounds were coming thick and fast, but they were being outstripped by new styles. Just as the dancers at places like Crackers were noted and respected figures, so the style-setters were stars. Boys – and despite it being a very mixed crowd it was still pretty much boys who set the sartorial pace – were names as well as faces. Micky Asset, the guy I met at the Bandwagon, was one, very much our local flagbearer, a dude who commanded consideration all over town. The Twins were, as their name might hint, identical twins, a pair of blond doppelgänger wide-boys from Aylesbury. These stick-thin lookalikes looked amazing in most outrageous stuff, cutting a sartorial swathe through London, all financed by flogging hot dogs from a stall in Trafalgar Square. Eric the surfer was another, a great-looking athletic guy who worked in the trendiest clothes shop in town and swathed his tanned body in the most cutting-edge gear, when he wasn't near naked on a board in the breakers, starting the craze for wave-riding in Cornwall. You'd go to clubs to hear those records, watch those dancers, but also to cast your eyes over these guys, to check exactly where things were going.

Things were going weird. Plastic sandals were first accompanied by Smiths jeans. These were the first pair of denims to really break the stranglehold of Levi's, as a street fashion icon. Straight-legged, in this time when every Joe was still proudly sporting flares, they were cut baggy in the arse, hanging down in a builder's crumple, with white stitching picked out on the seam, and a trademark hook of material curving round the hip, from which American construction workers could hang claw hammers. They also made a John Boy Walton dungaree. Smiths were workwear, authentic, blue-collar American workwear, only available in a couple of places and as such highly valued. Even more so were Ball jeans, similar cut to Smiths, but in a kind of light denim and an outrageous thirty quid a throw. They were the biscuit and the bollocks until jungle greens blew everything away.

Today combat trousers or cargo pants, to give them their new politically correct name, are ubiquitous, the casual trouser of choice for an entire generation of kids, Gap standards. When I first saw a pair on Micky Asset back in early '76, I couldn't believe my eyes and I couldn't buy them for want of trying. Jungle greens we called them; a tapered but baggy silhouette, accentuated by the plethora of pockets in odd places, there was no precedent for these strides. At first, before the inevitable copies appeared, they were genuine army surplus, to be acquired only from Lawrence Corner, where I'd bought my beret a few years before. But it wasn't as simple as turning up at this musty cornucopia of a shop behind Euston station, with its famously grumpy staff, and buying a pair, oh no. You had to make repeated, frustrating visits, had to wait for some squaddie the same size as yourself to discard his pants, so that you could proudly saunter along Burnt Oak High Road with your jellies on your feet, your jungle greens hanging down your bum, and maybe a string vest or a white collarless shirt. Dress like ou would either get openly insulted, or some guy would and ask where you got your gear.

iese days we are a pretty sophisticated lot; we get style sup-nents in our Sunday papers, fashion tips on the tele and buy our clothes with designer labels. The high street is rammed with purveyors of decent, affordable clothes in a multiplicity of styles. Not back then. Style in the mainstream British psyche of the 1970s was akin to homosexuality and fancy food, something vaguely distasteful that the French did. And the high street was a desert. Most people looked the same, looked cheap and nasty. If you stepped out of the herd, made any kind of statement, like-minded souls would stop and speak to you at bus stops, or in chemists' or cinema foyers. There were so few kids into this look, and it was so far away from the saggy, soulless mainstream, that an instant bond existed and you would swap phone numbers or arrange to meet solely on the basis of a shared taste in trousering. Waiting for the last tube home one night, after going to see the Crusaders in Victoria, a group of guys came over and asked about my trousers; they were straight-legged brown cords, nothing more remarkable than that, yet still worthy of note back then. We got talking, swapped details, and one of them in particular, Steve, Hounslow Steve, became a fast friend for a couple of years, even though we lived miles apart.

The flip side of this benign bonding experience is that you were far more likely to get abused or even attacked because of your clothes. I was walking back one night to Burnt Oak from Colindale station, as part of an elaborate fare dodge. I'd gone perhaps a quarter of the way when a car slowed down beside me, and the people inside started shouting insults about my clothes and hair. This wasn't exactly a new experience, so I ignored them and walked on. But as they stopped at the lights, one of them jumped out of the car and ran straight at me, aiming a kick, which narrowly missed, but threw him sufficiently off balance for me to have it on my toes and run. He pelted after me for a few hundred yards, hurling abuse, but I'd got sufficiently far away for him to give up. I walked warily on, blood pumping, senses heightened. Then, just as I thought I was clear, the car screeched up alongside again, forcing me to jump over a privet hedge. We began this elaborate game of cat and mouse, which lasted for a horrible amount of time and at one point saw me crawling on my hands and knees through front gardens. Finally they must have got bored and given up. I got home, covered in mud and perspiration, petrified and saddened, but not surprised. You knew all the time that there was a real possibility you'd take a hiding because of the way you dressed.

What I was wearing that night to provoke such a response involved a pair of pointy-toed winklepickers and a cap-sleeve T-shirt. *American Graffiti* had been a big hit at the movies, and there was a James Dean, rockabilly influence, with narrower, straight-legged trousers, plaid American shirts, flecked two-button jackets with wide lapels, and most notably cap-sleeve T-shirts. I didn't really have the arms for this style, which was a tight T-shirt with a very short sleeve to accentuate your musculature, but that certainly didn't stop me. I wore mine with pride, my skinny white arms dangling down like bits of string. Soon, though, they turned up on every market stall, embossed with a series of images on the back in raised fabric. There was a girl in fifties regalia sitting on a globe, there was a shark, there was a Cadillac car. There were a thousand stringy arms hanging from cap sleeves by the time we'd discarded ours.

The main reason cap sleeves crossed over is that Bryan Ferry wore them on the front cover of his first solo album. Street fashion rises up from below, like cream and damp, but certain celebrities can give it a major shove up. Ferry was undeniably cool, one of the very few pop stars who could carry any stylistic conviction, and he was also good at discovering what was going on down there in the damp basement of youth culture. The Roxy Music front man made a few well-documented forays to the funk clubs, and when he combed his hair into a quiff and donned a cap-sleeve T-shirt with a gold chain draped across the neck, it sent the whole look into the mainstream. So we moved on to the next one.

The mid-seventies, between the first explosion of the soul boys and the new spiky heterodoxy of the punks, was the period when the parameters were pushed way back, the wardrobe was tipped up and its contents flung in all directions. It was the time when I started to upset my mother. I was in the sixth form now, part of the small coterie of trendies who stood in stark opposition to the hippies, getting more and more daring in what we wore. The job in Soundrax gave me a few bob and a certain cachet, which served to egg me on. I'd grown to love the thrill of being watched as I strutted down the street in whatever was that week's latest. Even the insults and occasional assaults from neanderthals made me feel like I was clearly doing something right.

One Friday morning I had a stand-up row with my mum as I headed off to school looking smarter than I'd ever been in my life. I had been carefully acquiring the component parts for the dress attire of a 1940s staff sergeant from Milwaukee, scouring army surplus stores until I had compiled the complete kit: sharply creased lovat trousers, brown belt, khaki shirt with epaulettes, forage cap at a hopefully jaunty angle, and what I thought was the real winning touch, a tie tucked into the shirt, in the gap between second and third buttonholes. This was another image Ferry had paraded on *Top of the Pops* and I assumed my mother would approve – after all, she'd admired dashing GIs like every other young London girl during the war. Instead she said, 'You can't go to school like that, they'll send you home.' I kept my fingers crossed.

Uniform rules for sixth-formers were more relaxed, but they still had some, and I was constantly being reminded of them by teachers appalled at my increasingly bizarre apparel. This time, though, the powers that be decided I had gone too far. The minute I ambled into class, my form teacher told me to take off the hat and tie (they'd made me wear a tie for years, so I enjoyed that argument). I refused and was ordered to the headmaster's office. He gave me a severe dressing down for dressing up, and after reminding me that my education was at stake sent me home immediately, in disgrace. It had worked.

It was Friday and I'd figured that if I really provoked them I'd be able to scoot off to Crackers in my swankiest gear rather than do double English literature or whatever was on my timetable. I have rarely felt quite so pleased with myself as when I swanned up Tottenham Court Road, assuming everybody was checking my get-up. When I finally got into Crackers that afternoon, though, no one else was in GI gear, and rather than admiring glances I got a few sniffy looks from the top bods. I'd taken so long trying to get the total look that I'd missed the troopship. After a few anxious moments, I took the tie off and lost the forage cap.

Looks like that would come and go with ever-accelerating alacrity. One time I recall seeing the twins, those identical style icons, dancing around in skiing gear. Not contemporary, bright yellow, synthetic fabric Alpine casual wear – this was strictly vintage. Bobble hats, trousers tucked into beige socks, a biscuit-coloured crewneck jumper with a snowflake motif around the yoke, and an old-time, pull-over waterproof cagoule with a hood, toggles and a single large pocket on the front. One of them even had a rucksack on his back as he did the Latin hustle in the hottest year on record.

Even that *Heroes of Telemark* touch was nothing compared to the first time you saw a boy with a red wedge. The complete vision, starting from the bottom up, looks like this. Flat black lace-up winklepickers, a pair of shiny black, much pleated PVC pegs worn with a studded belt, a tight-fitting T-shirt with an exotic motif, a red bandana tied about the neck cinema-cowboy style, and a pronounced wedge, dyed in a solid, shockingly unnatural shade of pillar-box red. Oh, and pierced ears. Leaning against the bar on a

Monday night at the Lyceum, while the DJ throws out a hardcore jazz tune, this thing, this study in plastic and peroxide, looks both irredeemably odd and undeniably excellent. Then a new number fills the room, funky, crystal bright, hard-edged like it could cut as it flies around. This is dance music, but the voice is ersatz, theatrical and it's singing about Young Americans. Bowie's back. The PVC and pillar-box red boy moves away from the bar and performs a little shuffle, self-contained, self-conscious, aware that people are looking, enjoying people looking. He is definitely not a young American, but then what is he?

What he is, is a customer of Acme Attractions. Eric the surfer, that bronzed Adonis face, works at Acme Attractions, and for ages now, when you were in the queue at Contempo or maybe the toilets at Crackers, you'd hear whispers about this shop on the King's Road which did amazing threads, where the real arch boys shopped. First time I tried to track down Acme Attractions, first time I can ever recall walking down the King's Road, not a part of town I knew or felt comfortable in, I couldn't find it. It was supposed to be in a basement somewhere. The original address was actually Antiquarius, one of those leftover, late-sixties hippy flea markets, where the first incarnation of Acme Attractions was little more than a stall. I never located it at my first attempt, but instead spotted a very odd shop selling Teddy-boy gear, drapes and creepers and bootlace ties and such, further up the King's Road by World's End, and wondered whether we were in for a Ted revival. That shop was Let It Rock, which became Too Fast To Live Too Young To Die, which became Sex, which became the home of the Sex Pistols. But not yet.

By the time I finally found Acme Attractions it was in a proper shop all its own, with a small but revolutionary selection of schmutter, mixing second-hand, or what they called vintage gear, and designer stuff they had made themselves. It also had a jukebox with a ranking selection of sounds chosen by the guy who seemed to run the place, a scarily funky dread called Don Letts, who dressed in a leopardskin waistcoat and a full set of locks, mixing up heavy dub reggae with funk and old clothes with new, in a truly heretical way. There were also two designers, Helen and Jeanette, who were fine-looking, distant and aloof. And for reasons which seemed obvious at the time, they had a complete chromed-up mod scooter parked in the corner. Indeed there was a definite retro feel to the place, with lots of forties, fifties and sixties bits, old demob suits, scarlet swinging London hipsters, James Dean leather jackets, put together so that it felt terrifyingly modern, way out, confrontational, new.

I stood around in the shop for ages absorbing the considerable attitude, looking at the few punters who came in, studying those estimable shop assistants and that magnetic gear. What I really wanted was a royal blue mohair jumper, a hirsute, lustrous V-neck creation which positively exuded Acme swagger. Mohair jumpers were next in line for iconic garment status, but that day I had neither the wherewithal nor the belief to get one. Playing safe, I bought another pair of plastic sandals, albeit in some bright, fluorescent colour, heading back to Burnt Oak a little singed by the experience.

The first thing I did after my visit to Acme Attractions in early 1976 was get my ear pierced. For some reason I had it done on a market stall in Chapel Street, Islington, hard by the pie and mash shop, and I recall the rather mystified girl saying that mine was only the third male lobe she'd ever punctured and the other two were an item. When I got home with a sleeper in my left ear I had to have that probably overdue conversation with my mum about her son's sexuality. It took some time to assure her that having my ear pierced did not mean I was gay. Even longer to argue that it wouldn't be such a bad thing if I was.

By the time I had a hole in my ear and a pair of pink winklepickers in my wardrobe, I was down to a couple of mates from Burnt Oak and about the same from school. There was no aggression against me on home turf, but most kids simply weren't prepared to go that far, and what you wore defined you so clearly that it predicated who your close friends were. I was starting to get to know like-minded, similarly attired lads from all over London and I felt like Jack the Lad in the process. One of the truly liberating aspects of the scene I was now moving in was the way that gay guys were just an accepted part of the fabric. Here was an almost exclusively working-class milieu, full of tough urban kids of every colour, many of them faces on the football terraces as well as on the dance floor, and yet you just knew that some of the best dancers and nattiest dressers fancied each other, almost as much as they fancied themselves. It wasn't openly gay, but it could be pretty camp and in its way, in its time, remarkably tolerant. Those who couldn't tolerate that drifted away.

For me, just as I'd enjoyed the confusion spread by my long hair in hospital, four or five years before, so I loved the ambivalence of walking round in bright orange plastic sandals, with a big chunky wedge and a pierced ear. Much of the daytime that sweltering summer, though, I had very little on, save a pair of swimming trunks and a practised pout. It was blisteringly hot day after day, for months on end, standing pipes in the streets because of the water shortage, so our time was spent at lidos. These crumbling old 1930s outdoor pools still fringed London then, and were packed with city kids trying to enjoy the heat. Over at Finchley Lido there was even a coterie of very cool bods who took primitive ghetto-blasters and held urban beach parties. I tried to figure out how I could look trendy, send out signals, in a pair of swimming trunks, so I tried wearing white socks with my Speedos, as a sign of soul-boy allegiance. Regrets, I have a few.

Musically I was also exploring other areas. Throughout my soul phase I had still gone to gigs with mates from school, furtively turning my back on the clubs for a night. Suddenly there was a slew of exciting new bands playing in grotty boozers. Some of them like Kokomo, a large vocal group full of old jazzers, covering Bobby Womack tunes, were actually acceptable for a soul fan to like. Others though, like Kilburn and the High Roads, a bunch of swaggering, theatrical cripples led by the magnificent Ian Dury, or the maniacally monotone Dr Feelgood, deranged St Vitus's dance sufferers from Southend, were far too raw, too down and dirty, for the clubbers. The old schizophrenia was at work. I was Burnt Oak boy in the clubs, Orange Hill at gigs. The grammar school boys liked a bit of rough, while the real street kids preferred the polished plush of the clubs.

This tension, this pull and push, between a born-again, rocking live gig scene and a radically dressed-up club scene, wasn't just something experienced by me. It was as if a disparate set of desires and cultures were on a collision course, and two worlds, which had been forever separate, were about to crash. We were on the brink. I took to buying the *NME*, which up to that point had been a magazine I hated, because it avowedly hated soul music. But every week there was tell of some boiling new band, some angry ruffians with stolen guitars and well-honed sneers, who were shaking it all up. The Hammersmith Gorillas, Eddie and the Hot Rods, young, passionate exponents of steamy, three-minute r'n'r. We even had our own local legends: Bazooka Joe, a constantly evolving beat combo which included Danny Stern's brother Peter, a certain Adam Ant, and for a few rehearsals even Mick Jones, later of the Clash.

To add to the excitement and tangible sense of something imminent, new looks, each further and further out, were coming out of the clubs. Crazy colour hair had become big, not just pillar-box red, but blue and orange, or bleached brilliant white. The scene-makers started teasing their wedges out into quiffs and spikes. I wasn't prepared to lose my precious wedge, and didn't yet have the bottle to reach for a bottle of peroxide. I was still a schoolboy living at home. But I was anxious to try this new bright, white style. Somebody told me of a neat little temporary lightening technique, which involved tipping most of the contents of a tin of talcum powder on to your head. This was supposed to make your hair lustrous white for the night, but in fact just made me cough furiously while looking like I had chronic dandruff. Another supposedly good idea was to squeeze a lemon on to your bonce and then let it bleach naturally in the sun, for that streaked, healthy look, à la Eric the Surfer from Acme. I tried that too. One afternoon at Mill Hill baths, I took along a lemon, cut it in half and squeezed it over my head, exposing my locks to the scorching sun. My ginger hair did indeed develop lighter streaks. Unfortunately I forgot to wipe the lemon juice off my forehead and the citric acid took off a complete layer of skin, leaving me with nasty sunburn. God knows I tried.

But it was hard trying to keep up with all the different fashions now tumbling on top of each other, each provocative new twist provoking the next one. The barriers had been breached and there seemed to be no bounds. By late summer '76, kids dancing in soul clubs were way beyond. I had opted for a neo beat-boom look, tab-collar shirt, skinny tie, V-neck sweater over narrow, sharply creased trousers. Fetish wear had come in, overtly sexual, bondage, rubber and plastic, all zips and chains, exposed erogenous zones and constricted flesh. It was fairly commonplace to see a boy dancing away with a pierced nose, red plastic strides, a tight rubber top, personalized with a slash or a scrawl, his peroxide hair dripping sweat, which is running into his make-up. Something new, some hybrid, some warped mutation was undoubtedly crawling out.

Then one night, maybe September 1976, I went out with Micky Asset and a couple of other lads to a tiny subterranean den called Louise's, a lesbian cellar in Poland Street, Soho, named after its Sapphic host. None of the guys I went with were technically lesbians, and in fact I didn't think I'd ever seen a girl's girl, but word was out that this place was in. Despite the sartorial tumult of the preceding months, I still wasn't prepared for what I saw inside.

When you first walk into a nightclub, especially if it's new to you, it always takes a while for your eyes to tune in to the half-light, the smoke and the haze; still, dark corners, leaping flashes. You're blinded for a second or two, blinking to pull focus, trying to home in on something, get your range. When I first walked in here, I didn't so much blink as freeze, as if spiked by some icy, time-warping drug which disorientates and yet snaps you into intense concentration, a slack-jawed, slow-motion drug which floats you around, robbing you of speech, yet burning images on to your consciousness. Fuck. I was a boy just turned seventeen, a kid still too scared of his mum's reactions to dye his hair, a good boy studying for his A levels at a nice suburban grammar school – and it felt like I'd walked into Sodom. It was exhibitionist heaven. Heaven is a scary place.

I don't know who was actually present that night, but I can run down some of the likely candidates. Siouxsie Sioux and Steve Severin, soon to be from the Banshees; Siouxsie with her peephole bra and stilettos, Severin all starched gothic glamour. Catwoman with her cartoon pointy hair and dog-collar, a *Marvel* comic matron. The so pretty boys, Billy Idol and Adam Ant, pouting and preening. The guitarist Marco Pirroni, stout, not so good-looking but seriously clothes-obsessed. Jordan, the statuesque assistant from McLaren's shop now called Sex, who starred in Derek Jarman's movie *Jubilee*, wore a beehive on her head, drew geometric shapes on her face and exposed her buttocks. Michael Collins, her co-Sex-worker with a striped mohair and multiple rings in his ears. Johnny Rotten and his muckers, John Ritchie (Sid Vicious) and John Wardle (Jah Wobble), Dickensian scruffs straight from Snow Hill. The notorious nocturnal invert Philip Salon, camping it up disgracefully in rubber. A beautiful boy called

Berlin, dark and elegant, always silent. Glen Matlock, who also worked in Sex and always looked like the art school mod he was, and his fellow Pistols Steve Jones and Paul Cook, all hooligan grins and leather strides.

It was the Sex Pistols and their retinue, the coterie who became known as the Bromley contingent, only a few of whom actually hailed from that bit of outer London, but all of whom shopped in that King's Road Teddy-boy emporium, which now sold fetish gear. A couple of them, Cook and Jones, actually came from Shepherd's Bush, from precisely the area my family had left a few years before. And to my deep amaze there were also a few painted faces from even closer to home.

In one corner of this tiny room swamped in vivid darkness and incandescent with decadence was a little Burnt Oak squad. Steve Marshall, a boy I'd actually been in the same year with at Goldbeaters Junior Mixed Infants, a nice boy who occasionally went out, but up until now had largely been seen running errands for his mum. Here he was in the most terrifyingly trendy club in London, dressed in what appeared to be one of his mum's dresses, only ripped up, and worn with big boots with studs on. By him in the corner was a staggeringly beautiful, although dangerously young girl known as little Debbie, because she was, little that is, under five foot, maybe still under fifteen, with brilliant white peroxide hair cut into a spiky crop, black eye make-up, full bondage gear draped around her tiny frame and a school tie around her neck to accentuate her illegality. Last time I'd seen Debbie she'd been bouncing through the estate in a flared fifties Teddy-girl dress looking every inch the Sandra Dee. Now she looked like the star of an arty German porn film.

And there alongside her, perhaps predictably, but still shockingly, was Jean Reddy. My old skinhead friend had coloured her still short hair gunmetal blue, and was sporting trousers with blue plastic pockets with zips in, which showed her bum, and a T-shirt with a photoprint of a pair of tits on the chest. She was wrapped around a lithe, spiky-haired beauty in a spider's-web mohair jumper, a collection of hairy holes with nothing else underneath. Jean was smiling the smile of the happily damned.

Welcome to punk rock.

10

PUNK WAS a trouser revolution. For all the crashing glory and rabble-rousing bile of the songs, it was the clothes that really pulled so many pent-up kids in from different cultural corners and pushed the scene to such inflammatory prominence. Before anybody picked up a guitar or sat behind a drumkit, before a single staccato note was played, they strolled into a clothes shop and pulled on a pair of strides with the legs tied together, or stuck a safety-pin into a ripped-up T-shirt with a slogan scrawled across it. Punk was born out of the frantically bubbling stylistic stew of the mid-seventies, one of many startling assemblages which emerged at the same time, and one which struck a chiming chord before any chords were played. The look came first.

It was shortly after that scarifying night at Louise's, when I saw Steve Marshall, his eyebrows completely shaved off, proudly walking through Burnt Oak wearing a T-shirt emblazoned with a pair of cowboys with their ample dicks hanging out, that I first heard the name the Sex Pistols. He said, 'You've got to come and see this band, they're fucking terrible, but somehow they're fucking brilliant.' I remember the words exactly because they were exactly right. Much of the audience at early punk gigs was made up of people whose musical taste, like mine, was towards well-made, well-played funk ecords and a bit of highly polished glam dance from Bowie and Roxy. Most of them rarely went to see bands at all, and some of them weren't particularly into music. They were drawn to the Sex Pistols and the Clash and all the rest of the emerging gang by the way they looked and the attitude their attire embodied. It was the almost narcotic pull of their shocking glamour which drew you in. The barbaric howl took some time to tune into.

I also remember Steve Marshall's words with deep regret, because I didn't take up his offer to go and see the Pistols at Middlesex Poly in Hendon, one of their earliest gigs and a short bus ride from Burnt Oak. In fact I've lied many times and told people I was there, invented elaborate stories about seeing Jordan or Siouxsie spraying Anarchy on the walls of the gents' toilets while Lydon sneered his way through a butchered version of 'My Generation'. They did do it. I didn't see it. But I'm not the only person who's fibbed about seeing the Pistols in the early days. You could fill Wembley with the number of bods who claim to have been at St Martin's art school, the El Paradiso strip-club or even the Screen on the Green, whereas in fact the early audience for the Sex Pistols, for the as yet undubbed 'punk' thing, was made up of no more than a couple of hundred people and an even smaller inner coterie of scene-makers. It's a textbook example of what can happen if a group of like-minded souls get together, bonded in opposition to the mainstream. Especially if they are wearing bondage. The punk rock cultural *coup d'état* was the equivalent of Castro and the crew of the *Granma*. This was a putsch led by a small, hardened band of hairdressers and shop assistants.

I can't remember exactly why I didn't go to see the Sex Pistols with Steve Marshall. I had a new girlfriend from school, with whom I was madly in what felt like love, and she frowned upon my increasingly 'weird gear'. Perhaps she wanted to go to the pictures instead. Perhaps I was frightened. Certainly I'd been compelled, by seeing the Bromley contingent and Jean Reddy in their finery, to seek out Sex, but it took me a couple of weeks to pluck up the courage to do even that. Finally I headed on my own, as if facing some stern test, to World's End, where that old Rock and Roll shop had been. The latest incarnation of Malcolm McLaren and Vivienne Westwood's retail adventure was an altogether more imposing emporium; it was just about the weirdest, scariest place I'd ever seen.

The windows were all blacked out, covered with a grill because they were constantly getting smashed, and a huge pink, rubberized sign simply saying SEX hung above the place. I remember standing outside for ages, trying to build up the courage to go in. There was a phone box, one of the old-fashioned red ones, right by the shop, and I hid in there for a bit, trying to see if anybody I recognized went in, so I would feel more comfortable. I wasn't so much scared of the clothes, it was more that I was terrified of appearing like a witless suburban soul boy who'd come to have a peek, which is of course exactly what I was. I thought that if one of the people I knew from the clubs, no matter how vaguely, went in, then I could stroll in, say hello to them and it would be obvious that I was part of the scene, down by law.

Even though I was dressed very oddly by conventional standards – earring, big chunky wedge, narrow trousers, winklepickers and, despite the heat, the mohair jumper I'd finally got round to buying – I knew that this was the next level up, and I didn't want to look like a clumsy Sex virgin. I must have waited for about half an hour in that phone box. The only person I saw go into the shop was a straight goer, a businessman obviously out to buy some accoutrements for his hobby. Finally I decided to brazen it out, but the minute I entered the place, all black leather drapes and rubber curtains, wild slogans scrawled across the walls, dark mysterious areas and blinding neon, with these dirty, taboo clothes everywhere, I shrank, my head sinking into my shoulders as I tried to blend in with the blood-red carpet.

I mooched as invisibly as possible, peeked around a bit, saw Jordan, the big beehived manageress, a B-Movie sci-fi fetish mistress, and got even more intimidated. Little Debbie, the diminutive Burnt Oak girl, was there, looking fantastic in fishnet stockings and a bondage parachute top, absolute Sex, yet absolutely aloof. Rather than making it better that I'd seen somebody I sort of knew a bit, it made it worse. Debbie was a couple of years younger than me and from the same estate, yet she was bang in the centre of all this, a real face. I felt a little ashamed that I'd missed the boat. It was maybe September 1976 and I was worried in case it was too late to become a punk.

I also fell instantly in love. In one corner, on a plinth, was a pair of boots, a pair of black bondage boots: ankle-high, pointed, with thick rubber soles, big fold-over tongues, and metal plates and spikes sticking up from the uppers. This was the most extraordinary, the most desirable piece of footwear I'd seen since I'd first bought a pair of fragrant brogues in Kilburn half a dozen years before. Despite convincing myself I had missed the oily punk speedboat, I also knew somehow that pretty soon I'd possess a pair of those boots. They were thirty odd quid, which was absolutely horrific. Even T-shirts in Sex were fifteen pounds or more. I was used to paying three or four quid at most for a shirt. This was the first time I'd really come up against full-price designer wear, and I knew I'd have to go there.

Where I went first was to get my other ear pierced. It was in a jeweller's on the King's Road, and I felt I was making a suitably grandiose statement, an offering to this new sect, in its holy land. Originally it was my left ear which wore a ring, but having another one put in the right was more than doubly provocative. In 1976, it was generally accepted that having your right ear pierced was a signal, a deliberate advertisement of the fact that you were gay and open for trade. It was also a red rag to the neanderthals.

The King's Road on a Saturday at that time was a chemistry lab of looks. Soul boys in their bright pegs and plastic sandals. Acme-fed sixties revivalists, all thin leather ties and Chelsea boots. Kids in demob suits and trilbys, Bowie boys, fifties Americana freaks shopping at Johnson's in Ken Market for long fleck suits or leather jackets, and the deeply trendy Sex bondage crowd with their situationist slogans and straps everywhere. There was also a small but stern gang of neo Teddy boys. They too had originally bought their clothes from Malcolm McLaren and Vivienne Westwood, but didn't much like these odd interlopers, theatrically curling their lips at the assorted nonces and nancies. This tribal gathering was a fluid affair, with little pockets of each sect strolling around staring and stealing, somewhere between the Italian *passagiato* and a do-it-yourself catwalk show, but exclusively for teenage fashion victims. And apart from the Teds, who saw themselves as keepers of a true flame, there was a high degree of sartorial interaction.

I'd go to the King's Road on Saturdays with a couple of mates from north London and just float from shop to shop, not buying anything much, window-shopping, posing, ogling, secretly saving up for those boots from Sex. It was a more glamorous and highly charged version of 'doing the rounds', our old Burnt Oak ritual, only now we were in the company of cliques from all over town and further afield. There was a gang who came down from Birmingham every week, heavily into the New York Dolls, all teetering glam, slap and silk. The most startling mob, though, were a dozen or so lads from South Wales, tough valley boys from the Rhondda who would get the first coach up to London on Saturday morning and saunter up and down the King's Road, making people's jaws drop. Chains hanging from their noses, hair dyed and plastered over made-up faces, leather strides, jackboots, Nazi regalia, Communist insignia, anything to shock. These lads were further out than the most outré Londoners, yet even the Teddy boys would leave them well alone. I met a couple, one called Chris Sullivan, a beefy but poetic lad the same age as myself from Merthyr, who I hit it off with immediately, and Steve Harrington, later to be known by his *nom de punk*, Steve Strange.

By late summer '76, but before the Sex Pistols badmouthed Bill Grundy on prime-time TV and punk rock was really unleashed, you could sense the impending onset of something, feel the distant rumble. But at this stage, with a dozen different looks and styles clashing and competing every Saturday up and down the King's Road, quite what it was, what shape it would take and most importantly what it would wear, nobody knew.

The portentous fashion parade which took place every weekend on the King's Road throughout 1976, where largely ritualized clashes started to occur between Teddy boys and the newly named punks, had a lot in common with another London extravaganza, which ended in considerably more serious trouble that steamy summer. August 1976 was the first time I went to the Notting Hill carnival. I'd gone with a couple of guys from Burnt Oak, as much as anything because I wanted to explore the old neighbourhood, to see what had become of Notting Dale. It was just at the point where this part of west London was becoming cool, and the carnival was breaking out of the strict confines of the Caribbean community. I wanted to see what the fuss was all about.

You could smell the tension. My aim was to run around seeking out memories, leap about to a bit of reggae and try jerk chicken and maybe a spliff. But from the moment we got off the bus and walked through the solid police cordon to the front line, the pressure bearing down on you was almost physical. We were outsiders in every way, a point made by a charming gentleman in blue serge, with a riot shield and baton, who first sneered at my clothes and then asked me why I wanted to be here with 'all the niggers'. The boys milling round the boom-boom sound systems smoking weed, drinking Dragon stout, throwing languorous shapes, were not much more welcoming, but they were cool.

We weren't alone as outsiders. There was a fair contingent of London's fashion crowd, the proto-punks, trying and failing to fit in. For a while we mingled, grooved uneasily, but as the day became dark, so small gangs of 'sticks men' moved in – raiding parties of thieves and pickpockets, darting among the crowds. Then came the police swinging those batons indiscriminately, breaking heads. War in Babylon.

It went off big time, massed battles up and down Ladbroke Grove and little private skirmishes in every side street, to a soundtrack of biblical roots and culture reggae. The police were like a fury unleashed, snarling and enjoying themselves, the heirs of those 'Keep Britain White' Teddy boys and their ethnic hatred. The local rudies, sons and cousins of those first swaggering chaps in the Roger Mayne pictures, were going to give as good as they got, going to make a point after all those put-upon years. I didn't stick around long enough to see it all, but the fighting raged and raged. This was a clash which would not end here. The torrent of energy and desire and frustration which became punk was part of the same faultline, the same subterranean welling up, which exploded through the streets of carnival 1976. A new England forged from fury.

A picture from the '76 carnival riots graced the cover of the first Clash album when it finally emerged a year or so later. The Clash were the first punk band I actually went to see, and I fell. The combination of their perfectly realized urban warrior image, courtesy of Paul Simenon, and their diamond-crushing two-minute vignettes of romantic rebel defiance, shouts of white riot, from Jones and Strummer sent me weak at the teenage knees. It was a while before I then saw the Pistols, and although they were ravishingly right, perhaps the best-looking band of all time, it was guttersnipe vaudeville. If I had to choose, I was a Clash boy but, whichever way, I didn't have to decide which side. I was a punk.

The whole nation was about to tumble, or at least that's the way it looks now in retrospect, as punk rock would leap out from its hiding places, storm down from the hills and conquer the bastions of cultural conservatism, freeing the people to pogo in the streets. Actually it wasn't anything like that. For the first nine months or so it was still a dicey business being associated with this new craze. The music press, still staffed by old hippies who hadn't yet taken their flared strides in, were dismissive of these overdressed garage bands and their oily followers. The screaming tabloids, enjoying a nice juicy moral panic, egged on their readers to abuse pimply youths who dared to look different. We had Teddy boys chasing us up the King's Road, and the yeomen of England insulting us on a daily basis. Punks were famed for gobbing, but I was spat at more than once by people who looked like bus drivers. We were refused service, not just in pubs, which was normal for all of us, but in bakers and chemists. We were outcasts, we were news. We loved it.

Punk was a culmination of years of a largely working-class, organic, self-regulating, clothes-obsessed counter-culture. It was not a collective, intellectualized response in the way hippy had been, but a hedonistic, narcissistic one, from kids who had found a way to enliven their lives in a stale and gloomy England. By the end of 1976, the most tumultuous, the most preposterous, the most consistently creative year in this entire tale, it finally felt like we were throwing off the shackles of that horrid, hide-bound land. Punk was a culmination, it was the crescendo at the end of the pyrotechnics display. This place was convulsing with excitement, alive with creativity, like just maybe that dreary bloody war was finally over.

After my débâcle in Sex I'd consciously reactivated my old friendship with Jean Reddy. Jean still lived at home with her mum on the Watling Estate, but had left school and joined the in-crowd. She was openly gay, the first person of either sex I knew to come out, and hanging out with her and her glamorous girlfriend felt fantastically daring and thrilling. I hung lapdog-like round those two, for the reflected kudos and credit that might bring. I also got to wear her cast-offs. As a cheap way in to the sanctified Sex look, I bought some of Jean's old gear, including her jeans, the ones with blue plastic pockets and zips in the bum, and a couple of the very early Seditionaries T-shirts. Just enough to make it look like I'd been there from the very beginning. I also tried my hand at do-it-yourself couture.

Not until you've ruined your mum's kitchen table and a couple of perfectly decent T-shirts, and narrowly avoided blinding your dog, while trying to spray-stencil 'Under Heavy Manners' or some such Clash-inspired logo do you realize how difficult it is to make your own clothes. I know the punk look was supposed to be ragged and ripped, but you still had to look just so. In its way Punk was just as demanding and precise, just as precious about clothes as the most elegant mods or the most authoritarian skinheads. Thankfully Graham Smith, my arty mate from school who had dived right into the fray alongside me, was actually good at this sort of thing. He mastered silk-screen printing and ran off a load of excellent T-shirts bearing the very *de jour* legend 'We are all prostitutes.' It was a steal from a Subway Sect song, a band we'd adopted after seeing them support the Clash at a disused fleapit cinema in Harlesden.

As well as supposedly studying for our A levels, Graham and I were going out at least twice a week, often more, to gigs all around town: Generation X at a pub in Edmonton, the Damned at a college in Uxbridge, the Nashville Rooms in Kensington, the Roundhouse in Chalk Farm. HQ, though, was the Roxy, in a deserted Covent Garden, a post-floral wasteland enlivened only by this one wonderfully grungy dive. Don Letts, the leopardskin Rasta behind Acme Attractions, was the DJ, mixing the handful of punk records with some deep-down dub selections, an unlikely musical alliance which eventually led to that whole punky reggae party. Hearing reggae for me was reassuring. The first record I bought had come from Jamaica, and it brought home the fact that punk, despite its apparent nihilism and its theatrical rejection of everything which had gone before, was actually in the tradition. This was important to me, as I'd just carried out a major volte-face, from soul boy to punk rocker, as had half the people in places like the Roxy. I suspect that after a hard night getting your ears pounded by the Vibrators, or some such bunch of second-rate noise rockers, quite a few went back home and secretly soothed their jagged souls with a bit of cooling soul. Officially now, though, there was no turning back.

The clearest sign of making the great leap was buying a leather biker's jacket. I got mine from a proper biker's shop too, Lewis Leathers in Great Portland Street, where smudged petrol-breathers parked their Kawasakis outside and talked in that private language of twin carburettors and tons. It was the classic Marlon Brando in *The Wild Ones* leather, cross-over zip, epaulettes, buckle front, and it was the single garment which would carry me most consistently through the next couple of years. When I first pulled it on, first smelt and felt the hide, I experienced a guilty frisson. At heart I've always known that I'm a mod, and here was I donning the most emblematic of all rockers' attire. Punk was like that. Punk made me do it.

Punk never made me cut my hair though. Although spikes were definitely the order of the day, and although the scene would all too rapidly fall into a rather dreary regimentation, for the first few breathless months, before the rules were established, punk was truly anarchic, and the wedge was part of my own take. I exaggerated its lines, letting the fringe fall further over one eye, as it became more virulently asymmetric. Others had their own accommodations to make. This was when I saw what was clearly an old hippy in a pair of flares with a bit of string tied round the legs to make them straight, in an unknowing twist on the Victorian street Arab style.

Finally I saved up enough money to walk into Sex and walk out with my legs tied together. The rebel line has always been that you didn't buy clothes from Sex, you stole clothes from Sex. I'm sure some did, and I'm sure Vivienne turned a blind eye if one of her chosen children wanted to help themselves to a new bit of kit. But I was no tea-leaf, and I wasn't anywhere near close enough to the inner sanctum to get any kind of dispensation. So I saved hard and bought a bondage suit, plain black, zips up the legs, a towelling nappy clipped on behind, the cross strap allowing you just enough room to swagger, the top a baffling conundrum of straps and loops and rubber buttons. This was actually a beautifully made, high-fashion garment designed by the most exalted couturier this country had produced in decades. Punk, for all its street tough propaganda, was as much salon style as gutter glamour. And beneath this actually rather elegant whistle, a genuine twentieth-century design classic, was a pair of those boots. Clunking, powerful things, the metal studs gleaming out, the intent clear for all to see. Vivienne said that she made 'clothes for heroes', and bowling out of Sex in my full bondage for the first time, blinking into the glare of the King's Road, fronting it for all to see, I was fully aware of the transformative power of schmutter. Dressed like this you had to keep your head high and shoulders back, you had to step out. Dressed like this you felt ennobled, empowered. It's why warriors wear uniforms, why Scotsmen wear skirts. It's what my brother Barry must have felt when he first got that suit more than a decade before.

Somehow during all this turmoil I filled out UCCA forms and then took exams and passed. It's a cliché now to bang on about how you were the first member of your family ever to be university-educated, but I was. I was also the first member of my family to wear a dog-collar and it happened at about the same time. The former made my mum very happy. The latter made me a slightly odd soul at the LSE. I knew the London School of Economics was supposedly a hotbed of left-wing radicalism, which suited me perfectly, and I knew the London School of Economics was in London, which was absolutely essential. There was no way I'd even contemplate leaving my home town just at the point when it was becoming really exciting and QPR finally had a decent side. Three years just over the road from the Roxy learning about perpetual revolution felt just about right. Danny Stern, my ebullient school partner to gigs, was also bound for the LSE, so I wouldn't be alone, while Graham Smith, now my best punk friend and designer of splendid T-shirts, was just up the road at art school.

I walked into university on my first day in 1977, up the steps of the main entrance, past the Maoists and the Trots and the various far-left lunatics proffering tracts and prophesying the imminent collapse of capitalism. I was wearing a fairly subdued version of the current uniform: Dr Martens, Levi's, a mohair jumper and a biker jacket adorned with the logo 'Culture', my favourite reggae band. I looked round to see if there were any other similarly attired souls whom I could latch on to, but everybody else seemed to look like a refugee from 1971, long hippy hair, flares, even the occasional attempt at a beard. Punk clearly hadn't made it as far as this hotbed of rebellion.

On the noticeboard, among the advertisements for the rugby club and the swimming team and the alphabetti spaghetti of political parties, the WRP, the SWP, the IMG, was a sign which read 'Punk Rock is Fascist', and announced that there would be a debate on this motion in the student union, two days hence. This I thought, is going to be fun.

11

WE WERE OFF to see the Clash at the seaside. They were playing in Hastings, part of the White Riot tour, which took them from 1977 into 1978. I say we, because I was travelling with the gang of mates I'd quickly acquired at the LSE, and we were part of a larger gathering of London punks heading south for the gig. We went to every Clash performance within striking distance of town, sometimes hitching, occasionally staying overnight, crashing on someone's floor, maybe getting a lift back with the band, proudly calling them Joe and Paul and Mick. We were teen groupies, I guess, but because of the ethos of the times and the ethics of the band, it felt like we were all in this together.

Our crew had all been at the epochal rainbow gig of course, where the sheer, wanton energy of the event had turned into a mini white riot and pretty near lifted the ornate art deco roof off the house. Not in my head, but in my muscles and in my nerve endings, I can still feel the gut rush of people ripping up seats and sending them crashing and flying through the air, to that joyous machine-gun rattle. The noise and the physicality and the sweet force of abandon, of absolutely letting rip. It must have been like that for my cousin and his Teddy-boy mates back in the hide-bound fifties, tearing up seats to *Rock Around the Clock* for the sheer, senseless hell of it. As a grown man, with all the censorious reserve of age, it is hard to imagine wanting to kick and crash a chair in a mix of excitement and rage and pleasure, but we did. Maybe it was all the crap, all the built-up corrugated iron, sugar shortage, early closing crap. Maybe it was just fun.

The first friend I made at the LSE was on that first day. I was standing alone and defiantly posing in the bar, when this guy came up and asked if I knew when the Clash were playing next. He was a boy up from the country called Iain Hill. He was clearly a bumpkin, but he was a fellow QPR fan, so I treated him gently. The next one was a lad who I stalked. Time and again I saw this figure, usually heading resolutely for the library, wearing the same mohair jumper as myself. After trailing him for a while I eventually cornered this well-dressed, if diligent soul and suggested we sort this out. We couldn't go around wearing the same sweater, we'd have to work out some sort of rota. He was Graham Ball, a west London boy who came complete with his own boisterous mob of hardcore, ex-soul-boy Clash fans from Ealing. Graham was contemplating leaving university at that point because he felt so isolated from all the flared hippies and despaired of ever making like-minded and attired friends. I talked him into staying and he ended up with a fine First.

The third of the LSE musketeers was Steve Dagger. He arrived a little later, after some chicanery involving switching courses, and was obviously a fellow sartorial traveller. Dagger was the son of a print union father of chapel, out of Holborn, just around the corner from college. Steve carried with him a coterie of likely lads from the Angel in Islington, Arsenal boys who were all veterans of seeing the Pistols at the Screen on the Green, their local cinema. Dagger himself was a Spurs fan with unswerving soul-boy tendencies, including a bottle-blond wedge, which he still wears to this day.

As well as the gang of fellow first years at the LSE, I'd also become fast with a coterie of lads from outside college. The O'Donnell brothers, Jimmy and Ollie, second-generation Irish roustabouts from a clan up in Archway, had grown up around Johnny Lydon and followed the Pistols from the very off. Now they were the most unlikely and laddish hairdressers, working at Smile, the salon in Knightsbridge where I'd first had a wedge cut. Ollie attended to my barnet and had the most voluble gob in London, while Jimmy had the best biker's jacket. Both were absolutely fearless when it came to clothes. Chris Sullivan, that valley boy I met on the King's Road, had first come up to London in search of clothes as a fourteen-year-old, and had now settled here. Built like a prop forward, but studying fashion at St Martin's, he was the most clothes-obsessed character I'd ever met. Within a few weeks he'd moved in with me and my mum, bringing with him his mountainous collection of second-hand schmutter, everything from spats to cowboy hats, gaucho pants to dinner jackets, puttees to cummerbunds, all kept in scores of black bin-liners.

Finally there was even a girl in the gang. Melissa Caplan, a Golders Green lass, studying at the same art school as Graham Smith; she was an absolute provocation, hair dyed flame-red and pulled into spikes, face painted like a podgy Mondrian, space warrior clothes she'd run up on her mum's sewing machine. Melissa would flaunt past the good burghers and the side-lock-wearers of her deeply conservative Jewish neighbourhood without a flinch. She was brave and inspiring, and her large, irrepressibly loud mum always had good food in the fridge late at night. Bar Graham Smith, who now had trendy art student status, I'd all but jettisoned my old mates. Burnt Oak boys weren't good enough for me any more.

Mellisa Caplan wasn't Clash-bound, nor was Sullivan. They were both too art student for sweaty rock'n'roll, but about twenty of us had taken a train to the seaside and were careening out of the station in our best 'Cockney boys we are here' regalia. There was a police escort waiting for us, well, a couple of local bobbies, about the same age as ourselves. They told us they'd had reports that we were coming, and had been dispatched to make sure we didn't rip it up. 'We don't want you fighting with the local punks,' said one of these young old bill. There was a general murmur of incomprehension from within our ranks; why would we want to do that? He looked us up and down, staring intently at our garb. 'You Teddy boys versus the punk rockers, we've heard all about it.' Of course this was met with derisive laughter, but as I looked at what we were wearing, I realized his mistake was understandable.

By this stage – with the Sex Pistols riding high in the charts, lurid tales on TV of tribal wars raging up and down the King's Road, safety-pin T-shirts turning up ready ripped on market stalls, and punk couture spreads in *Harpers and Queen* – the whole thing had gone cartoon. It had made that journey from seditious underground scene to tabloid obsession, getting watered down and mucked up in the process. So, without any kind of planning, what we were wearing had shifted to accommodate that fact. Most of the obvious, over-the-top accoutrements, the shock tactic apparel of early punk, had been ditched in favour of a pared-back, classic rebel rocker look, which mocked the Teds even more cleverly. Almost all of us were wearing black leather motorcycle jackets, many adorned with studs and biker patches. There were lots of threadbare Levi's with chains going to pockets, and pointy fifties winklepickers, a few pairs of chunky motorcycle boots, some brothel-creepers, and even a drape coat, the irony of which was clearly lost on this seaside copper. The hair was now mostly dyed black rather than bright colours and there were indeed a few tumbling quiffs in with the spikes.

When we finally made it to the centre of town, our escort still lazily in tow, the local punks, terribly excited by the Clash coming, turned out to eye us up. They were indeed sporting plastic bin-bags and safety-pins; one had a condom hanging from his ear while another had coathangers attached to his school blazer. They were all blood-dripping Hallowe'en theatricality, pantomime punks, bemused by our sartorial sobriety. They really didn't know which side we were on, so we teased them for a while, singing Gene Vincent songs, poking fun at their do-it-yourself amateur theatrical attire. This made our policeman a little jittery, despite the protestations of true punkdom we'd made earlier, and he threatened to nick us all.

Once it was established that we were on the same side, the local punks were full of rapt questions about the scene in London, about the band, asking us what was coming next, who we rated, where we bought our gear. For the first time, after years of feeling like a little kid on the scene, going right back to having my shaven head patronizingly patted by grown-up skins, I knew what it felt like to be a face. In the soul clubs I'd been a schoolboy, sneaking in and hanging out at the back. As a punk, I'd always been in awe of the real scene-makers, the Sex crowd, the Bromley contingent, always been one of the ingénues. But now, on a windy day in a grotty seaside town, I was part of a crowd which had kudos and reverence. You know that scene in *Quadrophenia* where Sting, woefully miscast as the ace face, stands up in court in his leather coat looking just so, and nonchalantly pays his fine, well, it felt a bit like that. For the first time I fully understood what drives this culture on. Kids who would otherwise be ordinary can become stars, even if only in the eyes of a few of their peers hanging by the end of the pier. Then when the band arrived and actually acknowledged a couple of us by name, well, our reputation was set. I'd just started to get the sense of being part of the punk in-crowd, just felt I'd really arrived, as punk, at least in its dynamic fashionable phase, was about to end.

My first taste of television stardom came at about this time too. A couple of days a week I used to get up at the crack of dawn and get the tube to Dollis Hill, a nondescript suburb of north-west

London. There I'd meet up with a couple of the guys from the LSE, Iain Hill and Danny Stern, and about 10,000 trade-unionists, lefties, agitators, paper-sellers, and a slightly baffled but admirably resolute group of Asian women. The venue for this gathering was Grunwicks photo lab, a dreary breeze-block processing plant, where a year-long strike for union recognition among the almost exclusively female and sub-continental workforce, who had to endure terrible conditions, had become a *cause célèbre.* The aim was to shut the plant down until it accepted unionization. I went to Grunwicks because I believed in it. I still had the left-wing views bequeathed by my father and had only just taken down the Che Guevara poster from my wall. I was studying history and political thought at the most famously lefty institution in the land, and going to Grunwicks gave you big brownie points in the eyes of the reds at the LSE. I went to Grunwicks because it was exciting, in the way that football matches with an edge – local derbies where it could boil over at any minute – are exciting.

This time, though, it was even more dramatic; this was to be the final push to close the scab plant and win the dispute. The miners, the élite guard of the proletarian militia, were coming to support the blockade, their flying pickets led by Arthur Scargill. So too were the steelworkers, the other stern northern stalwarts, both of them due to be smashed to history sooner than anyone could have imagined. This was due to be a big day. I attached a red star to my black leather jacket and joined the throng.

The streets all around were nervously packed with people in donkey jackets and boots, many of them doubtless students and social workers trying to look like the real thing. There were also lines of hard-eyed coppers in riot gear, the hated Special Patrol Group (Sinister Parasite Gang to give them their popular Grunwicks name), the same paramilitary force I'd seen wielding their batons against the dreads at carnival the year before. Here was a snapshot of a still deeply riven land, none of the wounds and sores of the early seventies healed, but temporarily plastered over by a few years of a mollifying, if incompetent Labour government. Here was a foretaste of what was to come, as the class friction which had grated and rasped throughout my youth would finally reach a crescendo and a conclusion through the unlikely auspices of a Grantham grocer's daughter.

Suddenly they were coming. The news ricocheted round the throng, the miners were coming, and the big push to blockade the gates was on. The miners were coming and so were the SPG, their shields and batons ready to repel. It was like Spurs versus Arsenal, like the fighting at Notting Hill, only more so. All around battles broke out, police and pickets scrapping, two sides of an argument, which had simmered for generations, going at it with little mercy. There was a major shove, I linked arms with whichever comrade was nearby and pushed a little feeble push, not really meaning to go anywhere. But somehow, by absolute fluke, I felt myself being carried right to the front of the line, right in front of the gates, an inadvertent member of the class warrior vanguard. There were fights and skirmishes and arrests and blows going on all around me, and as I stood in the middle of this maelstrom, I saw the camera pointing right at me.

I didn't know I had smiled a nervous smile, before going all attempted stern and militant. I wasn't actually good at stern and militant, and I was actually shitting myself. On the nine o'clock news that night, watching with my mum and Chris Sullivan, I just looked like a bemused schoolboy caught in the glare. My mum told me off for getting so involved, but I suspect she was secretly rather proud, knowing that my dad would have approved. Chris Sullivan asked if I wanted to borrow his Russian-looking, Trotsky-style greatcoat, in order to appear more accurately Bolshevik next time. There wasn't a next time: the great push had failed, and the dispute was lost.

Appearing on the TV news gave me a certain limited kudos

at the LSE, but in 1977 it was the music press that really mattered. The *NME* was the bible. Initially they'd displayed a snotty superiority to punk, all the old hippy rock writers looking down on the overdressed young upstarts and garage bands. But editor Nick Logan had recruited Tony Parsons and Julie Burchill, via his famous 'hip young gunslingers wanted' advert; these two charismatic proselytizers captured the spirit of the time and the *New Musical Express* had become the splenetic voice of the new punk thing. Now that I'd hidden my soul and jazz records away, the *NME* was the paper I had to read, waiting at the newsagent's for the delivery on a Wednesday afternoon to see what Parsons was ranting about this week. I wanted to be that lay preacher. I started to tell people that I was going to write for the *NME*.

It was the rival rag, the *Melody Maker*, which turned up at the Soho punk club, the Vortex, one night while I was watching Siouxsie and the Banshees. They had dragged along Keith Moon, the soon-to-be-deceased drummer from the Who, to write a feature about his night on the town with the punks. Moon was a famous old-school hell-raiser, and the idea was to plonk him among the spiky young things and see if any sparks flew. Well, they very nearly did. This rude, drunken old bloke with a mock posh voice came barging his way into the club and happened to knock straight into me, spilling the one drink I could afford to buy that night. I told him he was behaving like an oaf and that he should apologize immediately. He said, 'Do you know who I am, old chap?' I said I didn't care who he was, and he announced with a flourish that he was Keith Moon from the Who and that he was going to burn my leather jacket with his lighter. Of course I was impressed by who he was. The Who were mod idols, Shepherd's Bush aristos, but I stuck firmly to the punk party line and told him that the Who were old farts who meant nothing to me and that if he burnt my jacket I'd be forced to hit him. After a couple of seconds staring aggressively into each other's eyes, while a photographer's flash went off, Moon suddenly threw his arms around me, declared that he admired my bottle and brought double brandies all round. We spent the rest of the night as the best of mates.

That Thursday the cover story of the *Melody Maker* was about Keith Moon's night out, and the centre spread included three pictures of Keith Moon and me in mock confrontation. I had somehow been selected as the representative of the punk generation in a clash with our forebears. I was insufferable for a few weeks. The glory was slightly tarnished by the fact that the writer got my name wrong and for some reason called me Eric. But it did have a genuine effect upon me.

The most important lesson punk taught was 'You can do it.' Learn three chords and you can be in a band, spray a shirt and you're a designer, tie your legs together and you're a hero. The literary equivalent of all this was the fanzines, which had sprung up to chronicle the scene. Urgent Xeroxed missives, the most prominent of them was *Sniffing Glue*, produced by two working-class south London teenagers, Mark Perry and Danny Baker, who you always saw out and about. Punk pulled back the curtain on celebrity, revealing that these were just ordinary kids up on stage, not the distant idols that rock had previously paraded before us. Getting to know bands on first-name terms, shopping and drinking in the same places as the Sex Pistols and the Clash, meeting the guys and girls who wrote fanzines, seeing Parsons and Burchill at gigs, actually appearing in one of those weekly music papers, receiving kudos from small town punks – all of this started to make me believe that I could actually make my life out of this culture I'd already spent so long immersed in and obsessed by. I started to say at this point that I wanted to be a writer. I told my mum that I was going to write for the music papers and she said, 'But Robert, they have people who do that.' Indeed they did, people who couldn't even remember a simple name properly, people I was increasingly rubbing shoulders with, and I thought that I could be one of those people.

A fellow undergraduate, John Sweeney, now one of our leading war correspondents, asked around to see if anybody wanted to contribute to an alternative LSE magazine he intended to edit, to kickstart his career as a journalist. I said I'd write a piece about the music scene. It was now mid-1978 and I wrote what I thought was a stinging tirade against the way punk had been hijacked by the masses, sold its soul and lost its style. Just as the rest of the students had decided that punk wasn't fascist but fab, so I wrote a piece proclaiming that it was passé, and had squandered its energy by becoming mainstream. Amid the militant egalitarianism of the LSE student body, my overt élitism was a truly provocative stance, and when the one and only issue of *First Issue* came out it gained me a certain notoriety. I loved that of course, but I also meant it. Within a year punk had burnt itself out, all the radicalism and individualism had gone and a dreary conformity had replaced it. Punk was now the new orthodoxy. You suddenly got hundreds of identikit punk rockers, who'd learned the tenets second-hand from tabloids, descending upon the King's Road, all Mohawk hairdos, cider bottles and gobbing for the tourists. It was postcard punk. Punk had come from the gutters, but had originally been about reaching for the stars.

Despite being a short-lived conflagration, punk had changed everything. There was no going back to the days when everyone looked like an extra from *On the Buses* and listened to the Eagles. It had unleashed a huge, latent desire among British youth to be part of some tribe or other, had awakened a creativity largely dormant since the swinging sixties. As punk spun centrifugally out of control, so a series of sub-sects shot off from the wreckage. The rockabilly look, half-heartedly espoused by me and my mates at Hastings, became a full-blown tribe. These were the boys who would become the Rockats, the Stray Cats and the Polecats, all feline struts, tattoos and rebel yells, flecked pegs, open-neck shirts and cut-off Levi jackets. Very cool for a couple of weeks.

One of the more amusing progeny of the original punk beast was the emergence of a kind of Hammer Horror gothic thread. Taking their lead from the likes of the Damned and the Banshees, this had always been an element of punk, but now it became goth, a style all its own. The goths were sweet suburban kids pretending to be the un-dead while studying for sociology A levels. Oi, though, was deeply ugly.

I first saw a hint of a neo-skinhead, neo-Nazi strain when I went to see a band called Sham 69, playing in Acklam Hall, directly under the Westway, less than a mile from where our house had been. They had a charismatic, rabble-rousing leader in Jimmy Pursey, shirt off, skinny torso contorting, Hanway's answer to Iggy Pop. He probably wasn't a Nazi, but he attracted a following of ugly, skinny white boys who probably were, throwing salutes and screaming insults. They played a stripped-back, below-basic version of punk rock which took away all the wit and the subtlety and the élan and replaced it with stomps and shouts. Their clothes also peeled away the class from both punk and skinhead, to which they paid a dubious homage. (Sham 69 refers to the year skinheads first emerged.) It was big boots, skinny jeans, braces and crops, a look soon adopted by overtly fascist bands like Screwdriver, who rode the rising tide of National Front support as the country grew ever more depressed, divided and volatile.

Oi was the aptly monosyllabic grunt of a name for this barbaric rearguard action. As an active member of the Anti Nazi League, I would come up against its followers on street corners many times. This was when the teacher Blair Peach was killed by the SPG at an anti-racist demonstration. This was when the predominantly Asian area of Southall was set alight during a riot at an oi gig in a pub. This was when you could just feel the tensions pulling and snapping.

Another far more positive strain of the post-punk virus, fermenting in a petri dish somewhere, was the mod/skin revivalism, which would become two tone. There had been a little modish scene running parallel with punk throughout, a trend first exhibited at Acme Attractions and popularized by the Jam in their suits and two-tone bowling shoes from Shelleys. Concurrently, there was also a kind of glam skinhead thing going on. Very different from the ugly recidivism of oi, this was a jaunty Maddy boy business, all skanking ska music and oversized Dr Martens from Holts in Camden Town. You could also buy old stock Harringtons and Crombies, from the Last Resort, a sixties emporium on Petticoat Lane where Melissa Caplan, with her Bridget Riley gear and psychedelic hair, was the shop assistant. This is where the producers of the proposed movie of *Quadrophenia* came to recruit extras.

They should probably have gone to the Midlands. London and Manchester had been the two British punk cities, while the midlands had always been a bastion of heavy rock. But somehow in Birmingham and more specifically Coventry, a bunch of kids informed by punk, but enthused by ska and reggae, had forged a sound and a style which fused those two into a black-and-white, Anglo-Caribbean, high-energy hybrid. I wasn't ready for revivals, still had a no-going-back attitude, but two-tone was really a breath of fresh air in an increasingly stale atmosphere.

A couple of years later the Specials would memorably sing about London becoming like a ghost town, and it wasn't just their town. 1977 had been the year of the great punky reggae party, but 1978 was the hangover which followed. London shrank back into its shell. The Roxy closed down, Acme Attractions became Boy, flogging punky tat to King's Road tourists, the Sex Pistols killed themselves, the Clash became a stadium rock band, and all the energy emanating up from the streets, which had made London shimmer for the last couple of years, just seemed to ebb away. New wave was the new thing, insipid middle-class pop bands like the Police and XTC.

The main, deeply unattractive, fashion trend, as the glow of early punk faded, was a kind of sartorial miserablism. Emanating originally from the north country, championed by John Peel and all the other old prog rock hippies, and epitomized by serious-sounding bands with names like the Gang of Four, the Fall, Joy Division and Echo and the Bunnymen, their music and their look was militantly dour. It was a conscious rejection of all the designer frippery and heroic narcissism of the London punk scene, which also managed to eradicate all the creativity and fun. This was bed-sit depression chic, with the aim being to look as ordinary and as glum as possible. Hair cut like a schoolboy, faded black jeans, a C&A sweater and a long green trenchcoat, perpetually done up against a metaphorical wind blowing nobody any good.

Mid-1978 is one of the few times when I can't really recall what I was wearing on a day-to-day basis – I guess it was just jeans and a leather jacket. I was into politics, into football, into university, into the girls at university. Danny Stern, who was always a pioneer, picked up on a truly nascent skateboarding scene, growing his hair and going for a baggy, beach-bum Californian cool, but I could never do Californian and never balance on anything. For me, I distinctly remember thinking that maybe the whole caper had ended. I still loved music, though, and took up an invitation from Jean Reddy to attend a musical soirée. I went with Jean, Melissa Caplan, Graham Smith and Chris Sullivan to see David Bowie at Earls Court. *Heroes* had been one of the few non-punk records you were allowed to like during the revolution, and I wanted to make up for missing Ziggy Stardust half a dozen years before by seeing the return of the Thin White Duke.

I dug out an old pair of baby blue Acme pegs and a baggy white cotton shirt, twinning them with the studded Seditionaries bondage boots, which still looked fabulous. The gig passed by in a bit of a haze; Bowie was in one of his transitional phases, and it all felt a bit overblown and saggy after the blitzkrieg of punk. But the future was there. I didn't know it at the time, of course, but in among the vast, nondescript rock crowd there were little gatherings of renegades and malcontents. Philip Salon, one of the early Sex contingent, was present, with a gaggle of giggling boys, camp as ever. Steve Strange and some of the Welsh mob were there; so were Chrissie Hynde, Marco Perroni, Rusty Egan and a few of the old soul faces who had bypassed punk completely. Micky Asset was there, the Burnt Oak mover and shaker I'd so looked up to, still looking strong. It was almost shocking and certainly inspiring to see people dressed up again, defiantly flaunting and posing.

A few weeks later we got invited to a party at a flat somewhere in town. I was standing in the kitchen, interrogating the fridge, when a vision in triplicate entered the room. Here was Philip Salon again, only this time in a full white wedding dress, with bovver boots on his feet and a policeman's helmet on his head, flanked by two disgracefully young boys. One was wearing full tartan bondage, but adorned with numerous scarves and hankies, all silk and chiffon, with a huge pompadour crown on his head and make-up to match. The other was some kind of multi-coloured Dickensian urchin, with a ripped and patched frockcoat and a stovepipe hat, theatrically bashed in. These two boys, younger certainly than myself, were up from south London, and proceeded to prance hilariously round the room. One was called George, the other Jeremy, and along with their outrageous mentor they made the most startling tableau I'd ever witnessed in a crowded kitchen. Boy George and Jeremy Healy were certainly part of what was to come.

Somehow on the grapevine of trendy London I heard that one of the original designers behind Acme Attractions had just opened a shop in Covent Garden, the old punk playground. I went along to check it out and immediately the old vibe was back. They called it PX, the name of American army stores. The décor was stripped back, all white and stark, with Kraftwerk playing mechanically in the background and Steve Strange theatrically manning the till. The clothes were a bit Dan Dare, a bit space Cossack – padded shoulders and stand-up collars, piping and sashes and stuff. After the studiously glum look of northern new wave, PX was liberating beyond belief. I bought a blue, skin-tight T-shirt with a silver sash running diagonally across it and shoulder-pads fit for the NFL. I had no idea where I was going to wear it, as there was nowhere to go. Then, as I left the shop, Steve Strange said, 'We're starting a new club at a place called Billy's in Soho, Tuesday nights, come along.'

The 1980s were about to begin a year and a bit early.

12

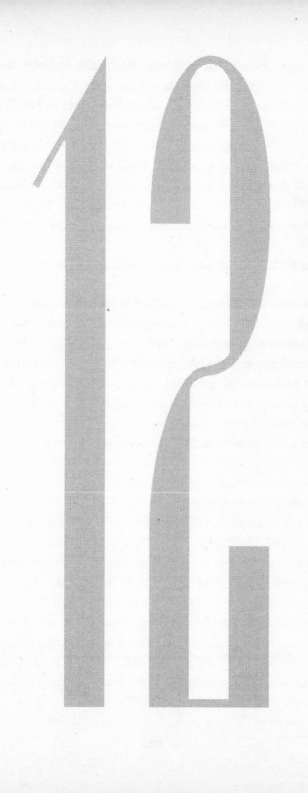

SOHO HAD long been London's Tenderloin, a hunting-ground in more ways than one. A charismatic enclave of twisted alleys and ancient thoroughfares, connecting dilapidated but still dignified Georgian terraces, where De Quincy had squatted in a squalid basement to dream his opium dreams and Marx had dodged his landlord in a garret and dreamed of revolution. Soho was the home of the British music scene, beret-wearing jazzers crowding together in Archer Street, cradling their horns and hustling for gigs at Ronnie Scott's or the Hundred Club. Soho was the home of the British film industry, eager runners clasping tins of stock, legging up Wardour Street and penning phantom scripts in smoky pubs. Soho was the home of the beats and the bohos, writers and painters, poets, actors and charlatans, inverts and outsiders, crowding together in the French House and the Colony Room, away from little England's puritanical gaze. Soho was where the gangsters, Maltese and Italian, East End and Up West, had fought for turf, and where the mods had graduated from the coffee shops of Old Compton Street to the Scene in Ham Yard, swallowing pills and stealing poses. Soho, known in tawdry books as the black mile, was Sex. Soho, in my suburban mind, was impossibly sexy. But not in early 1979 it wasn't.

The lust industry was still there, but like almost all of our industries it had been eroded by decades of ineptitude and deep-felt puritanism to a few handwritten signs and half-hearted red lights. Soho, before the 1980s unleashed a torrent of well-timed hedonism and yuppie regeneration, was the sole domain of dirty old men in macs, shuffling dismally to clip joints, and miserable dirty book shops, which could barely deliver the little they promised. There were still a few grumpy restaurants, serving up stodge to businessmen, and a handful of weary discos with sticky carpets and a clientele of oleaginous lotharios. Soho was the saddest example of the way in which inner London had been eviscerated by urban blight and flight. A place of nightlife, where the night had no life.

Then, as the new, yet seemingly already exhausted year emerged, there was the rubbish. Foully ripe with that sweet, clawing stench of putrefaction, providing home to rats who scampered unhindered, it piled up in the streets and poured from never emptied bins. Strikes and more strikes was the story, until those who should have been laid to rest piled up like the litter. This, it was proclaimed, was our winter of discontent.

We were having the time of our lives. You'd see us, if you knew where and when to look, moving from shabby shadow to shadow, little peacock clusters, our plumage an affront to a still judgemental town. We moved in groups, for safety and for reassurance, as to walk alone through the night dressed like this could still provoke violent enmity. There was a definite thrill to it, sticking two sartorial fingers up at the dreary conformity, giggling with collective vanity at the power to provoke and enrage. Tuesday night, the deadest time in this always near moribund playground, was the night we were invited out, to gather at Billy's, a small, unspectacular club down a suitably unmarked stairwell. Above it was the Golden Girl, a grubby whorehouse, where tarnished brasses lazily tempted the seedy mac men. The girls would occasionally give a whistle as we walked by, and we'd shimmy and blow kisses, confident that we had made it to our destination in one piece. And what pieces we were.

Tuxedos and wing collars, padded shoulders and cummerbunds, riding boots and Sam Browne belts, leather caps, silk scarves, rubber T-shirts, diamanté brooches, taffeta gowns. That first night at Billy's, I had on my quarterback PX top, a pair of voluminous white linen harem pants which Melissa had made and a pair of Kung Fu slippers from round the corner in Chinatown. I had no idea what I was supposed to look like, but we all knew you had to *look* and make people look. Steve Strange was on the door, camply clocking your get-up as he let you in and took your two quid. For the first few weeks he didn't have to try too hard to keep people out. The very idea of a one-off night, where an outside promoter fills an otherwise empty club with his own punters, was entirely new. The logic for the club owner (in this case a wide black guy named Vince) was obvious. On Tuesdays he couldn't even attract sufficient lotharios and nurses to make the place viable, so why not invite this weird Welsh shop assistant, who claimed to have lots of friends, to take over and take a share of the takings? There were maybe only thirty or forty elaborate souls at most, gathered up by the bush telegraph, to answer the call. Billy's wasn't a big place, a couple of dark rooms and a shiny mirrorball, and the few who gathered there on the first few Tuesdays could find a corner each to lurk in, bits of their extravagant outfits protruding from the murk.

Rusty Egan was the record player. He'd been a minor punk face and the drummer in a band with the former Sex Pistol Glen Matlock, called – most provocatively in this time of dour militancy – the Rich Kids. As yet there wasn't much choice for the selector. A staple of Bowie and Roxy, Kraftwerk's Germanic machine music, and a touch of slick Euro-disco, like Georgio Morodor's pulsating 'The Chase'. The sound was electronic, Teutonic, avowedly fake, a fabulous respite. From the murky corners of the club came a few dancers, posers rather than hoofers, throwing shapes, sucking in their cheeks and extending their lithe limbs for all to admire, proto-vogueing. I'd gone in my Chinese space-cossack attire with Chris Sullivan in monocle and spats, Ollie O'Donnell as a tartan Teddy boy, Melissa Caplan as a psychedelic swinger and Graham Smith as a mod matelot. Billy's was like a do-it-yourself, teenage version of a Neue Sachlichkeit painting, *Cabaret* on a student grant. I knew from the very first moment, before even reaching the bottom of the stairs, that this was it.

The nucleus of what would become known as new romantic, which would go on to define the 1980s stylistically, which would shift the tastes and the desires of an age, (and which would be derided like no other) was weaving its way through the wreckage of the winter of discontent to get to Billy's on Tuesday nights in 1979. This cadre in ridiculous clobber has been portrayed as the extravagant over-reaction to punk's ripped and torn anti-style. But that is to completely misunderstand both movements. Almost all the kids, and there were few people in Billy's over twenty-one, who made it past Steve Strange in those early days had been punks. They'd been the eager-eyed young ones at the back, too young to really make a mark or form a band, but they'd been punks in the glorious early days, when punk itself was an underground, individualistic, overdressed style statement. Billy's was like Louise's only more so. Billy's was for those who'd tasted the thrill of wearing clothes for heroes and wanted it back.

WE WERE a generation of British youth who had lived our entire lives in the glow of pop culture, and been through every teenage sartorial twist from the twist onward. We were innately versed in every nuance of every look and trend, and were now prepared to go beyond them all by stealing and borrowing bits from everywhere. The past was a dressing-up box. The 1970s started with skinhead brutalism and ended with the playful post-modernism of a handful of clothes-obsessed narcissists in a basement.

At the time I would have found it downright insulting if anybody had said that I was part of the same gust of zeitgeist as Margaret Thatcher. I was aware that there was a neo-liberal, meaning rabidly right-wing, strain of thought running through the academics, if not the student body at my university. My tutor was Ken Minogue, a free-market ideologue and one of Thatcher's theoretical advisers, but I was still an avowed lefty. But there is no doubt that the ache for change, which became a raging inflammation once it was embodied in the nipped tweed suits and sculpted WI hair of Thatcher, was also what drove us to don ridiculous outfits and preen and scheme for all our worth. Individualism as a response to class branding, me as a rejection of us, dressing up as an alternative to feeling down. Big Bang barrow-boys in red braces and yellow Porsches, Boy George and Margaret Thatcher were all riding the same shock wave.

Punk had been a thrashing spasm of brilliance, but despite its apparent nihilism had actually shown that even here, in 'sick Britain', you could accomplish something. The handful of self-obsessed, self-confident exhibitionists gathered at Billy's on a Tuesday night had learnt the lessons of punk and were determined to create shining lives for themselves, or at least look good trying.

After a couple of months, Steve Strange and Rusty Egan had a falling out with the owner of Billy's. The place had got a little more popular as word spread, and Steve began his gleeful act of rejecting anyone who wasn't sufficiently spectacular. But there still weren't more than sixty or seventy regulars and no one was really making money, so we were evicted. Robbed of our home, it seemed very likely that this nascent new scene would fizzle out. Nobody in the press had noticed, there wasn't much of a buzz, just another little post-punk sect, all dressed up, and now with nowhere to go. But then Steve and Rusty found a wine bar on the edge of Covent Garden, called the Blitz, most bizarrely adorned with posters and photos from wartime London and a few gas-masks and tin hats.

The old soul-boy owners did the same deal that Steve had done at Billy's. On Tuesday nights Steve would control the door, Rusty Egan would play the music and George O'Dowd would work the cloakroom. No one yet called him Boy George, because the idea of a boy who dressed like a girl and swore like a trooper didn't need explaining to the kind of people who went to the Blitz. This place was about to become arguably the most influential club in London's nocturnal history.

Excuse me a list. I'm just going to run through the litany of people who you might have seen on an average Tuesday night at the Blitz in mid-1979. Around Steve Strange and Boy George were most of the people who were with them in Visage and Culture Club; Marilyn, who by now was planning his own gender-bending pop assault; Adam Ant, who moved from punk to pirate here; Toyah Wilcox, about to lisp her way to celebrity; Jeremy Healy, who I'd first seen on the arm of Phil Salon, and who would lead Haysi Fantayzee, to a few chart hits before becoming a superstar DJ. Kirk Brandon from Theatre of Hate was there along with Midge Ure, whose Ultravox would have one of the biggest Blitz-inspired hits with Vienna, a portentously pretentious song which seemed to capture the essence of a *fin-de-siècle* post-socialist era; Sade, then a fashion student at St Martin's; Chris Sullivan and Christos Tolera (who'd lent me the electric blue wedding suit), both soon to be in Blue Rondo à la Turk; most of the members of a band called Animal Nightlife, who were hugely hip; Mark Moore, who would become S Express, and all of Spandau Ballet and their manager. That's just music.

From the world of fashion, John Galliano is probably the most famous and enduring Blitz alumnus, but you can add David Hollah and Stevie Stewart, whose Bodymap label was one of the most influential and globally successful of the 1980s. Likewise Stephen Linnard, an old Goldmine regular who was a star designer, fond of boasting that he earned more than Margaret

Thatcher, and his mate the famed mad hatter, milliner Stephen Jones. Karyn Franklyn, writer and long-time presenter of BBC's *The Clothes Show*, was a regular, as was Iain Webb, fashion editor, Kim Bowen, now head of Australian *Vogue*, and Dylan Jones, currently editor of British *GQ*. Most oddly of all, David Claridge, who found fame as the voice of Roland Rat on *TVAM*.

Michael Clark, arguably Britain's greatest, and certainly its most controversial modern dancer, was a denizen, as were the film and video director John Maybury, the conceptual artist Cerith Wyn Evans, and a host of people who went on to be influential in their chosen fields. When they were at the Blitz none of these, bar perhaps Midge Ure, was any kind of success or celebrity. In fact, if you were a celebrity, chances were you wouldn't get in, as Mick Jagger famously found to his cost when Steve Strange theatrically backed him for being too old and dowdy. The queues started to wind despairingly down the street and the egos of those inside started to inflate.

The Blitz was a hothouse. Like the Two I's on Old Compton Street in the late fifties, or the Crawdaddy for the beat boomers of the sixties, the Blitz was one of those places where a critical mass is reached and a scene solidifies into something far larger, propelling the people there into prominence. A place where an amazing competitiveness but also a sometimes catty camaraderie develops, which drives everybody on. We'd arrived a handful of over-dressed kids skulking in the shadows and ended up a year later lauded and laughed at in equal measures, as the leaders of a movement which was shaping the sounds and styles of our generation. Yet we were still essentially a penniless set of students with a ragbag of DIY outfits, battling through jumble sales with old biddies and haggling in charity shops. Melissa moved into a now notorious squat on Wardour Street, a gorgeous but perilous old Georgian town house right in the centre of town, where among others Boy George had a room strewn with tat and bodies. I spent many nights there avoiding the missing stairs and the falling masonry, while still living in Burnt Oak with my mum, sharing a room with Chris Sullivan, who proudly refused to wear the same outfit twice.

One night Chris would dress as the Milk Tray man, all stretch black ski-pants, black polo-neck and balaclava, the next he'd be a 1920s-style film cameraman with plus-fours, a sleeveless cardigan and an oversized check cap back to front. Frank Sinatra, W.C. Fields, Dizzy Gillespie, Tom Mix, Rudolph Valentino and, perhaps most bizarrely, Mahatma Ghandi – all of these provided sartorial inspiration for Chris, who played a game akin to *Stars in Their Eyes*, where he'd rummage in his pile of dustbin-bags and emerge as the style icon of his choice. I could never quite bring myself to wear a loincloth and sheet in order to make an entrance at a night-club, but getting ready in the same room as Chris Sullivan certainly drove you on.

I cut off my beloved wedge. By the end it had mutated into something far more odd, as one side grew down below my chin in a long, asymmetrical fringe. When we saw a new band from up north called the Human League, whose lead singer favoured just such a style, I rushed to get it chopped off. At this point the need to appear unique was paramount. Ollie O'Donnell at Smile decided I should go for what he called a Buzz Aldrin, a savagely precise NASA-style flat-top, which with a few minor variations became my haircut of choice for the next few years. I also got a new suit, my first actually tailor-made, by an old East End boy in Whitechapel. It was a dog's tooth Edwardian-style job with high rising strides, wide shoulders and a Max Baer* back. One night

* Max Baer won the world heavyweight championship in 1934, but secured an even more impressive honour when he had a piece of clothing named after him. He was a famously dapper man, and had a special jacket designed with a pleated back and a half belt to encompass his large shoulder muscles without stretching the fabric. He went on to be a minor movie star, and his son Max Baer Junior starred as Jethro in *The Beverly Hillbillies.*

I'd twin that with a stand-up collar, bow-tie and ill-fitting patent shoes from a charity store. The next it might be a swirling Cossack shirt with a pair of rubber riding boots I bought in PX and a big diamanté dangler lent by my long-suffering mother. She used to tell the perplexed neighbours that we went to lots of fancy dress parties.

And in a way we did. The Blitz on Tuesday was always the highlight of the week and you had to make a massive effort to appear amazing. Melissa would start dressing at around lunchtime, Chris would be rummaging as soon as he got up (also around lunchtime). I would have spent much of the week before, making mental notes on what effect I intended to create that Tuesday. There was never one Blitz look, but whatever you wore you had to stand out, especially for the people standing outside desperate to join the party. Impressing them was your number one duty. You always arrived with your gang, swanned past the crowd outside with as much show as possible, using your rank as a Billy's original to waltz in, kissing Steve theatrically on the cheek as you did so. It all seemed very starry, but chances were, once you got inside, you'd have no money for a drink. We used to nick bottles of wine from the storeroom and open them with a penknife in the loos. The Blitz was all about show, and we were the main attraction.

But this wasn't just a once-a-week business, and having made a name as a dresser you had to keep it up. I never saw George or Steve Strange out of slap, never saw Chris out of character. A new-found social whirl began to flow around us, as our reputations spread and we started to get invited to fancy dos, particularly by the older, arty crowd like Derek Jarman and Andrew Logan, who wanted the pretty young things to grace their soirées. One event that sticks in my mind is what may well have been the first ever warehouse party, the forerunner of all those illegal raves which would send paroxysms of apoplexy through *Daily Mail* readers throughout the 1990s.

Thatcher had embarked upon her scorched-earth policy towards Britain's anachronistic industrial infrastructure, causing a massive rise in unemployment and a huge stock of empty commercial and industrial premises. One of the most notable of these in London was the area of riverside right by Tower Bridge, known as Butler's Wharf. Today it's the centrepiece of Terence Conran's gastro-design empire, and a series of hugely expensive apartments. Then it was just one of an endless array of disused hulks lining the old abandoned docks. So, in a wonderfully piratical piece of capitalist improvisation, a small gang of old soul boys broke in, set up a sound system, printed up some tickets and flogged them for a fiver each to hundreds of eager hedonists. Nobody, to my knowledge, had ever done this before. Where the dour post-punk, green-coat brigade were making sulky records about Thatcher's wasteland, we were dressing up and dancing in it.

The perpetual adrenaline surge of vanity and creativity which was unleashed as the 1980s approached, allied with a propensity for cheap alcohol, meant that I don't recall actually standing still and taking stock at any moment during the Blitz era. It was such a rush, such a torrent of perpetual motion, a buzz of being in with the in-crowd and flaunting and flouting, that there was no time for introspection or analysis. Certainly there were times when it would have been wise to take a look in the mirror and take stock. How did a boy who'd first been inspired by mod, who'd been Reggie Elms's skinhead brother, end up dressed as Robin Hood in the girls' toilets of a club, watching two guys in gowns and make-up snogging? But the thrill of being there, of being on the guest list, of being recognized, was all I'd ever wanted. There would be time later to understand it all; we were far too busy loving it.

Now I can see that the Blitz was actually the coming together of two different strains of sartorial thought which had previously been poles apart. White socks meet white faces. On one side were the straight, usually male, predominantly working-class London kids, of which myself and Gary Kemp and Steve Dagger, Ollie O'Donnell et al were part. Boys who would be at the Blitz one day and on the terraces the next. There was even a little firm of Blitz regulars from Hackney who were hardened Tottenham terrace fighters and members of a far-left street-fighting gang called Red Action! On the other side of the equation were the likes of George and Steve Strange and Marilyn, the gay gang, the art students and the fashion fetishists, who had been strictly Bowie. They had that theatrical, camp extravagance, and a battle-hardened bottle, which meant they could wear anything without fear. They'd been outsiders all their lives, a brand of defiant flamboyance stretching back to Quentin Crisp and beyond. There was always an uneasy tension between the two camps; I couldn't stand George, and I'm sure the feeling was mutual, but we were part of something together.

The looks, and just as importantly the attitudes, which emanated from the Blitz were a combination of those two elements. Of course it was the more outré and outlandish stuff which tended to get photographed and noticed, but for every boy dressed as a girl, or done up like a pierrot or a pirate, there were guys in dinner jackets or biker jackets, sixties ratpack suits or forties demob gear. Most of the time I wore whistles, and even went through a period when I was trying to look like Perry Como in open-neck shirt and pastel sports jacket; another couple of weeks when I opted for Burlington Bertie foppery, frockcoat, fob chain, cravat and cape.

Because the Blitz was less than half a mile from the LSE, we often used to gather early Tuesday evening in the student bar, where the drink was cheap. Myself, Graham Ball and Steve Dagger were all bona fide and we could invite a few friends. So you'd have the bizarre spectacle of a dozen or so Blitz kids, done up like extras from a dozen different costume dramas, mingling with the Trots and the sociologists, who still clung to old hippy flares or those skin-tight elasticated jeans which were such a blight upon the age. They also had a collection of haircuts that time forgot: mullets and perms and even the worst hair-do of all time, that hippy busker thing, cropped short but with wispy rats' tails hanging down the back. Quite what they made of us I'm not sure; but one time when Chris Sullivan came down in jackboots, jodhpurs, black shirt and tie under a full-length heavy leather Rommel coat he'd bought in a Berlin market, the lefties were convinced that the Wehrmacht were attacking.

It was even odder on the occasions when I never made it home after the Blitz and slept at the LSE. At the very top of the building there was an old library with a few leather sofas and a couple of musty portraits of J.M. Keynes and the like, which hardly anybody ever went to. If I'd been up until dawn at some post-Blitz party I'd sneak up there when the building opened for a couple of hours' kip, before going to a comparative political structures lecture at ten o'clock. But this meant I'd have to go to the lecture and spend the rest of the day in whatever get-up I'd been sporting the night before. Walking round Britain's premier centre for the study of economic science, dressed as a cowboy or a Clan chief, certainly raises your embarrassment threshold. I'd just have to front it out when they stared and pretend I'd put all this on for their benefit.

When I got a part-time job as a play-leader for the Inner London Education Authority I took to keeping a set of civvies in my locker. My work involved looking after junior school kids after school and in the holidays. My school was in King's Cross, one of the most savagely deprived and tough areas in the country, and it was not wise to take on those fantastically gobby kids in fancy dress. It was yet another marked contrast between the glamour of the clubs and the rest of my life. I loved working with kids and kept on almost until the ILEA was abolished by the job-snatcher a couple of years after I finished at the LSE.

It was in the London School of Economics, in the lecture hall, sitting next to Steve Dagger, making notes about Pareto's iron law of oligarchy, that Steve said something which in hindsight was rather important. He nonchalantly mentioned, 'I'm managing a band.' Dagger has a very matter-of-fact way of speaking and he said that as if he was announcing that he was going to have pizza for lunch instead of a burger. I pointed out that he was a poor undergraduate politics student like myself. But he insisted. Gary and his little brother Martin Kemp had formed a band with a few other guys they knew from school, and Steve, who was a far more diligent student of pop culture history than he was of politics, had decided that he would be their Andrew Loog Oldham. 'Gary can play guitar, Martin plays bass, I'll play the telephone.'

A few days later Steve rang up half a dozen movers from the Blitz and invited us to see this band of his at a rehearsal rooms in the Holloway Road one Saturday afternoon. I didn't expect much.

13

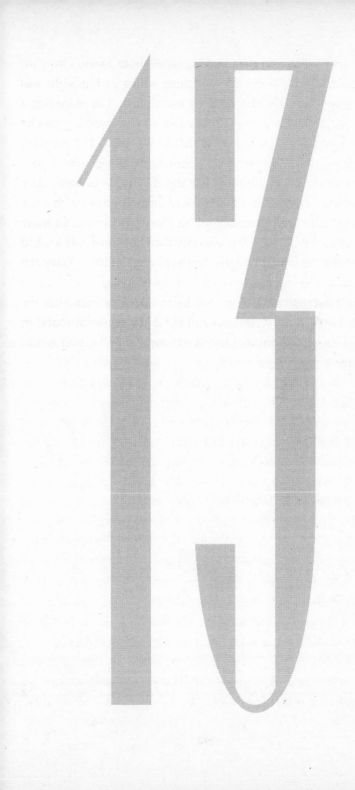

THE HOLLOWAY ROAD is one of the most resolutely grotty in all London. As 1980 approached, Islington was already well on the path to gentrification; the elegant terraces of Barnsbury and Canonbury were being bought up and done up by lawyers and journalists and the like. The acronym yuppie hadn't quite made it to these shores yet, but young urban professionals in all but name had already altered the social make-up of the rough bit of London the Kemp brothers had grown up in. Over in Fulham, where there was good access to Chelsea and the Home Counties, rugby-shirt-sporting public-school boys and their green-wellie-wearing wives parked their hatchbacks outside once lowly riverside cottages. The club crowd had begun the regeneration of Soho and Covent Garden, breathing life back into the night. But the Holloway Road was still the Holloway Road.

Even today it's one of those noisome arteries, furred up with traffic and lined with shops selling kebabs and second-hand car batteries. Whatever the weather, the Holloway Road is full of puddles of dirty water dripping from the railway arches. It's not an auspicious place. It's certainly no place to drag a dozen members of the club cognoscenti, with hugely inflated ideas of themselves, far too early of a Saturday morning. This, we thought, as we climbed through a grotty warren of fetid dens lined with amps and broken bits of old recording equipment, into a truly manky old rock'n'roll rehearsal room with black walls and even darker vibes, had better be good.*

Gary Kemp had been a mate for a while now. We'd been on nodding terms from punk days, and got talking at Billy's and the Blitz: I knew he came from a very similar background to myself, went to a grammar school, had been through the whole soul thing, and now worked on the print. He was perhaps the most prominent, certainly the most voluble member of a group of Islington lads we called the Angel boys, which included his remarkably good-looking, although still very young brother Martin, who was best mates with that Greek kid Christos, who had lent me the still infamous electric blue suit. Through Steve Dagger, a school friend of Gary's, we got closer still.

Looking back, I wouldn't be remotely surprised if Steve Dagger had ordered Gary to keep schtum about being in a band until it was all in place and they were officially unleashed. Certainly music and acting had been a major part of Gary's life since he'd joined Anna Scher's Islington finishing school for would-be EastEnders as a kid, and joined a series of power pop bands from about the age of fourteen. I had no idea of any of this, no idea this group of his had been rehearsing away for months, wondering how they could attach themselves to the now rapidly rolling Blitz bandwagon. For them, there was a lot riding on this Saturday morning rehearsal, but for myself and Chris Sullivan and Steve Strange,

---

* A decade before, this had been 'The Black House', a black consciousness meeting-room, social centre and haven for radical black power activists. Michael X, a would-be British Malcolm X, originally known as Michael Defreitas, who'd been a pimp and Rachman enforcer, started the place with money donated by John Lennon. But it all ended nastily when Michael X was charged with extortion and eventually hanged for murder in Trinidad. The place still bore a powerful darkness.

Melissa Caplan and my old school mate Graham Smith, who'd been invited to this dump on the Holloway Road, there was a high degree of scepticism.

Once Gary and Martin and the other three started playing, however, it was obvious that they could actually do it. They knew which way to point their instruments, the tall bloke at the front with the foghorn voice could hold a tune in a kind of pub sing-along manner, and what's more they had songs. The one that immediately stuck was the one that started 'de de der de de de der de de de der de de de'. Two fingers on an electronic keyboard, and then that big saloon-bar voice booming portentously on about being 'beautiful and clean and so very very young', while the beat did that metronomic pounding Euro thing which was the requisite rhythm for dancing at the Blitz. N1 rococo disco. Gary and Steve had clearly assembled a group of people, dressed them up in vaguely trendy gear, a black leather coat for the singer, pegs for the guitarist with the wedge, no one could see the drummer. Martin didn't need any help, he was a born dandy and the one who you naturally looked at. It all looked and sounded about right.

After the show Gary went on to Graham Smith about doing some photos 'in a German expressionist style', all moody shadows and shapes, as he dropped the names of trendy Bauhaus designers we should have heard of. Melissa was asked about designing some clothes, Steve Strange and Chris Sullivan were roped in to organize gigs, while Steve Dagger took me to one side and said, 'We need a name.' At that point they were lumbered with a terrible moniker, the 'Gentry' (kind of rich kids in tweed), and he knew they required something better. We all went to a skanking old Irish boozer just up the road from the rehearsal studios and over a pint of lager I suggested they call themselves Spandau Ballet.

The genesis of the name lay in a trip to Berlin, where I'd been to with a football team from the LSE that summer. I played for something called the Cosmos, a fairly useless leg-breaking full-back in a maverick side full of ringers that Danny Stern and Iain Hill had set up for a lark and to stick two fingers up at the sporty types at the school, who took everything so seriously. We wore the most lary strip we could find, lemon-yellow with a lime-green sash, very South American. We were posers, but had a few decent students and a couple of excellent ringers. We beat the second eleven, narrowly lost to the firsts, got a reputation for flair (apart from me), and somehow ended up getting invited on a tour of Berlin.

This was when it was still divided, and also just about the hippest city in Europe, what with Kraftwerk and Bowie's well-documented association. The prospect of standing by the wall and playing spies at Checkpoint Charlie, eating Russian caviar and dressing up in dramatic cold war gear, meant that Chris Sullivan, Graham Ball, the O'Donnell brothers, Graham Smith and a few other Blitz mates came along even though they weren't going to play any football. We were certainly the most extravagantly dressed group of supposed sportsmen ever stopped and interrogated by machine-gun-toting border guards. I stepped off that train at Kurfürstendamm wearing bondage trousers (there was a minor punk revival thing going on), with white socks and loafers and a skin-tight satin top with a Lenin badge on it.

While in Germany we lived in anarchist squats in Kreutzberg, paid homage to Bowie and Lou Reed, went to lots of stern-faced night-clubs, visited the East and lost a couple of games due to terrible hangovers. We also went to see Spandau prison, where Rudolf Hess was the only prisoner. Among a mass of graffiti on a nearby wall were the words Spandau Ballet. I thought that would make a nicely nonsensical name for a band should I ever need one. Suddenly on a Saturday afternoon in the Holloway Road I did. Dagger agreed it was good, evocative and provocative, and Gary, who has never been scared of being pretentious, agreed that it somehow matched the spirit of the moment. So when Chris Sullivan organized a warehouse party in Battersea, in an old print works where Toyah Wilcox rehearsed, the band, making their official début performance, were called Spandau Ballet. The invitation was designed at my mum's kitchen table in Burnt Oak. We nicked a line from a David Bowie song and described the evening as 'A Crash Course for the Ravers'. And that's exactly what it was. I introduced the band on stage, attired for the occasion in all-black, urban guerrilla gear, sweating profusely under a polo-neck jumper and woollen beanie hat but refusing to take it off and spoil the effect. Once Tony started belting them out in an armoured, full-length leather coat and Martin shook his quiff, I could see Dagger's mind working overtime and the pound signs flicking across his eyes as his plan clicked into place. Spandau went down really well with an audience who up to that point didn't really have a group to call their own. And the party was truly wild.

When at about four in the morning the Metropolitan Police arrived to find at least 400 revellers crammed into a warehouse, the whole gaudy pageant of London street fashion – women with shaven heads, boys in priestly vestments and rabinnical robes, toy soldiers and gay sailors, spacemen, cowgirls and Theresa, a legal secretary who was always attired as Marie Antoinette, complete with wig and beauty spot – they didn't have a clue what to do. Eventually they nicked one poor soul, an old mate of mine from Orange Hill called Mark Bradshaw. He'd drunk too much, fallen akip and woken up with a copper prodding him. For some reason he too borrowed a line from a David Bowie song, leapt up and shouted, 'This ain't rock'n'roll this is suicide,' at the policeman at the top of his voice, and ended up with his arm up his back as a result. I remember being selfishly concerned, because he'd borrowed my rubber riding boots and I thought I might not get them back if he went down.

I was now in my third year at the LSE and hadn't really thought for a moment about where it was all leading. I vaguely considered doing a Master's as a delaying tactic; I'd assumed everything would fall into place and some sort of career would present itself. And then it did. I'd told my mum, with a truly pretentious flourish, that I wanted to be a man of letters, and she seemed disappointed. She said, 'With your education you can do better than be a postman.' I'd told just about everybody that I could write, indeed, that I would write for the *NME,* and then one day Steve Dagger called my bluff. Yet again we were sitting at college when he informed me that Spandau were planning their next performance, another invitation-only affair, and that the plan involved me. Obviously he wouldn't allow any music journalists in, as that would shatter the air of élitism, and besides, they might write nasty things, but the band needed to start generating some column inches. So I would write a review of the evening, take it along to the *NME,* they would print it, Spandau would become a successful band and I'd be a music journalist. Easy.

I went along with all this just to keep Dagger quiet. Spandau played on the Saturday night and yet again they were spot on for the carefully selected audience, who provided more of a show than the group did. It wasn't too difficult to make the connection between Spandau and the scene. Musically they had that combination of funky dance rhythms taken from soul and the Germanic electronic feel, with just a touch of the arrogance of punk. Stylistically Gary and Martin at least were a pair of preening council estate coxcombs who'd always walked that walk, and they enthusiastically assembled a look. Tartan, which I'd first wrapped around myself as a Rod Stewart fan, was one of the kaleidoscope of styles which was being paraded at that juncture, and Gary and the boys swathed themselves enthusiastically in a plethora of plaid. Martin was out collecting kung fu slippers, Sam Browne belts, high-collared shirts, anything to ensure that Spandau looked like the house band of the Blitz.

On the Monday morning after the gig, Dagger said to me, 'Where's the review?' Obviously I hadn't written one, so he marched me round the corner to his mum and dad's council flat and stood over me while I hand-wrote a flowery tribute in biro on lined school-style notepaper. He then walked me the mile or so to Carnaby Street, where the offices of the *New Musical Express* were. If he hadn't been with me I would have skulked off, as I was still convinced that this whole endeavour was ridiculous. The *NME* had attained holy status during punk and, even though the music scene was in a definite lull, it was still the most influential journal aimed at a youth audience and the sole arbiter of all things trendy. It seemed very unlikely that they'd print a review of an unknown band by an unpublished writer who couldn't even type.

When we got to Carnaby Street, there was the usual dribble of Scandinavian tourists buying policemen's helmets and punk wigs from the souvenir shops and even a couple of postcard punks pouting theatrically for them. Steve walked me right to the door of the office block which the *NME* occupied, and told me to go up the stairs, physically blocking the doorway so I couldn't turn back. I didn't have a clue what to do next, so clutching this by now rather dog-eared bit of paper, I walked into the cramped reception, where for some reason Danny Baker, who'd progressed from *Sniffing Glue* to the *NME* and was one of their star writers, was sitting answering the phones. I asked him what to do with a live review and he pointed rather dismissively to the live editor, a youngish guy sitting at a desk piled precariously high with records and papers, just across the office.

Having got this far, I loved the idea of writing for the *NME*. This place was remarkably unglamorous, but that made it less scary. Nobody involved appeared that much older than myself, and indeed the live editor, sporting some kind of awful Man at C&A top, was far worse dressed than me. I realized that I would need an edge, as they must get sack-loads of unsolicited schoolboy scrawl. I stood by his desk and as he reluctantly looked up to acknowledge my presence I blurted out the words, 'Your paper's shit.' As I said it, I half expected him to have me physically thrown out, but instead he just looked rather nonplussed. So I regaled him with this rapidly blurted speech about how there was this amazing scene going on that the *NME* knew nothing about, and how dare they call themselves hip if they didn't know about the Blitz, and this band called Spandau Ballet who everybody was talking about, who combined the music and the look that was changing the face of, etc., etc. And when I couldn't think of anything else to add I slapped my piece of paper on to his desk with a flourish. Now I was sure he'd throw me out.

Instead he read the piece, said it was good and that they'd run it with a picture next issue. I was amazed. In a daze I walked back down the stairs to where Steve Dagger was still waiting. He asked me what happened, and still shaking my head I said that they were going to use it in the next issue. Steve just looked at me and said, 'See.' We walked back to college.

£15.63 I got paid for that review. It ran the next week and very quickly started the process of Spandau signing a major record deal and becoming a hugely successful band. From that point on I shelved the idea of postgraduate study and told people as often as I could that I was a journalist. I still had my job as a play-leader, still lived at home with my mum, but I was a music journalist for the *NME*, no less.

One immediate effect of the *NME* article was that Steve Dagger got a call from Janet Street-Porter, the old Fulham mod who'd made the first television documentary about the Pistols for her LWT series *Twentieth Century Box*, which had launched them to public prominence. She now wanted to do a similar thing with Spandau Ballet. Steve organized a gig at the Scala cinema, a small arthouse behind Tottenham Court Road run by an old Islington schoolmate of his called Steve Woolley.* Janet would film the gig,

---

* Steve later formed Scala pictures, produced dozens of good movies, such as *Company of Wolves*, *Mona Lisa*, *Scandal*, and oversaw *Absolute Beginners*.

still only the band's fourth, but she wanted the show to be as much about the whole Blitz phenomena, the fashion and the lifestyle, as the group itself. So they asked if I would mind them basing the programme around me and a couple of days of my life leading up to the gig, as some kind of spokesman for the movement. They didn't have to ask twice.

At this stage almost all the clothes worn by the still relatively small group of people based around the Blitz were either second-hand, or for the more elaborate pieces, self-made. Half the kids were fashion students and they made stuff to sell to the other half. There was a kind of cottage industry, in reality more of a squat industry, as the likes of Melissa and Simon Withers and Stephen Linnard ran up bizarrely complicated garments which invariably involved straps and flaps and fasteners, came with sets of instructions and took hours to put on. Simon Withers made some fantastically complex wraparound trousers which appear in all the early Spandau photos and look a little like something Greek soldiers wear beneath their skirts. I had those. Melissa made these kind of tabard things, all in one, vaguely medieval, that pulled over your head and tied between your legs. I never had one of those. This DIY creativity was essential because there weren't any shops appealing to this audience. And then there was.

A shop called Modern Classics, a tiny one-off boutique owned by a gently taciturn but highly intellectual designer called Willie Brown, opened at the very end of 1979. He started this place in what was a forgotten corner of inner city dereliction and crime known as Hoxton. This was a part of town no one ever went to, but Willie Brown, taking advantage of dirt-cheap rents, opened this shop in a little alley off Old Street where almost everything else was boarded up and abandoned, and filled it with some of the most remarkable clothes ever sold. His big thing was Russian Constructivism, the artistic movement which had accompanied the early flowering of the Bolshevik revolution, resulting in a dramatic modernist style of painting, poetry, theatre design, architecture and – although this had been largely overlooked – fashion. Mayakovsky, Malevich and Rodchenko all wore the Constructivist uniform, a kind of Stakhanovite futurist suit, all poppers and pouches, with baggy, almost jodhpur-like trousers and short blouson jacket. Somewhere between Casey Jones and Leon Trotsky, militaristic but practical. Willie Brown faithfully reproduced this stuff from the few drawings which remained, and Gary Kemp and myself bought a suit each. Mine was in heavy-duty beige and brown cotton drill, with Soviet symbols, good solid proletarian stuff. We even made a trip to Oxford to see a tiny exhibition on the works of Mayakovsky, which inspired me to write some supposedly dramatic poetry to accompany Spandau's performances. We thought we were so very arty.

So when *Twentieth Century Box* said they wanted to make this programme, we suggested that they film me shopping at Modern Classics and getting my hair cut by Ollie O'Donnell at Smile. Hair and clothes, the true basis of a music scene. They also filmed the band preparing for the gig by humping their equipment into a Ford Fiesta parked outside John the drummer's dad's council flat in Kentish town. This programme was supposedly about the trendiest, most glamorous group in town, and we all looked exactly like the penniless herberts we really were. For some reason Janet decided to shoot the whole thing in black and white, presumably to make it look more sophisticated. For my part I camped it up furiously in a second-hand beret and tatty ballet pumps. It just made us look even more laughably down at heel, more like the charity shop charlatans we were. When they got to the gig though, and the whole fantastic parade of Blitz regulars arrived at the cinema in their excessive raiments, George as Widow Twankey with a kimono and chopsticks, nicked from the local Chinese, in his hair, the show did take on a 'happening' feel.

Gary and I had decided that I would again introduce the band on stage, only this time reciting some of the Constructivist-inspired poetry I'd written. Thankfully, in an act of some considerable sartorial restraint, I went on stage in a classic black, sixties ratpack-style suit I'd bought in a charity shop – white shirt, thin black tie, polished black shoes, even a pin in my breast pocket keeping a hankie in place. I read out these words:

From half spoken shadows emerges a canvas
A kiss of light breaks to reveal a moment when all mirrors
are redundant
Listen to the portrait of the dance of perfection . . .
Ladies and gentlemen, the Spandau Ballet.

All right, I know. You can't imagine how many times that clip has been shown on TV, my flat top bristling in the light, my supposed friends giggling with delight at every airing. And when the first Spandau album, *Journeys to Glory*, came out a few months later and an even more pretentious bit of my terrible teenage verse adorned the Graham Smith designed neoclassical sleeve, well, that was it. The image of me as awful poet and poser was firmly established. What did I care? I was now a professional writer (I'd written one piece) and at the very centre of one of the grooviest scenes London had witnessed in a decade or two. During this period I also had my finals to contend with. The very last exam I would ever sit fell on my twenty-first birthday. I celebrated by buying a kilt.

This was no ordinary kilt, though. Willie Brown had taken the basic shape of a Scotsman's skirt and simplified it, changed the fastenings, lessened the pleating and also taken away the plaid. So what you had left was actually a wrap-around knee-length gentlemen's skirt in heavy grey wool. It was an alarmingly expensive item, but I got my first proper discount because we'd given the shop exposure on TV. I also got my first experience of walking along the streets with my inner thighs rubbing together, which as a man is a unique and unsettling sensation. Ride the London underground in a skirt, no matter how artfully minimalist and fabulously hip, and chances are people will react. They did.

There's a couple of other early Spandau events which are worth noting. One was their first foray out of London, when Steve Dagger booked a performance at the Botanical Gardens in Birmingham. He'd chosen Birmingham because it had a club, Barbarella's, which was rumoured to have a similar kind of scene to the Blitz. He also booked a charabanc to ferry up fifty of the London club crowd to make sure there was some support. I was used to travelling to far-off cities in coaches for football matches and this was remarkably similar. Except that the mob crammed into the bus, with the beers at the back and the music blaring from the front, included every ludicrously attired club queen in town.

When we got to Brum we spilled out like dolls from a toybox, lording it large over the locals as we sashayed between the palm trees. But it was obvious that there was a genuine scene going on up here too. The style was more glittery and even more theatrical, a kind of glam goth thing, with silk and chiffon in all directions. They also said that they had a band of their own, who had taken their name from the same film that had given Barbarella's its title. I remember looking at them huddled together in a corner with headbands around their mullets and instantly dismissing them as no-hoper provincials. They were Duran Duran.

BIRMINGHAM convinced me that this scene of ours was going to spread beyond the closed confines of the Blitz and become a national phenomenon. The gig, which tipped the balance for Spandau Ballet, was the one they played on a battlecruiser. The final Spandau event in the summer of 1980, the last time they would play to a selected, invite-only audience, was on board HMS *Belfast*, moored in the Thames by Tower Bridge. Steve had conned his way on to the ship, which could be hired for private soirées, by claiming that it was an end-of-term affair for Oxford undergraduates, and only at the last minute mentioning that there was 'a quintet' playing. Come the night, though, the clamour for tickets was hysterical and the scenes by the riverside chaotic as hundreds of London's finest jostled to get on board.

One group of buccaneering, ticketless lads from Ealing, led by a piratical character known as Dave Mahoney, a wild libertine who went on to run illegal clubs and cause mayhem for the next few years, procured a rowing boat from somewhere and scaled the ship, *Treasure Island* style, whooping joyously as they did so. Philip Salon, who had been around since Louise's and before, arrived in perhaps the single most bizarre outfit I'd seen up to that point. He was attired in one of his collection of wedding dresses, but this time he was festooned with fairy lights, like a walking Christmas tree. When he finally forced his way through the mêlée and got on board, he asked where the nearest plug point was and proceeded to plug himself in, sitting there happily flashing away. The band played amid all this, squashed into a space which looked like the set of *Eraserhead*, all pipes and levers and wheels everywhere. At one point I walked up on deck to survey the scene only to hear one of the startled old salts who ran the place exclaim, 'I've just seen two geezers dressed as bleeding spacemen buggering each other in the boiler room.'

This time Steve Dagger had invited all the major record companies, and you could see them in their satin tour jackets with the sleeves rolled up, slack-jawed in the corners. Almost immediately after the gig, though, the band was invited to play in St Tropez for a couple of weeks at some swanky Eurotrash club. They invited me along as well, as a kind of favour, and we enjoyed a fortnight trying and failing to find girls who looked like Brigitte Bardot, while we pretended to be used to such smooth, continental sophistication. When we got back Steve had a list of calls on a notepad at his mum's flat. It read like a Who's Who of the British music industry. Every major record company had rung up, and within a few weeks the band had signed to Chrysalis in a record-breaking deal.

I also had to set about securing a future. My mum bought me a second-hand typewriter from an ad in the *Evening Standard*, a real clunking metal-and-ribbon job, and I went back to the *NME*, bolstered by the fact that I had first tipped them off about Spandau Ballet. I produced a couple of further live reviews for them, but got into big arguments because I wanted to write about fashion and clubs and clothes, all of which they still hated with a rockist vehemence. I had a couple of meetings with the benign if slightly melancholic editor, Neil Spencer, who seemed to understand where I was coming from and took something of a shine to me. We'd talk about old mod styles and tunes, while he admitted that the *NME* wasn't really the place for me. One day he took me into his office and said, 'Robert, why don't you go and see Nick Logan over the road, he's just started a new magazine which would be right up your street; it's called the *Face*.'

14

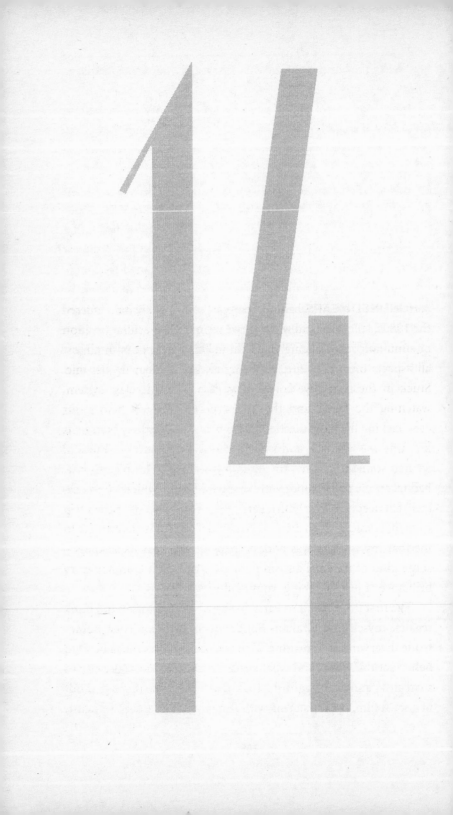

A HUNDRED YEARS behind, ten years ahead. As Britain entered the 1980s, still riven and warring, we were in the peculiar position of simultaneously lagging way behind our neighbours in almost all aspects of normal life, yet being ahead of them in just one. Stuck in the restrictive corset of an anachronistic class system, watching the fabric and the infrastructure unravel before our eyes, lacking the basic niceties of late-twentieth-century bourgeois life, this was the sick and sadly dated man of Europe. But still we had something. Even my meagre travels, which up until now had taken me to St Tropez with Spandau, Spain (which I immediately fell deeply in love with), Paris, Berlin and a school skiing trip to Switzerland (which I immediately despised), had revealed to me that my country was odd, perhaps ill, but that its sickness – some kind of national autism perhaps – gave us a compensatory brilliance at just one thing: youth culture.

The first time I went to Paris, in spring 1977, I was in full punk regalia, myself and Graham Smith in bondage and our home-made 'Everyone's a Prostitute' T-shirts, me also sporting a beret to better get the vibes. And what a fuss we caused. Paris, the city of surrealists and avant-gardists, looked at us as if we'd crawled out of a sci-fi film, openly staring with something like amazed disgust.

I went again as a new romantic a couple of years later, and myself and Chris Sullivan and Melissa stopped the traffic as cars screeched to gawp. Their city simply didn't create people like us. I too was amazed because they had coffee, proper coffee made from beans, which you could sit and sip outside elegant cafés, where waiters with aprons waited upon you while you discussed life. They had restaurants with white tablecloths and wineglasses and specialities on the menu, which ordinary people went to, and cool bars with sleek furniture which stayed open late at night. They had trains which worked and modern football stadiums with seats where civilized people of both sexes sat and talked tactics. They had arty movies and clothes designers and shops which sold elegant things to adults who liked stuff like that and wore Benetton sweaters over their shoulders as they strolled along broad boulevards, window-shopping with their neatly dressed kids. We didn't.

There was a savage social and generational apartheid at work here. The old and the young rarely mixed; the generation gap in this country was a chasm, with the mature and settled rarely venturing out after dark on to streets claimed by the young and feral. The English middle classes had retreated behind privet hedges, occasionally emerging to a cosy England of warm beer served in dun-coloured pubs festooned with horse brasses, which were closed most of the time. They had their own sports and entertainments. They had executive toilets.

The other half, my half, had caffs and red-tops and boozers with sawdust on the floor and brutal neon discos. We had football stadiums, where thousands were herded on to lethal, crumbling terraces and then left to their own devices. And left to our own devices we created a complex and terrible culture with its own rituals and rites, dress codes and songs, a mythology and a history. Football hooliganism, which was as much a facet of British youth's sometimes violent brilliance as any pop craze or fashion trend, was just one of the ways in which we were ahead of everybody else.

Like mod and punk and new romantic, we invented it. By 1980, the terraces, and the pubs and clubs around them, were terrifying places, where well-drilled, sharply attired firms left calling cards on their razor-cut victims. Cultured Europe looked on in mystified shock and awe as we rampaged through their towns every time an English club visited.

England was an untamed, dysfunctional, yet fiercely creative place. The French could do cuisine, the Italians could do furniture, we could do football violence and punk rock. And just as Europeans picked up on punk, years after it emerged in London, but never quite got it right, never got any pop culture really right (how could they in their modern comfortable countries with coffee?), so finally they also took to football hooliganism, the English sickness.

This sickness was also our saving grace. The two great creative engines of youth culture, music and fashion, have always been black America and working-class England, both siphoned off and segregated from the mainstream of their respective societies. And as the 1980s, a time of perpetual revolution, arrived, that's all we were good at – creating and exporting exciting, tribal youth cultures, good and bad. In 1980 this sickly land had three things to call its own; fighting at football, street fashion and the *Face*.

When, in an effort to get rid of me, Neil Spencer sent me across Carnaby Street to the office of Nick Logan, owner, publisher, editor and sole employee of the *Face* magazine, I had never heard of it. Not many people had. I guess I should have gone to the nearest newsagent's, done my research and drawn up an informed and detailed analysis of what I could offer it. But I didn't. Instead, armed with the powerful arrogance of ignorance, I just walked in and asked for a job.

Instead of doing my research, I did what I've always done before important meetings, which is decide what to wear. The very fact that it was called the *Face* made me confident that Nick Logan, who I had heard of because of his tenure of the *NME* in its finest phase, would care about clothes. He obviously had a mod sensibility, so I decided to go for some hip nightclub stuff, but with a few modish touches. I wore a pair of narrow-cut Black Watch tartan trews, with white socks and loafers and just a plain, loose-fitting white shirt. I don't suppose Nick Logan noticed for a minute what I was wearing. He was in a tiny chaotic one-room office which had been loaned to him by the owners of *Smash Hits* magazine, and it was so full of mountains of magazines and photos and stuff that he could barely see above it. This was literally a one-man operation, which had been started on the money he'd raised by mortgaging his house, and he had somehow managed to get to issue three on his drive alone. Nick Logan might not have been aware of my attire, but I immediately spotted that he had that old mod thing. He was trimly clad, sharp in the way that they always are, his hair was well cut, his clothes neat, his manner crisp, and the moment I walked unannounced into that room I knew I desperately wanted to work for this man and his magazine.

So I did the same thing I'd done at the *NME* a few weeks before, only in reverse. I said that his mag was fantastic (even though I'd never actually seen it) but that it would be even better if it ran a major feature on this amazing scene which was happening at a club called the Blitz. I said that this was where kids were breaking the style barrier with their daring looks, and that there was this band called Spandau Ballet, who captured the essence of this epoch-making . . . etc., etc. I even told him there'd been a major TV documentary about it all. I then waited, with everything crossed. He asked what evidence there was that I could write. I said that I'd written loads for the *NME* and that Neil Spencer had recommended me for the *Face.* He commissioned a major piece on Spandau Ballet and the whole Blitz phenomena.

The *Face* had originally been launched in April 1980 with Jerry Dammers from the Specials on the front cover, and had latched itself to the two-tone thing. Pork-pie hats and Fred Perrys,

Sta-Prest and Harringtons will always look cool, but like just about every tribal look at the time it was looking backwards. There were mods and skins and punks and Teds and rockabillys a-plenty, but none of them were going to make the *Face* stand out. Because there was no one else, and no other model to base it on. It was still essentially a music paper, written by exiles from the *NME* and *Melody Maker* and photographed by rock snappers.

Today the newsagents' shelves are groaning under the weight of glossy, visually elaborate magazines aimed at bright young things, every Sunday paper has a style section, and two-bob design shows are the staple of cheap TV. But not then. The only magazines for males were full of cars and naked ladies, and the serious press, still strictly monotone, never sullied themselves with visuals or popular culture. For most British people in 1980, style, like homosexuality, was still something vaguely distasteful. Within a year or two style editors were *de rigueur* and Boy George was a national icon.

And it was all the *Face*'s fault. It reflected a series of changes to the old pop order, maybe to the core of British society. It arrived at about the same time as the promotional video and, soon after that, MTV. From that point on bands had to care as much about the way they looked as the way they sounded. The *Face* also very quickly latched on to the fact that there was a small but influential constituency of people who wanted not just a lifestyle, but a life of style. They yearned for some of that chic, urban, continental élan they'd tasted on holiday. They wanted good things, which looked good. We were about to enter a sophisticated visual age, when life in Britain switched from black and white to colour. And it took an old mod like Nick Logan to spot that. But it took the visually exciting scene dubbed new romantic to give the *Face* its real *raison d'être.*

Now that the vast and varied early eighties London nightclub cavalcade is remembered by the name new romantic, it is perhaps telling that the first article to chronicle the movement, the one I wrote for the *Face*, issue 5, was entitled 'The Cult with No Name'. The term new romantic was coined by a guy called Perry Haines, a St Martin's student on the fashion journalism course, whose gimmick was wearing preposterously high Dr Martens. He wrote a few pieces for another new magazine, *ID*, a zeroxed fanzine for the fashion and art school crowd. At the time Perry used the expression new romantic, it fitted a certain section of the Blitz cognoscenti, those who that week were draping themselves in britches and ruffles. But the flouncy, Little Lord Fauntleroy look was just one of many that were paraded simultaneously. Inevitably by the time the term new romantic caught on, the groovers and makers wouldn't be seen dead in frills.

I'd intentionally called the piece 'The Cult with No Name' in an effort to avoid limiting the whole thing, to show that this was somehow a distillation of all the tribal styles there had been and an adherent of none. But of course such earnest subtleties were never going to catch on, and the far snappier new romantic sobriquet stuck. It did have a certain validity, in that many of the kids at the Blitz (and for a long time we were also known as simply 'Blitz kids') had a passionate, positive attitude to life. George may have been a hard-bitten warrior queen, Chris Sullivan was a tough valley boy, but like so many of those at the centre of the scene they had a gleeful, devil-may-care attitude. The atmosphere among that lary élite was a strident combination of hedonism, narcissism and youthful naïvety, which was perhaps romantic. But the girls' toilet at the Blitz at three in the morning, ankle-deep in foul liquids, crammed with drunken exhibitionists, some snogging, one throwing up, one snorting speed, another desperately trying to apply his make-up while swaying to Moskow Diskow, was not an especially romantic tableau.

Being splashed all over the pages of this hip new magazine catapulted Spandau. By the autumn of 1980 Gary Kemp had completed the first part of his journey. He'd gone from the boy in the council flat watching David Bowie perform 'Star Man' on *Top of the Pops* on a Thursday evening to being the act that kids in their thousands talked about in school playgrounds the next day. He was still living at home with his mum, though, as was I with mine. I'd tried to use that typewriter she'd bought for me, but it was as useless as I was, so my first *Face* piece, and indeed the next half a dozen, all about club fashion, were written out longhand on lined paper. Nick Logan put up with it, though, realizing that the momentum of the Blitz scene, which was now starting to mushroom into a major national and even international story, was carrying his fledgling magazine along with it.

Besides, I was cheap; I would have written for nothing. Everyone working for the *Face* back then pretty much donated their services. It was still selling only a few thousand copies, but to all the right people. And some of those people asked me to write for them as well. So I started getting commissions from other papers and magazines, while I made my first appearance as a guest on Radio 4, on some deadly serious cultural analysis show, as the mainstream media struggled to come to terms with this emerging popular culture. 'What do we mean by style?' was one of the ridiculous questions asked that day, in a stentorian BBC voice clearly unused to such frippery. I loved all this media lark, but the main focus for me was still on dressing up and going out. The early eighties was a ferociously good time to be on the guest list.

After the initial all-in-this-together flourish of the Blitz, the scene started to fragment. The split between the white faces and the white socks, the gays and the straights, really became apparent in the new looks which emerged. Vivienne Westwood, the true heroine of punk, returned with a collection that was undoubtedly influenced by this new night-club phenomenon. Part couture corsair, part deconstructed dandy, it was a swashbuckling riposte to the Blitz kids and many of them went for it. Simon Withers, who'd made much of the early Spandau stuff, went off to work in her design studio, and Philip Salon managed her new shop, bafflingly entitled Nostalgia of Mud.* It was in this gear that pretty punk Adam Ant, relaunched his career as a crooning Highwayman.

Steve Strange, cash-rich on the success of the Blitz, which now ran to full houses twice a week, would arrive drenched in Vivienne's latest creations as he courted record company executives eager to sign Visage, the act he'd got together to sell his face. Malcolm McLaren was also putting together a band, specifically designed to sport the new Westwood look. Malcolm had been to the same grammar school as myself, and whispers said that George O'Dowd, the notorious cloakroom attendant, was going to be the lead singer of Bow Wow Wow. Everybody who'd ever been a face at the Blitz decided that they could be pop stars too.

SOON THE CHARTS were full of my mates and the term new romantic spread like a disease. You started seeing execrable ruffle-covered shirts on the high street and harem pants in Top Shop. There was a certain pleasure in witnessing people leap from tight snow-washed denim jeans to flowing robes, but not enough to compensate for the fact that your scene was being sold wholesale. It also got somehow associated with the whole upper-middle-class, Sloane Ranger thing of nice gals in high, stand-up ruff collars and cuffs, and foppish chaps with fringes, which was so far from the truth. When Diana got married a few years later in that melting chocolate cake dress, its makers, the Emanuels, were described by some commentators as new romantic designers. The danger of the term was that it made it all sound limp-wristed and wan. But then

* The name was actually a translation of *nostalgie de la boue* – a French expression which first arose in the eighteenth century to describe an aristocratic liking for the clothes and style of the peasantry, a kind of sartorial slumming.

lots of money was being made by a few and they had every reason to continue the trend.

I resisted the temptation to stand in front of a microphone. I was already doing what I wanted. And I was never really into this new tricorn hat and frockcoat thing. By this stage, as a reaction to the high street excesses of the now definitely dubbed new romantic look, I was going out almost exclusively in suits. Chris Sullivan and I put on a club in the basement of a Swiss restaurant in Soho called the San Moritz, where I DJ'd and played Sinatra and Samba, jazz and film music, while the audience in dinner-jackets and dickie bows swooned and smooched. It was the most pretentious place imaginable, and I loved it beyond imagining. The St Moritz only lasted a few weeks. As the pace of change became insanely fast, everything at this time only lasted a few weeks. We then switched over the road to the Kilt, one of London's oldest discos.

It was late 1980 when we moved into the plaid-clad interior of Le Kilt, untouched since the sixties. There were antlers on the walls and tartan carpets, and the DJ booth was an old sedan chair with a couple of decks in it. It was wonderfully swinging London, falling apart and of course empty most of the time. But we filled it on Thursday evenings by returning to our soul-boy roots. Chris and I had both been funk kids, and we roped in Graham Ball, also an old Crackers and Global Village hand, and decided to put on a night of hardcore sweaty funk, jazz and Latin. Chris and Graham worked the door, while I sat in the sedan chair and played records. Technically I was a terrible DJ; my speciality was playing the wrong side at the wrong speed, but this was well before mixing became a *de rigueur* skill and you were judged by your talents as a selector rather than a mixer. A selection of James Brown and War, mixed in with Tito Puente and some of the new avant disco from the likes of Ze records, coming out of New York, hit the mark. But also we had a fiercely cool crowd, with a very defined look, which was always the real pull of the best clubs. We had queues round the block, *Newsnight* filming a piece about us, with reporter Robin Denselow having terrible trouble talking convincingly about 'hip young things making London swing again'. We also had more money in our pockets than we'd ever known. I spent it on trousers. Big trousers.

It was at Le Kilt that the zoot suit craze first really kicked in. Chris Sullivan had finished his fashion degree at St Martin's, and now he was designing suits in the classic late forties style, pioneered by the hepcats of Harlem. Baggy strides way above your waist and huge jackets scraping your knees, dangling key chains, berets, two-tone correspondent shoes, goatees and twirly moustaches. This fitted in with the jazzy style of music we were playing and marked a definite departure from the more camp extravagance of the gay crowd who were following Steve Strange to his new venue, Club for Heroes. I had three or four suits made on the proceeds of DJ'ing, never quite going for the massive, double-breasted zoots, which Chris sported. I was into a slightly toned-down version of the jazz look, boxy finger-length one-button jackets, pleated trousers with turn-ups. My favourite suit had a fine rainspot polka-dot in the fabric, and I scoured thrift stores for hand-painted kipper ties and long spear-collar shirts to go with them. Of course every new twist had to be chronicled in the *Face*. Finally between writing and running clubs I was earning enough money to give up the job as a play-leader. I was also increasingly aware that I ought to find somewhere to live.

Burnt Oak had become a truly sorry place. Ever since going to the LSE, I'd spent less and less waking time on the Watling. I had discovered a new world and raced away from my roots without glancing back. I guess that meant I hadn't noticed what was happening. Reggie had moved away, along with so many Londoners who were vacating the old estates. And for good reason. At some point a massive drug problem had engulfed the place. Beer had always been the poison of choice in Burnt Oak, and it was full of drinking men, prematurely aged from the bottle. But as the 1980s, a hard new era, unrolled, some of the generation of kids who I'd grown up with succumbed to a virulent new high. For the first time heroin, which had previously been an obscure hippy drug, became the route to oblivion for working-class kids, and as usual Burnt Oak was in the vanguard.

Smack took out a swathe of the guys I'd climbed trees with, done the rounds and sneaked into soul clubs with. The sharper ones escaped; Mickey Asset and a few of the other faces headed abroad, to the States and Australia searching for that beach thing. Others worked on a kibbutz for a while or bummed around Europe. Steve Marshall was loud and proud in the same clubs as myself, and Jean Reddy was living with her partner in town, occasionally turning up at clubs, always looking great. Many of the others, though, those who hadn't found a route out, fell.

A couple of guys died, one well-known character was sectioned in a mental home after freaking out on the High Street, a few were imprisoned, one after shooting his dealer with a shotgun. Many more just sank into a dreary opium haze, which robbed the estate of all the vitality and the wayward but sometimes creative aggression which had made it such a remarkable place to grow up in. Society was changing, and there was little place for unskilled but obstreperous urban lads. Burnt Oak, as a bastion of old-time working-class values, was dying. Somebody prescribed heroin to make sure it had a pliant, quiet death. It worked.

Unemployment was raging at record levels and the major industrial unions seemed set on the mother of all battles with the stern new lady of the land. She called them the enemy within. There was an almost palpable tension building up on the streets of the inner cities, particularly in predominantly black areas, where young second-generation West Indian kids had had enough of being treated as outsiders in their own land, persecuted by an openly racist police force. In Ireland a hunger strike had started among republican prisoners in the Maze, who were demanding political prisoner status. Combative, divided, tribal, extreme. The social and political schisms of Britain in the early eighties were mirrored in the plethora of youth cults, who would literally see each other as the enemy.

The *NME* and the worthy rock mob saw the overdressed dilettantes of the Blitz as emissaries from a foppish devil. They hated Spandau, hated all the bands which swanned along in their wake, and as I was increasingly seen as the spokesman for this movement, they hated me with an almost weekly vehemence, which manifested itself as constant jibes in articles and gossip columns. I loved it. They also resented the fact that the *Face* was rapidly replacing the *NME* as the arbiter of cool. Their crown was slipping, and people were starting to talk about the *Face* as the magazine of the new decade, taking its predictions and fancies as scripture. Nick Logan brought in a brilliant young graphic designer called Neville Brody, who sharpened up the visuals, and it seemed it could be true.

Abroad, people were also starting to really notice this resurgent London and clamouring to find out more. Nick Logan hated interviews so he always suggested I do the talking. Over a few weeks I was interviewed by earnest journalists from France, Italy and America, asking long questions about the socio-semiotics of silly clothes. We had to do the interviews in the pub round the corner from the *Face* as the office was so cramped and I could hardly take them to my mum's in Burnt Oak. The greatest interest came from New York, which had a similar, though less clothes-obsessed scene. At their behest a major music and fashion show was set up in Manhattan, to present Spandau and a host of the young cutting-edge London designers to the city. Obviously I was going to go too, to write for the *Face*, to DJ at the show and to lig my way around. I was put up in the Gramercy Park Hotel by the organizers, the first time I'd ever stayed in a proper hotel.

This wasn't my first time in New York, though. I'd been the year before with Sullivan and Graham Ball and a load of the guys, eleven of us staying in a one-room apartment on 11th and First, deep in the East Village when it was still a tough Hispanic neighbourhood. We'd turned lots of heads in pink zoots and bondage, made loads of contacts in the club world and I'd DJ'd at Danceteria, which had the slogan 'Fuck art let's dance.' It was the guys behind Danceteria who had set up this Spandau bash. This time there was a radical new New York scene, which had just started to break out. A British girl called Blue had opened the first downtown club playing rap music, which was the big thing up in Harlem and the Bronx. She had Grandmaster Flash and Fab Five Freddy, playing two records at the same time and talking over the top, and scores of these sweet uptown kids, politely queuing up in their baggy jeans, sneakers, baseball caps and bandanas to come into her club to spin on their heads. I went and watched, and came to the conclusion that it would never catch on.

There were some designers I'd never met involved, a collective fresh out of the art schools called Axiom, who were picked to parade their gear. To call them designers is a bit of an exaggeration, as none of them had much of a business as such, but they had tons of ideas and front and enough half-finished clothes to just about assemble a fashion show. We all arrived at different points and had to find places to stay, as this was being done on the cheap. We also had to find models prepared to walk the catwalk for nothing, so we went out to clubs to persuade pretty girls to model for the show, which would directly precede Spandau's début American gig. I'd had worse jobs.

We'd recruited a few willing would-be mannequins, and they had to meet at an apartment on Gramercy Park for fittings. I walked in to see half a dozen half-naked girls struggling to understand the bizarre creations they'd be parading in. One of them immediately stood out as being a rare beauty, a mulatto girl with her hair pulled back in cane-rows. She held herself with this mix of arrogance and elegance, which was mesmeric. I half thought I recognized her from somewhere, but went over to say how glad I was that we'd got a really great-looking model. I expected her to reply in some Brooklyn Latina drawl. Instead she cussed me in a voice which was nine parts Clacton, explaining none too gently that she was not a poxy model, but a designer, she was one of the girls from Axiom. She'd only deigned to model in the show because we'd been so useless at recruiting proper models. Her name was Sade.

15

WEARING TWO PAIRS of jeans at the same time was a trick – the ones closest to collapse, over the top of a slightly sturdier pair. Another one was wearing a pair of long johns under your jeans, so that they showed through the rips and gaps, a bit Burt Lancaster. Studded belts were good, so too were motorcycle boots, perhaps with thick socks turned over the top, like a ton-up kid in an old British black-and-white movie. There was lots of old punk stuff on display too. Cowboy T-shirts, the muslin ones with long sleeves that poked down below everything else, or really early Vivienne Viva La Rock shirts, showing length of service to the cause. Other essentials included a plain white cotton T-shirt (still bizarrely difficult to acquire) with the sleeves rolled high, a ripped classic American sweat top in plain grey or an old plaid lumberjack shirt undone to the waist. Quiffs and flat tops were in, loafers, or frayed espadrilles with no socks. Dancing shoes for hard times.

This dressed-down, ripped-up look came out of the blue, a flash reaction to what had gone before. There was a perfect illustration of the speed and apparent contrariness with which trends were zipping by. August Darnell, aka Kid Creole, had been a big hit in Britain, partly because he'd fitted in perfectly with the whole zoot suit, Latino swagger thing. Blue Rondo à la Turk, the band Chris

Sullivan and Christos Tolera had formed, primarily to display their wardrobes to the world, had signed a major record deal with Virgin. They were a wonderfully anarchic and energetic live band who played a kind of punk salsa, but it was never really going to work on record. When they received a barrage of negative reviews Chris suggested that they call their album 'They Shoot Clothes Horses Don't They', but Virgin, who'd spent fortunes on them, didn't see the funny side. August Darnell, who was a far slicker musician and more polished songwriter, did manage to make it through to the mainstream. In fact he was far bigger here, where there was a genuine fashion scene to go with the sound, than he was back home in the States. So his record company flew him to Britain to film a live concert, but for some reason they decided to do it in Manchester. As most of the hardcore be-zooted hipsters were down in the capital, they offered to ferry up a coachload of Londoners from the hottest club of the time, which was the Beat Route in Greek Street, Soho, to dress the set and dress accordingly. The Beat Route was a genuinely legendary den of every kind of iniquity. It was where Spandau Ballet had filmed the video for 'Chant Number 1', easily their most funky and club-credible record. It was where Steve Lewis DJ'd with a photo of Lenin behind the desk and where big baggy suits and fiercely raw sounds combined riotously every Friday night. So theoretically it wasn't a bad idea to pick fifty odd Beat Route regulars and offer them free drink and accommodation for the night in return for looking cool and Creole-ish for the cameras.

But in the few weeks between recruiting the Beat Route boys and them clambering on to the charabanc north, one of those seismic shifts occurred. The whole scene had shunted from cool to hot, getting much tougher and rougher, musically taking a lead from early hip-hop and radicalized funk. 'Money's Too Tight to Mention' and 'The Last Poets' provoked dancing in a kind of frenzy as the snakebite-and-speed-inspired hedonism hit hard, so that once again the perspiration ran down Soho walls and revellers slid down them. There was a logical, functional side to the hard times look, as anything vaguely dandified would be ruined. But it was also a classic élitist reaction against the spread of suited and booted wide boys into the mainstream. Modern romance grinning on *TOTP*.

You can just imagine the look on the faces of the Kid Creole film producers when the expensive coachload of supposedly sophisticated London scenemakers arrived, not in smart, voluminous zoot suits and kipper ties, but draped in this aggressively ripped and torn apparel. They were absolutely appalled to see a gang of leather-clad, rocking soul rebels who looked like they'd been put through a shredder and behaved like they'd been at the moonshine. All night the lary Londoners heckled the band, leapt disgracefully about and fell over.

'HARD TIMES', which came out in September 1982, was the title of one the most noted and notorious articles I ever wrote for the *Face*. It was a cover story, featuring the pert bottom of a mate called Lee Barrett, wearing a pair of ripped and frayed Levi's so that his skants showed through, a studded punk belt, cotton T, and a hankie hanging from his back pocket, gay cruising style. Inside there were more pictures of this deconstructed, low-down and dirty style, including the author in a cut off-Levi jacket and carefully tumbling quiff, trying desperately to look like Jimmy Dean, but looking more like Jimmy Somerville. I never could do scruffy properly. The piece was a stridently hectoring slice of trendy one-upmanship, chronicling this truly underground new look which had actually first emerged at a tiny illegal club aptly called the Dirt Box, in a one-room squat above a chemist's on the Earls Court Road. It acknowledged the fact that the attire was a reaction to new romantic frills, which had now made it as far as Bucks Fizz in pirate headbands, Boy George with his pop band Culture Club as the nation's favourite cuddly queer, and baggy suits in high street stores.

'HARD TIMES' began, 'Bear with me for a while: this first bit may be hard but it is important. Read it twice if you have to because this is something you are going to have to grasp before we can go any further. And that is the notion that youth culture now represents not a rebellion but a tradition, or rather a series of traditions that date back to the advent of the teenager and continue to grow along a compound continuum of action and reaction. Imagine a spiral that begins with a birth out of post-war liberation, it is cyclical, but the circle is never completed because it is also revolutionary; therefore patterns repeat but they are never quite the same.'

I wince now at the undergraduate pomposity of the piece, but still agree with its central theme: that youth culture, driven by a few clothes-obsessed kids at any time, is a self-referential, self-conscious story that repeats itself as it progresses – a tradition, which had a beginning, and may therefore have an end. The febrile speed at which things were changing in the early eighties, and the almost apocalyptic feel of the time, with its savage politics, paranoia and hedonism, was the whole thing racing towards its end. The explosive teen caper was burning itself out by constantly plagiarizing itself. 'HARD TIMES' was part classic rock'n'roll, part soul-boy swagger, part gay iconography, part punk. But, as the piece stated, it was also partly a reaction to the politics of the time.

This short article in the *Face* caused an almost unprecedented fuss, largely because it made an explicit link between clothes and politics. It stated that the almost pathological aggression of Margaret Thatcher's hard-line policies, which meant very hard times for many, was even having an effect in a world as far away from pit closures and racist policemen as you could get.* And that the sartorial and social antics of a few night-clubbers actually said

---

* This was when successful British designer Katherine Hamnett wore her anti-nuclear T-shirt to a reception with Thatcher at Number Ten, and huge, baggy slogan T-shirts were a massive craze. Their political impact was diminished when the bold-print-on-big-white-T style was purloined by the band Frankie Goes to Hollywood and they became known as 'Frankie Says' shirts.

something pertinent about the times. It read, 'Everybody who can feel is feeling pain right now. People are getting angrier, the optimism which once led to bluff and bravado is now an optimism that you can defy and you can dance.'

It stretched the credulity of many when I suggested that the attire of a few trendy nocturnalites had anything to do with the combative politics of Mrs Thatcher's assault on the various enemies within, the coming cull. But looking back, I still believe there was a lot of truth in it. The atmosphere during the early years of Thatcher's rule was so poisonous, so bitterly divided, that it pervaded every area of life. If you weren't for her, you had to be against her and she was against you. There was a defiance on the streets as well as harder music and harder drugs in the clubs, there were also more and more illegal warehouse parties as the shells of decimated industrial spaces were squatted and partied in. We were literally dancing in rubble and coming up time and again against the police. You could feel the forces colliding.

Inner city became a euphemism for run-down and violently troubled, as confrontations and conflagrations engulfed Brixton, Liverpool and Bristol. I was now living half a mile from Broadwater Farm, in a disused fire station with my half-Nigerian girlfriend. We'd originally squatted the place together, her brother, who was an old hand at such procedures, climbing into this imposing but long-neglected building in Tottenham. It was just about habitable, with three or four good-sized rooms above the old hall where the engine was kept, the remnants of a kitchen and a toilet outside on the balcony. Despite no longer having a pole to slide down, it was perfect.

After our first encounter in New York, Sade and I had got closer over the days as we prepared for the show. Her clothes, subtle, understated, with a touch of her African roots, were by far the most competent on parade and she was good at wearing them. The night after the event, 5 May 1981 to be precise, we ended up sitting in an old Irish bar in Hell's Kitchen, talking into the night, lining up drinks on the mahogany and going home together. We'd been together from that moment on.

The reason I can name the date so precisely is not because it's emblazoned on my heart, but because it's in all the textbooks. It was the night Bobby Sands, the first of the IRA hunger strikers, died. The first of Margaret Thatcher's bitter enemies dispatched. New York with its massive Irish population and marked republican sympathies had been waiting for the death with held, hardened breath, and now, on one of those nights when an entire town feels focused on one event far away, it engaged in a kind of angry, emotional wake. I too had strong republican sympathies; most of my mates growing up had been Irish, and to me Bobby Sands was a hero. But I also have no doubt that I played all that up, to ratchet up the emotional intensity of the night in an effort to get this girl to fall for me. It worked.

The day we got back I moved into her tiny house in Wood Green, a nondescript north London suburb. It was a short-life property, a temporary let from the council, and a few months later when they wanted their house back we found the fire station and moved in. Things were going remarkably well for me workwise, though none of it seemed particularly remarkable at the time. I'd got so big-headed that I took it all as my due. Within a year of leaving college, I was perhaps the most recognizable writer for the most fashionable magazine on earth. For money I had a weekly column in a London magazine, *Girl About Town*, a freebie given away to office workers who had to endure my strident opinions every Wednesday. I was appearing regularly on TV and radio, whenever they wanted some bolshy young git with a silly hair-do to comment on trends. Increasingly they did, as the media became more and more aware of the new fashion thing. I was labelled a 'style guru', a tag which always made me giggle, implying that I sat around in elegant rooms chanting fashionable mantras, rather than living in a squat in Tottenham. I was then offered a job presenting a television series, in fact I was offered jobs presenting two TV series in the same week. I was twenty-one.

One was called the Oxford Road Show, and was a BBC2 Friday-night half-hour pop and politics series produced from the Oxford Road in Manchester. The other was a new bit of ITV teen tele, which was much more of a straight pop culture format. I chose the *Oxford Road Show* simply because they'd asked me first. It was a mistake. The show was a live, studio-based, supposedly high-energy thing, mixing bands performing on the stage with discussions about unemployment and toxic shock syndrome with members of the mainly student audience. There was a resident comedian equally new to his job, who would perform diatribes about current affairs. It had nicked the old *Ready Steady Go* slogan 'The Weekend Starts Here', but this wasn't a good way to start anything, certainly not a career in television. When I travelled up to Manchester to present the first show, I had no idea what to do, but I'd worked out my outfit and thought I could bluff it through.

The first time we went live on air on national TV on Friday afternoon was the first time we'd stood in front of the cameras and it showed. I looked like a rabbit caught in the arclights and the murderous trajectory of cameras scooting everywhere, frozen. The whole thing was a hideous shambolic mess, wantonly under-rehearsed, but it wasn't entirely my fault. The producers had this concept of 'dangerous TV', as they called it, which is why they'd plunged us straight into the firing-line with little guidance. We just got shot down. The only things which were half decent were the suit I wore, a black fifties job, very Marlon Brando in *Guys and Dolls*, with a black shirt and silver tie, and the comedian, who was also making his TV début. He was called Ben Elton. Ben, also wearing a suit, one of those glittery baggy numbers with the sleeves pulled up which became his trademark, sparkled in that ranting street-corner Trot style of his. I just fell on my face when confronted with the prospect of interviewing a sofa full of monosyllabic kids about the brutal results of free-market economics. It was excruciating.

A few weeks later it had got a little better, but not much, and the head honcho from BBC Manchester made some terrible suggestion for yet another piece of 'dangerous TV'. Even though I had only a month's experience at this television lark, I could see that what he was suggesting would not make good TV, and I told him so. This man, a senior producer at the British Broadcasting Corporation, in a very bad corduroy jacket, replied, with a completely straight face, 'I'm not trying to make good TV, I'm trying to start a revolution.' Before puffing theatrically on his roll-up as a sign of solidarity.

It made me realize just what a genius Nick Logan was. He had genuinely revolutionized the magazine world and made a brilliant magazine in the process. Except perhaps I didn't fully realize this at the time or else I wouldn't have rushed off to be features editor of something called *New Sounds New Styles*. This was an attempt by one of the big publishing companies to cash in on this newly discovered audience for fashion and music, and make a *Face* doppelgänger. To lure me over, they used the one tactic Nick Logan had never tried – they offered me money. I spent it on more and more expensive clothes and on swanning around in them like the celebrity I now thought I was. *New Sounds New Styles*, which was full of fashion spreads featuring the most absurdly over-the-top stuff, all shaven-headed futurism and make-up for men, folded pretty swiftly and I was back knocking on Mr Logan's door. Surprisingly he seemed happy enough to have me back.

By 1982 the *Face* had grown a little and there were perhaps half a dozen people working full-time in the still cramped offices on Carnaby Street. I was never one of them. I flitted in and out, making sure I was present whenever we did enjoyable bits, predicting trends, suggesting features, ins and outs lists. This would usually consist of Nick, myself and a couple of others sitting round his office batting ideas back and forth, deeming this to be in, that to be out. Nick would say something like Russia feels right, I'd say CCCP logos, someone else would suggest fur hats and neat vodka and then we'd move on to something else. There was no more science to it than that, and little more thought. Yet the pronouncements of the *Face* were given incredible credence and shops would decide what to stock according to what we'd written. There was a degree of self-fulfilling prophecy by this point, and if we deemed something to be trendy then it became so.

The whole 'HARD TIMES' ripped jeans thing became horribly commonplace horribly quickly. You could almost see the nation's youth reaching for the razor blades to attack the knees of the their jeans, while sweatshops throughout the Far East must have worked overtime to carefully cut and fray millions of pairs of pristine new denims. You could always spot jeans which had been intentionally torn, though, they were just too polite, so there was also a major growth in the search for authentically old Americana, and shops sprung up importing sackloads of America's cast-offs. Somehow there's something unique about the way a cowhand's bum wears away a pair of denims.

Sade had pretty much given up on fashion after a series of putative backers had failed to materialize; she'd run up debts, and was looking for something else to do. Sade is good at things. If she took a photograph it would be a fine photograph, if she wrote a short story it would be an engrossing one, but I didn't know she could sing. One day we were heading to Wales, to Barry Island in fact, to see Chris's band Blue Rondo. A group of us had clubbed together to hire a minibus, and Lee Barrett, the bum in the 'HARD TIMES' pictures, was going to do the driving. He engineered that Sade and I were sitting next to him in the front and we chatted aimlessly if amiably until about Chiswick, when he suddenly asked Sade if she could sing. Without missing a beat she said that of course she could sing. I looked at her slightly askance but she just shrugged her shoulders. Lee then explained that, along with just about everybody else who'd ever been to the Blitz and the Beat Route, he was managing a band, a bunch of guys who'd written a few half decent songs in a vaguely funky Latin style, and they needed a backing singer. Sade looked the part, she agreed to go along to a rehearsal, and we headed west without much more being said.

When it came to the audition a week or so later, the rest of the band decided that Sade couldn't sing and Lee had to tell her she'd failed. She didn't seem too bothered, but Lee did. He'd already realized that although her voice might not yet be entirely up to scratch, she had something much more important. She had that stature I'd been so smitten with when I'd first seen her in New York. So he talked to the band again and pretty much pleaded with Sade to have another go. I still don't know what made her swallow her fierce Yoruba pride, but she agreed.

The band, at this stage called Ariva, with Sade wearing a pair of ripped jeans and a black vest, first appeared in public playing 'Smooth Operator' on the back of an open-topped lorry outside the Beat Route at three o'clock in the morning, as the punters turned out. It was an audacious stunt, the effect of which was limited by the fact that almost nobody emerging from the Beat Route at the end of the night could actually see. It was the start of a shameless process of trying to make sure that this lot were the next in line after the procession of Spandau, Visage, Culture Club, Blue Rondo, all of whom emerged directly from London's hyperactive clubland and were flogged as much on the way they looked as sounded. But once people were watching the band with all their faculties intact, it wasn't difficult to see that the star of the show was the supposed backing singer with the almond eyes, scraped-back hair and hoop earrings.

Nick Logan suddenly had a crisis. The back page ad on the

next edition of the *Face* fell through and he had nothing to replace it with. Even by this stage the *Face* was still in a fairly precarious position. The back page ad is one of the most important and lucrative a magazine has to sell, and Nick simply couldn't get anybody to pay for it that month, so he decided to put a picture on the back. He'd heard about Sade and the buzz currently doing the rounds, and he opted to put a full-page shot of my girlfriend in a tight, cocktail hour, black backless number where an ad should have been. It was the best advertisement imaginable. The record companies went bonkers. Sade was signed.

At about this point I got a call from the *Sunday Times* to say they wanted to run a profile on me in their glossy magazine. It was called 'The Face Behind the *Face*', and included a full-page colour head and shoulders shot, of my head and shoulders in one of their most preposterous phases. By now the 'HARD TIMES' look had transmogrified into something else. Denim was still big, especially vintage forties, fifties and sixties Levi's and Lee stuff, but now the aim was to find it in its most pristine condition, so as to distance yourself from the razorblade merchants. So you spent your time hunting for Lee Storm Rider jackets, the blanket-lined winter jackets with a cord collar made for the prairie in December. Or original Big E Levi's, where the E on the red tag on the back of the pocket was a capital, denoting that it was pre-1960. As had been the case from mod days onwards, all jeans had to have the correct red selvedge stitching on the inner seam of the leg. I was in my element again. By now I didn't blanch at paying £100 for a pair of Levi's with the right detailing on the red tag on the back pocket – I was the flash, know-it-all bloke from the *Face*.

Given that I'm obsessive, I couldn't let it stop at seeking out the right jeans. I went for the whole cowboy thing in a big way. Cuban-heeled gunslinger boots in fancy-stitched thick brown leather, with a chisel toe. Vintage jeans, worn, but still dark because they've so rarely been washed. A chambray shirt with pearl buttons. A buckskin coat, with fringes hanging from the sleeves, and a pair of tan leather gloves with a cinched wrist. I also owned a series of cowboy hats, both proper Stetsons from a bizarre shop in Essex which specialized in accoutrements for urban cowhands, and more commonly, straw cowboy hats, with the brim turned over. I discovered a great authentic suede Confederate cap in a shop in New York, which became my pride and joy as I exaggerated my bowling walk to suit this outlaw get-up.

Obviously I looked preposterous, but when you've recently sported a kilt and pixie boots, cowboy stuff actually seems remarkably sensible. And of all the looks I've worn, there is something eternally attractive, almost addictive about cowboy gear. I don't mean line dancing, bad country-and-western cliché cowboy togs, but Paul Newman in *Hud* or *Left Handed Gun*, Brando in *One-Eyed Jacks*, or Cormac McCarthy's *All the Pretty Horses* (the book, not the movie). I guess it is something to do with all those boyhood fantasies, but also the usually sublimated fantasies of manhood. Real, subtle, functional western wear is one of the few theatrical outfits a grown man can wear and not look ridiculous in. You would never have told Lee Marvin he looked silly in a stetson and a pair of jeans. Clint Eastwood doesn't look like he's playing cowboys when he pulls on a poncho. Travelling through the ranchland of northern Mexico as a *Sunday Times* travel writer in the 1990s, I saw countless grown men in this stuff: sombreros and sheepskins, denims and suede boleros. They were probably the best-dressed men I've ever seen anywhere in the world.* Of course it might not look quite the same in Camden Town.

To go with my collection of cowboy duds I needed a distinctive

---

* There's a sleepy ranching town called Jerez, in the foothills of the Sierra, which I believe is the best-dressed town in the world. All the guys wear complete cowboy outfits, giant sombreros, stack-heeled boots, even lassos tied at the waist. But instead of horses they ride around the dusty streets on pushbikes.

hairstyle, and Ollie came up with the Colonel Custer. This is the only time in my adult life that I've had long hair, long enough, that is, to tumble down over my shoulders, but worn slicked back and with the ends lightly permed, so that it curled in *Little Big Horn* style. If I'd been any good at growing facial hair I would have gone for the goatee too. The Colonel Custer was an attention grabber. It was the last statement-haircut I would ever sport.

It was during this particular bad hair period that the *Sunday Times* came to the Old Fire Station to write a profile of me, and again the photo lives on. Almost as embarrassing was my appearance on a new live Friday evening pop extravaganza called *The Tube*. It was filmed in Newcastle, so they flew me up to talk about the whole cult of vintage denim and the minutiae of capital E's, strategically placed rivets and red selvedge stitching. Once I got to the studio it became apparent why *The Tube* had such a reputation for wildly anarchic broadcasting, because almost all the guests were pissed. The drink flowed liberally back in the green room and I was more than a little cut by the time I went on air. My interviewer was to be Muriel Gray, a rather dour Scottish feminist who had little truck for such fashion frippery as selvedge stitching. She rather aggressively started grilling me on the details of all this, which seemed odd as well as off considering they'd invited me to come up and talk about it. I was starting to get a little pissed off as well as pissed, when she said something along the lines of, 'This is ridiculous, what's wrong with the jeans these people are wearing?' – gesturing at the Geordies in the audience in their stone-washed denims. I replied, in my best terrace fashion, 'You can't expect me to dress like northern scum.' And the whole place understandably erupted.

It wasn't the wittiest retort, I was merely indulging in the kind of northerner-baiting absolutely commonplace at football, where, as a Londoner, I have always been a soft southern bastard. But it didn't play too well with the good folk of Newcastle and I had to get a police escort back to the airport. A while later I went to watch QPR play away at Anfield and got chased all round the back streets of Toxteth for being that arrogant London tosser off the tele. They definitely had good cause.

Back safely in London things were on the move again, things which, with hindsight, have an enormous bearing on the story. South Molton Street, a pedestrianized parade of shops just off Bond Street, had always had strong fashion trade links. Anthony Price, Bryan Ferry's favourite designer, had his showroom there back in the seventies, and an upmarket boutique called Browns had been the favourite hunting-ground for well-heeled soul-boys and girls into swish duds. But in late 1983 two shops opened, the like of which we'd never seen before. They were the first in town dedicated to the new wave of trendy Japanese designers who were all the rage across the continent. Yohji Yamamoto and Comme des Garçons, names you had to learn to pronounce pretty quickly. The shops themselves were super-modern, minimalist and cool in a way we'd never experienced, and the clothes they sold were designer to the nth degree. This was an entirely new take, more *Vogue* than the *Face*. The style was austere, understated, grown up, the clothes almost intellectual in their complexity and a long way from the street. Deconstructed, bias cut, mixed fabrics, twisted seams, carefully assembled to show a kind of studied insouciance, arch and sophisticated. These clothes were also unbelievably, stupidly expensive. Designer labels had arrived. I remember looking at a pair of crumpled £200 trousers in boiled linen and thinking I'll never be foolish enough to pay those sorts of prices. Within a month I was wearing an embroidered Comme jacket with a ruched elasticated back which made those strides look cheap.

The second great arrival in London around that time was the Soho Brasserie. It's almost impossible to understand the shock waves caused by the opening of a simple Parisian-style bar and restaurant in the old tenderloin, selling bottled beers and citron pressé and calves' liver and bacon against a backdrop of tiled walls and white tablecloths. All we'd known was dodgy old boozers and crappy caffs and suddenly in 1984 we had this. The Soho Brasserie was ultra-cool in that laid-back continental style, and it was aimed not at fat businessmen but at bright young things. Soon you saw all the emergent media and music-biz types sitting together in their designer gear, Nick Logan conspiring with Tony Parsons, Peter York lunching with Julie Burchill. Nobody had ever had lunch before, not in London. But it wasn't like we were in London. It was like we were in some bourgeois, comfortable European city. This was when I first heard people talking about property prices. It was the start of something. It was very nearly the end of something.

16

My dog sleeps on Fila, my dog sleeps on Fila. La la la la. La la la la.

COVENTRY AWAY 1983–4 season. There's maybe seven or eight hundred QPR supporters being lazily herded by a small police escort through the low-built suburban-looking streets leading up to Highfield Road, Coventry's ground, on a Saturday afternoon on the way to the game. It's the usual motley collection of football fans: misshapen middle-aged men with beer guts, a few real old timers who've been doing this for decades, dads with their sons held tight by the hand, a surprisingly sizeable sprinkling of middle-class types, a handful of couples, a smattering of nerdy trainspotter boys in scarves and anoraks, talking statistics. But the bulk of the mob is just that, QPR's mob, a firm of lads from their late teens to their late twenties, who are there to put on the show.

Most of them are not fighters as such. Although this is a vicious era, when the mass ends of the seventies have been distilled down to a more ruthless, more organized hardcore of tightly knit, Stanley-knife-carrying cadres, QPR are not a particularly violent crew. There's probably no more than a dozen front-line committed fighting boys, and usually they're not boys at all, but men in their thirties, borderline psychopaths, who never got over the thrill of a punch-up. Most of these jaunty lads being chaperoned through a nondescript Midlands town on a Saturday afternoon could have shoved back if push came to shove, but they were not out for blood. They are, though, definitely up for it. And *it* means putting out, strutting through the streets, scaring passers-by, singing during the game, gesturing with their hands held low by their sides, winding up the opposition mob, who are equally up for it. And in the spring of 1984 *it*, more than anything else, means wearing the right gear. It means being a casual. And QPR have something of a name for it.

So there's approaching four hundred swells from Shepherd's Bush and Northolt and Harlesden and such places, and they are dressed. They are dressed in a litany of labels, they have the latest Diadora Gold or Adidas Forest Hills on their feet, a few even sport Gucci loafers, the ones with the gold bar across the upper that cost upwards of £120. These are worn with parallel Lois cords or the bottom half of a Kappa tracksuit; it could be the Fiorucci jean with a slit, stepped bottom, that's just come in. Above that a Gabbici top perhaps, or a bit of old-school Pringle, a Lacoste polo-shirt with the crocodile on the foldover, beneath a highly desirable Patrick cagoule or a Chippie parka. This is all topped with a neat, short, carefully groomed hairstyle, perhaps a deerstalker hat, and a touch of tomfoolery. Nothing too flashy. The overall look, as the name suggests, is smart casual, that awful expression bouncers use outside suburban nightclubs. But it has to be absolutely spot-on casual, precisely right in a world where labels and garments come in and out with alarming alacrity. The aim is to be one step ahead, to display your prowess, your spending power and your pace.

And these label-laden coxcombs from west London are doing just that, at the front of the column, singing and bowling and giving it large, when they round a corner near the ground. Suddenly they're confronted by their opposite numbers, a gang of Midlands youth in their finest designer sportswear, arrayed across the narrow street, blocking their path and looking for a confrontation. The London bunch stops with a jolt and the herd concertina into them. You've now got two large groups of opposing likely lads a few feet apart, with the small police escort still trying to catch up and work out what's going on. For a second or two, the two sides stand snarling at each other, rapidly eyeing the opposition up, working out the odds, looking for the angles. Will it kick off, who will throw the first blow, who will run?

In the tiny space of time it takes for these kinds of calculations to be made, the QPR boys have been scanning the Coventry ranks for signs of weakness. A flaw is spotted, and by that inexplicable collective thought process which exists among football crowds, the telepathy of the terraces, a chant rises up from the Rangers ranks, a hundred or so minds thinking alike and then singing in unison: 'My dog sleeps on Fila, my dog sleeps on Fila, La la la la, La la la la.'

They'd seen that some of Coventry's top boys were sporting Fila, an Italian sportswear label which had once been the business but had gone out of fashion in London at least a month before, and were laughing and lambasting them for such gauche sartorial tardiness. Instead of launching themselves at the cocky cockneys in a fit of rage, the Coventry firm started looking each other up and down, perusing their togs and looking closely at what Rangers were wearing. And as it dawned on them that they'd been outdone in the style stakes, you could see their faces drop and their will for the contest wane. They'd been beaten and they knew it. As the desire for a fight seeped away, they slipped away too, fading into the side streets as the Rangers boys carried on to the game cockahoop with their victory. (On the pitch we lost 1–0, which I had to look up, whereas the glorious sartorial success remains vivid in my mind.)

Casual was the real style wars, a raging internecine conflict where what you wore was a weapon. It was a striking return to the fanatical clothes élitism of mod, played out largely against the backdrop of the mass culture of the football terraces in a moribund phase. Casual was a return to classic working-class sartorial values, a cycle reasserting itself, but also a dramatic sign of changing times, a logo-crazed celebration of consumerism in Thatcher's new England. It was also the first major clothes-based youth cult which, although I watched with fascination and sneaking admiration, followed and chronicled, I took absolutely no part in.

Casual first appeared as early as maybe 1980–81. While me and my arty mates were getting dressed up and written up, in our ludicrous costumes at the Blitz, kids younger than us, on the council estates and in the inner city playgrounds of London and Liverpool were already arguing the toss over the coolest trainers, seeking out very specific makes of exotic European polo-shirt or tracksuit, showing off that they had the nous and the bunce to get the latest. It's tempting to say that casual, in its purest form, had no starting-point, because it had been with us since time immemorial. It's Jack the Lad showing off.

Certainly, when I first saw kids proudly parading in their shell-toed Adidas and their Lacoste shirts, I was transported immediately back a decade to 1970 and myself as a ginger suedehead in Golas and a Fred Perry, gazing into the window of a sports shop, desperate to buy a Slazenger golfing jumper. Indeed Slazenger jumpers and golfing tops were a big part of the early casual wardrobe, as was skiing kit, tennis and athletics gear. Anything, which bore a fancy continental name: Tacchini, Ellesse, Lacoste, Kappa, Diadora, even Fila. Anything which was more expensive than the run of the mill, bog-standard version. Most importantly, anything which was hard to get hold of, which had in-built kudos because you couldn't just buy one in your local branch of Millet's.

Back in the eighties this sort of sportswear was not ubiquitous on the high street, it wasn't in this country at all for most of the more outré labels. There weren't shops full of enticing trainers and fancy tracksuits with alluring labels designed to separate desperate young kids from their cash. The first exposure most British youngsters had to this stuff was when their football teams played away in Europe. That's one of the reasons why Liverpool was such a hotbed of casual excess. Liverpool FC were the dominant English team, indeed the leading side in Europe, throughout the late seventies and eighties, and every time they played away in the European Cup, thousands of quick-witted, light-fingered young scallies were let loose on unsuspecting cities in Italy, France, Switzerland and Belgium. These were the kinds of deeply bourgeois places where you could find cool-looking, top-of-the-range trainers, ski-wear or running suits on every corner, and where they weren't too hot on security. So every time the Reds were in town there'd be a tidal wave of shoplifting, and a raft of new styles for the wide boys to flaunt and flog back home.

Down in London a similar thing happened with Arsenal. It being the capital, there were a few shops which sprang up specifically to cater for this new craze. In the same way as the middle classes were starting to be hungry for the trappings of continental civility – extra virgin olive oil, espresso coffee and bottled mineral water – and the big bang braggarts were hooked on Porsches, Don Perignon and tables at swish new Conran restaurants, so working-class boys identified their own chic objects of desire. Of course they went for clothes. Lacoste was the first label to break through. It was actually a rather ordinary French make of casual wear, most specifically cotton three-button polo-shirts in a range of pastel shades, but that little green crocodile became a veritable fetish. Soon every market stall was full of snide Lacoste, fakes manufactured for Essex in Thailand. Kids were carrying razorblades to slice off the croc from the real thing and attach it to their dodgy Tesco top.

This label-mania soon spread and sped up, with a constant

supply of new trainers or tracksuits now being imported in, to feed the collective clothes Jones. 'Taxing', which had always gone on, became an epidemic, a kind of gutter excise, as kids throughout the land had the sneakers taken from their feet, and the papers were full of lurid stories of taxing gangs prowling the inner cities. One week it was Adidas Trim Trab, the next Diadora Borg Elite, each pair always ten quid more than the last. Each big-town team had a hardcore of lads who were bang into the gear, and Euston station on a Saturday morning, as the London firms gathered to get on trains to far-flung northern grounds, was like a hyped-up catwalk show, stroppy boys strolling round the concourse so everyone could enjoy their labels, like some sort of Olympic, synchronized swaggering team had arrived in town.

QPR, whose home ground is in Shepherd's Bush, the old mod heartland, had a top reputation for up-to-the-minute gear because they had a shop right by the stadium which was one of the leading importers of this stuff. It was called Stuart's and had actually been around in the seventies as a soul-boy emporium, limped on through the lean years, but came back to the fore when it hooked on to the casual craze. Each week new consignments of schmutter would arrive from Italy and France and fly out of the shop within moments. On Friday afternoons before a game you would literally get queues of kids stretching up the Uxbridge Road desperate to hand over ludicrous amounts for specialist attire for sports they'd never dream of playing, in order to look just so at the sport they went to watch.

There were other elements feeding the casual craze. One was the growth of hip-hop in the states. Black American kids were also heavily into sportswear and there was a link between the burgeoning ghetto style of New York and the predominant working-class look in London and Liverpool. There was always a fairly high proportion of black British kids into the casual scene. But really it harked back more to the smooth soul-boy style of five or so years before, before it went weird and punky. Indeed, soul was the chosen music of the casuals. But music didn't really matter much. Casual was perhaps the most purely clothes-driven cult of them all. It was all about the right stuff.

Another lineage to the craze, which went back further than the old soul boys, was the wide boy. It was Del Boy. As well as exotic makes of sportswear, the casual wardrobe always had a smattering of would-be gangster chic. In the late seventies there'd been a short-lived lust for leather shoes with lurid gold-plated tips on the toe and heel, a bit of cheesy foot jewellery worn with camel coats and slacks by geezers who talked out of the sides of their mouths as they ducked and dived. And the slickest casuals always had the air of the minor league villain about them. Some of them were. So they wore Farah flat-fronted strides, with metal Pierre Cardin belts. Gabbichi Italian knitted short-sleeved shirts with large collars, contrast piping and a G on the breast pocket. Pringle diamonds or Benetton lambswool sweaters in lemon or salmon – even better, Scotch House cashmere – with perhaps a Burberry scarf and a fly-fronted mac. They looked somewhere between the cast of *Goodfellows* and Arthur Daley's lary love child.

It was the more obvious tracksuits and trainers, though, which made the news and began to filter through to the mainstream. By about '84, every third-rate, third-division football thug in a gang with a silly name – Luton's 'Migs' (Men in Gear), or Cardiff's psychopathic 'Soul Crew' – turned out in their livid high-street regalia. The market was flooded with flamboyantly nasty combustible shellsuits in lurid colours and patterns, and these quickly became a uniform for the kind of people whose main sporting interest is shouting obscenities at police vans outside courtrooms. Also, bizarrely, British pensioners, who had once displayed a high degree of sartorial restraint, began to sport these abominations. Spot a Saga Holidays group at an airport in the late eighties and it looked like a convention of retired runners or footballers fallen on hard times, legions of arthritic mutton dressed like Paul Gascoigne. To this day in eastern Europe the Mafia still proudly sport trackies as a sign of their status, and there are 'No tracksuit' signs on hotels and bars in places like Bulgaria and Slovakia in a futile attempt to keep out the criminal riff-raff. Blame it all on casuals.

By 1987, when Harry Enfield invented his tracksuit-wearing, wad-waving 'Loadsamoney' character, it was all over bar the shouting. And there was lots of shouting. But casual didn't just go away, it started to mutate and split. In the north, Liverpool, where it had arguably begun, and also in Manchester, there was a classic reaction against the overt shiny designer regimentation of casual, which some called 'the scruff'. You still had to have the right gear of course, but the look now was vehemently downbeat. A pair of worn, old-school Stan Smith trainers or scuffed Kickers. Flared beige cords, worn too long and just fraying at the edge, a loose-fitting sloppy-Joe T-shirt, maybe with Pink Floyd or some other old hippy logo on it, and a cagoule or skiing jacket worn with the hood up, over a scalp-close crop.

This was the slacker ethos which would later evolve into the whole baggy, acid house, Madchester style that dominated the nineties. But it began in Liverpool as a snub to casual excess at some time in about 1985. That was precisely the gear that many Liverpool fans would have been wearing at the Heysel stadium in Belgium, when the all-conquering reds played Juventus in the murderous European cup final on 29 May 1985. It was the end. The final, tragic nail came in ninety-six coffins at Hillsborough in 1989. Those vast, unruly standing ends had been rookeries, where a disreputable, but often thrilling other-world was forged. Some of it was about violence, but more was about stature and kudos and communality and dressing and singing and having it larger than the rest. From the point when I'd first been taken to football by my dad in the mid-sixties, right through to the late eighties, it had been a crucible of gutter creativity, a dynamo of all that wayward, peacock brilliance. But when the bodies started piling up, it had to stop. The dismantling of the football terraces and the clothes culture which went with them was one of the major reasons this gaudy teenage cavalcade, which had started a generation before, with Teddy boys stomping in their drapes through war-concussed slums, started to slip away.

Way before Heysel and Hillsborough, before the whole football thing effectively killed itself, there was another reaction to the tracksuit-and-trainer casual scene. Whereas in the north the chaps started to scruff up, London, doing well out of Thatcher's raging free market, went the other way. The mid-eighties saw the advent of a slew of designer boutiques, often in the most unlikely locations, flogging top-notch, top-dollar designer labels to equal those overpriced Japanese emporiums of South Molton Street. These places went way beyond the junior élitism of spotty herberts in Ellesse and Lacoste.

Tower Bridge Road in Bermondsey, deep Millwall country, is a rough old area. This was where the term hooligan first originated in the nineteenth century, and to this day it is still pretty sprightly. But on any given day in 1985, you could stroll through the council estate and take your pick from three different lavishly expensive designer emporiums. These places certainly weren't stocking Fila, they weren't even too concerned with the likes of Stone Island, Chipie or Henry Lloyd, the mid-range casual wear which was slowly taking over from the now derided and lampooned sportswear for the average casual. These little shops right in the middle of what looks like a textbook scene of urban deprivation were rammed with Giorgio Armani, Ralph Lauren, Jean Paul Gaultier, Dolce and Gabbana, Gucci and all the other totemic fashion houses which have become so ubiquitous now, but were almost unheard of then.

Fifteen years before Posh and Becks, way before super-rich footballers were routinely seen parading in their *pret à porter* creations, working-class football fans in south-east London were eagerly splashing out on this stuff to go and stand on the terraces and taunt lesser-dressed mortals. When Hoddle and Waddle were still wearing dodgy mullets and tight, elasticated denim, market traders and plasterers and spivs who sell tickets outside the ground were swathed in the most expensive clobber money could buy. They were the future. They were now.

In 1985 I went down to Bermondsey to write a piece about all this. I was proudly sporting £200 crumpled linen trousers from Yohji Yamamoto and thought I could flaunt it over these slum draggers. I walked straight into *Bermondsey Vice.* This was a Millwall equivalent of Don Johnson and crew, in oversized, unstructured Armani suits with silk T-shirts beneath and the sleeves rolled up, Gucci loafers worn with no socks, wealth worn with no qualms. In flash cocktail bars the talk was of whether Italian labels were better than French, and as the imported beer and champagne flowed, the cocaine, directly from South America, was produced with no inhibitions. The fact that the bar was not on Ocean Drive, but part of a decaying pre-war estate plagued with broken drainage and burnt-out cars, didn't seem to strike anybody but me as remarkable. At about three in the morning the owner of the bar wrapped his cashmere jumper round his shoulders, threw over the keys and told us to lock up at our leisure. This was working-class boys doing well and claiming their piece of the plush modern action. These boys didn't want street fashion any more. This was arguably the full stop at the end of a long and thrilling story.

I too had inevitably succumbed to the lure of these shiny sartorial baubles and padded designer shoulders. I didn't shop in wide-boy boutiques, didn't join in the heady casual race, but almost without noticing I was sporting more and more expensive clothes made by famous houses like Comme, Gaultier and Yohji, rather than any kind of truly alternative streetwear. What was actually happening was that the more savvy designers were cleverly tapping into the stylistic energy of Britain's streets, nicking ideas, refining them into international brands and selling them back to us. Gaultier forever popping up in London clubs, studious Japanese types with notepads in Camden market. British youth culture was becoming a feeder system for *haute couture.*

As I was getting a bit more affluent and my girlfriend certainly was, it felt like time for a little refinement. So of course I went for it, bought into it. After a couple of years of plugging away, Sade had become an overnight success. 'Your Love is King', a song written in the kitchen of our fire station, had been an instant hit, and *Diamond Life*, the album it came from, became the biggest-ever selling début album worldwide by a British female artist. She was huge. The refined sound Sade and her boys constructed has come to be seen as indicative of swish eighties yuppie values, yet perversely it was made by a mixed-race girl living in a squat in one of the roughest parts of London. Sade had class even when she didn't have a penny. There is always a gap between finding success in the music business and any money actually coming in, so there was an amazing period when Sade was one of the biggest stars in the world and we literally didn't have a pot to piss in. Winters in the fire station were rough, and I remember one day, when the toilet out on the balcony had frozen solid again, Sade, who had a limo waiting outside to take her to *Top of the Pops*, had to pee in a bucket.

For a period I rode on her immaculate coat-tails, and we rode all over the place. It was a time of constant trips to New York, Paris and Tokyo, picking up clothes wherever we went, shopping in all these new temples, layering label over label. I remember the tiny thrill of pulling on cashmere for the first time in a snotty shop and saying I'll take that. In both colours. I was moving away from what I really knew and what I really loved. I distinctly recall spending fortunes on a Ralph Lauren copy of a classic tan suede cowboy jacket, which had to be flown specially from Chicago to New York.

This was no longer exactly 'HARD TIMES' attire. It was my charcoal grey double-breasted, wide-cut, big-shouldered Jean-Paul Gaultier suit which the villain figure wore in the 'Smooth Operator' video, Sade's second enormous hit. The clamour to get a piece of the girl was deafening, and it soon became apparent that Sade hated the fame which went with her job. She shied away more and more. I had no such qualms.

Being Sade's boyfriend became my prime profession for a while, and I was pretty good at it. Suites at the Georges Cinq, long black cars at your beck and call, weeks away recording in the Bahamas hanging out with rock stars, and full carrier-bags from every coveted house in the world. It all seemed pretty good form to a boy from Burnt Oak. We had newspapers offering fortunes for lurid stories, and making them up when we refused to co-operate, paparazzi climbing trees to try to photograph her in the new apartment we'd just moved into. The hounds were unleashed. Desperate to keep her dignity intact, Sade retreated into a tight huddle of her oldest confidants and our relationship edged away.

THIS WAS the height of the emerging media-land, and the sweet taste of honey was everywhere. Its epicentre in Soho was buzzing with the matt black brio of the elegantly avaricious. My city, traditionally a place of shameless trade, was now fully awake and doing business after its post-war lull. The Soho Brasserie was no longer the only cool bar and restaurant in town, there were dozens of swish new places to hang out and carouse, and more artfully minimalist clothes shops by the week. The *Face* was no longer the only magazine, every page was glossy, every section style-obsessed. In 1985 the Groucho club opened specifically for the proliferation of media types, so now I could flaunt all this newly acquired designer stuff while bragging about 'various projects', networking and rubbernecking in a club of my own. Most evenings myself and a likeminded group of urban insurgents, wrapped up in whatever were the appropriate labels, gathered in Dean Street for a spot of diligent indulgence. We'd plot and air-kiss at Groucho's before floating over to the new Soho hangout, the Wag, run by Chris Sullivan, where I was perpetually on the guest list, as was just about every model and pop star, fashion designer and designer drug dealer. It was all very 1980s.

This was a harsher, sharper place, let loose and running rampant. The comforting social divisions which had been solid, which had informed every aspect of life, which had indeed been so central to the story of post-war working-class kids, excluded from the mainstream, creating their own vivid, clothes-based culture, out in the pumping periphery, were all breaking down. The miners' strike was a bloody last stand. I was part of Red Wedge, an arty attempt to revive the left with good graphics and pop gigs, which got mired in the clawing miasma of Labour Party bureaucracy, doomed to fail by dullard apparatchiks. We were going through the convulsions of a social revolution forced through by a militant Tory who was anything but conservative. And I was busily debating whether Antwerp had better designers than Milan. My friends and I, with our rampant individualism and solipsism, our lust for success and the trappings of modernity, our rejection of the stifling old straitjacket in favour of fancy jackets of every kind, were no doubt part of that merciless drive.

By the summer of 1986 we had done something. We had burst through, tipped up the hierarchy, made the knowledge of the street – the raucous, romantic nous of ripped jeans, oversized suits and silly hair – into a currency of great worth. The *Face* held its fifth birthday party at a studio in Covent Garden. It was a splendid affair, with hordes of desperate wannabes outside, flashlights popping, burly security guards on the door and every trendy media type from all round the world, downing cocktails of every colour. This was a shameless celebration of how far we'd travelled. As I slowly waltzed in, milking it in the latest stripy Paul Smith suit, a beautiful girl with a plummy West London accent and daddy's money oozing from every flawless pore begged me to get her in. I looked at her, said 'Sorry, darling' in my best clipped accent and carried on in.

But as it all got more self-satisfied, more sophisticated, so the energy diminished. We were never really sophisticated, and all the expensive élan in the world can never truly equal the rush and thrill of the joyously naïve. I was getting older, growing up, but so was the whole scene, transmogrifying into something more assured, less creative. Also I suspect I was tired of the chase, battered from a break-up, bored by the same old. So I headed off. Out of a London in the throws of becoming a very different city, I headed to a place which was experiencing an even more dramatic transformation. Bound for Barcelona to write a book. When I came back a year and a half later, the whole saga, and certainly my part in it, was approaching the endgame.

17

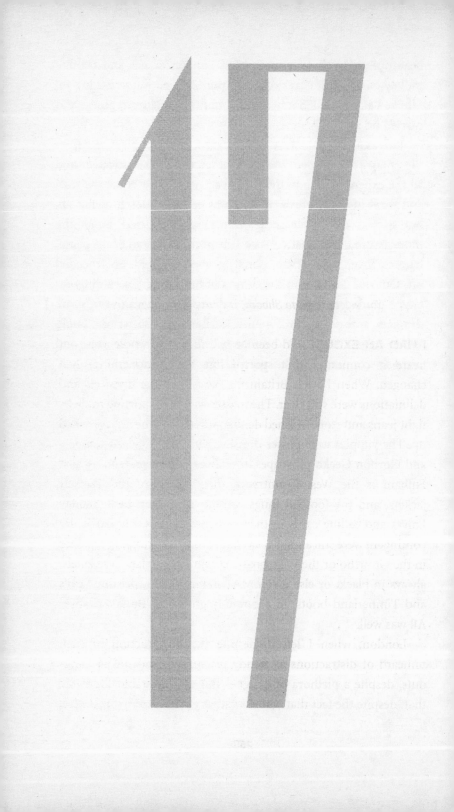

'You've got to go to Shoom, it's full of slum boys on E.'

I HAD AN EXCUSE. I'd been away and so hadn't seen or even heard it coming, hadn't spotted just how much things had changed. When I'd left Britain for Barcelona, the divisions and deliniations were still clear. The masses were still sporting mullets, tight jeans and stone-washed denim jackets with the sleeves rolled up. The yuppies were power-dressing with their Dallas shoulders and Gordon Gecko pinstripes, the Sloanes were pretending that Fulham is the West Country in their Barbours and Hackett jackets, and the football thugs continued to keep their Stanley knives and calling cards in their designer casuals. My particular contingent were still a small if swelling minority, lounging together in the Groucho or the Wag, boasting avant-garde Japanese labels, always in black, or else green MA1 flying jackets, pristine Levi's and Timberland boots, in a carefully groomed 'Buffalo Stance'. All was well.

London, when I left it, despite the introduction of such unheard-of distractions as trendy restaurants and media hang-outs, despite a plethora of designer this and desirable electronic that, despite the fact that whole swathes of the once dying centre, from Soho to Clerkenwell, Islington to Notting Hill, were being trendified and regenerated by a new-found fervour for slick urban living, was still ostensibly the ridiculous old tribal, vital city I'd grown up in.

The Catalan capital, after forty frozen years under the shroud of Franco, and yet to be homogenized and neutralized for the Olympics, was a splendid place. In 1986 this really was the city that never let you sleep. Despite that, a year after settling in an art nouveau apartment just off the grand *modernista* avenue of the Paseo de Gracia, and spending half my days escorting visiting friends to the Gaudís and my nights taking them to wild after-hours clubs, I managed to finish a novel entitled *In Search of the Crack*. Published by Penguin, with a cover drawing of a Soho street by Chris Sullivan, to reviews which could charitably be called 'mixed', it was a far too thinly veiled account of me and my compadres' adventures in the heady nocturnal London of the early eighties, complete with clothes-obsessives, warehouse parties, bizarrely named bands and a doomed love affair with a gracious, yet tempestuous beauty.

Mission accomplished and funds diminished, it was time to come home. But home was moving away. The hot new night-club was Taboo, a studiedly decadent, militantly homosexual soirée hosted by a chubby Australian with a fake egg on his head. Leigh Bowery was the most extreme of all the new generation of queer exhibitionists, who'd followed on from George and Marilyn and always seemed desperate to outdo them. There was something which struck me as simultaneously admirable and stupid about the outlandish Taboo kids with their tragic flamboyance. The whole rabid scene was the Blitz replayed as exaggerated farce by a generation which regretted it had been born a few years too late to be at the original. Leigh Bowery despised me with a vehemence which I can only assume was born of jealousy, and he made a big show of getting me thrown out of Taboo one night. Being expelled from a nightclub by a man painted gold and purple with a prosthetic hump on his shoulder was one of the more surreal experiences of my time. But it was also indicative that my time in the clubs, in the whole caper, was fast running out.

At this point, when Boy George was having his heroin problems splashed all over the front pages, and so many of the old club cognoscenti were paying the price for living solely for tonight, there was a fatal nihilism rife in London, especially among the young gay crowd at Taboo. The official new, post-Aids gay way was safe sex and pink pounds, sensible cropped-haired men strolling hand in hand along Old Compton Street in tight jeans. But those covered in paint and prosthetics at Taboo chose instead to go out in a dolled-up, drugged-up blaze of glory. Kids caked in theatrical slap and opium residue were dying on floors as the party dragged on around them.

Aids, an acronym I'd first had explained to me on one of those early eighties New York sorties, took out some of the finest. Going to funerals became an all too common occurrence in the second half of the decade. One of the most prominent was when Ray Petrie died. Ray was the mercurial *Face* stylist responsible for the whole Buffalo Boy look – which blurred the lines of sexuality without camp androgyny and was the antidote to the designer-label mania of the time. He put ruggedly pretty guys – young Marlon Brando lookalikes his favourites – in flying jackets and trilby hats, baggy jeans with their underpants showing. He showed Barry Kamen's underpants in a launderette in a Levi's ad and changed the way the nation looked. But the very fact that a multinational corporation like Levi's was now so wised-up on street style was yet another sign of the way the creativity was being utilized, sucked in and spat out. Ray's funeral was an immaculately attired wake for an age.

The lethal combination of smack and Aids was part of the downside of the second half of the eighties. The other drug which was wantonly common at the time was ecstasy. The big fib now is that ecstasy first hit London some time in the summer of 1988 and after taking one pill the whole loved-up, dressed-down, psyched-out acid house scene was born. Truth be told, ecstasy had been seeping through the blood system and soaking the brain in seratonin at trendy clubs on both sides of the Atlantic for at least five years. Ecstasy was perfectly legal when it first inveigled its way into London's underground nightclubs and was a major factor in the softening of the whole zoot suit and 'HARD TIMES' scene. It's hard to be sharp when you're out of your head on E, which makes you want to shed inhibitions and clothes. It's why so many of my friends suddenly found themselves in patently inappropriate marriages. This sensual, but entirely untrustworthy combination of chemicals was to play a major part in the next and final twist in this story.

By the time I'd returned to London and resumed a career as a journalist, broadcaster and none-too-successful novelist, I felt a little alienated from what was happening, but then not much was happening. There was a veritable whirlwind up in the heady reaches of media-land, with Soho soirées and slick members' clubs proliferating, people acting like a remake of *The Sweet Smell of Success.* But down there, where things cook, it was all quiet. Or so I thought. I recall interviewing Peter York for the *Face* in the mid-eighties and he predicted that the next youth revolution would be more about Atari than Elvis. In the long run he was right. The youth culture game, which began with Elvis, would end with Gameboy. But there was one last blast to come, and I never saw it coming. Ten years after punk had crawled out of the gutter and the boutique, a decade after a small, élitist clothes-based scene had gone dramatically overground and gone on to define an age, it was to happen again. Only this time it really did appear to change everything, because everything had already changed.

Acid house, rave, call it what you will, was simultaneously the last distant ripple and reverberation of the story which had started in Notting Dale with those Teddy boys fighting their way out of torn slums, and also the sign that it was all over. The generation of kids whose first great night was spent at some mass rave in a field somewhere outside the M25, wearing baggy, lilac clothes with smiley decals, gurning inanely to repetitive beats, was the first generation to completely sever the ties to their drape-wearing forebears. All the old élitism and tribalism, the angry, excluded creativity and the lineage of style semiotics stretching right back to blue suede shoes, meant nothing to them. And they were first spotted at a club called Shoom.

Debates of the 'How many angels can fit on the head of a pin?' variety have raged long and hard about where the house scene first emerged. It's that north versus south thing again. Manchester probably has the best claim musically. DJs there picked up very early on the new electronic dance beat coming out of Chicago. This was house, the pulsing, hypnotic successor to funk and disco. Stylistically the look, all formless and functional, was a continuation of 'the scruff', the Liverpudlian riposte to designer casual excess, which would eventually end up as that caricature baggy business with flapping jeans and soppy floppy hats, which was arguably a northern soul variant anyway. But in terms of the whole culture of acid house, the ethos and the lifestyle, which was the last and I believe the final, indigenous addition to the litany of great British youth style sects, it all began in an old gym in deepest Bermondsey, South London. At a club called Shoom.

Or maybe it was Ibiza. When it first emerged in late 1987, the rave scene, which was to cause such panic attacks among *Daily Mail* readers and to herald a tectonic shift among the nation's and arguably the western world's youth, was actually known as Balearic beat. Its origins lay not so much in the gay black clubs of Chicago, or even the Scally clubs of Lancashire, but in the vast, balmy open air gatherings of Ibiza Town and San Antonio. The Balearic island of Ibiza had been a summer destination for British club kids going back to the sixties, when it was hippy holiday central. I'd first gone in 1981, when Spandau played there, and had been back many times.

Going to Ibiza to party was certainly no new thing. But in the summer of 1986, while I was residing in nearby Barcelona, a group of London club DJs spent the summer there, shedding clothes, inhibitions and hard-learned cultural assumptions, as the rum and coke and the ecstasy mixed with the soft Mediterranean air to produce a chilled-out, loved-up, communal vibe. The music they were grooving to was unthinkable back home, mixing the pumping electronic rhythm of house with the cheesy stadium rock of Simple Minds or the cod flamenco of the Gypsy Kings. Clothes-wise – well, obviously on a hot island not too many were involved. The neo-hippy brightly-coloured, loose-fitting draw-string trousers, vests, sandals and beads of the sybaritic Balearic beach bum was the basic uniform. Smiley badges, as a kitsch-me-quick symbol of e'd-up euphoria, were part of the Ibiza tip. And one of the British record-players tripping out to this seductive cocktail for a few weeks was a south London lad called Danny Rampling.

Danny was an old soul boy, certainly old enough to know that you couldn't get away with stuff like that in trendy, élitist London, which was still stuck on suits and labels. But when he bucked every trend by opening a club called Shoom that winter, specifically to try to replicate that whooshing good times Ibiza vibe, the kids he attracted were not old. This was a new intake, fed up with the suited and booted 'you're not correctly attired, you don't know the catalogue number of every James Brown tune, you can't come in our club', élitism of Soho. This was not a generation who had boasted Sta-Prest and Salatio box-top loafers in the playground. They hadn't queued up outside Crackers or shopped at Acme, these were not veterans of the punk barricades or the three-day week. They couldn't care less about that stuff.

They wanted to go out on a Friday or Saturday night, take some happy drugs, pull on some bright loose-fitting gear, pull a boy or girl and dance. They had come of age in an entirely different England.

I was standing in the Wag one Saturday night in the winter of 1987, in my usual spot, upstairs in the back bar, waiting for the craic to kick in, gently tapping my £300 Oliver Sweeneys to some old-school jazz-funk tune, but aware that it wasn't really happening. This just didn't feel like the place to be. An old friend, Spike – one of London's best one-nighter entrepreneurs, who'd run legendary clubs and parties for years – said to me, 'You've got to go to Shoom, it's full of slum boys on E. They're dressed like hippies and they're loving it.' He then went on to briefly describe this scene, which had been happening for a week or two up a back alley on a council estate somewhere in deepest Millwall territory. Maybe an hour later he said that a little posse were off down there and did I want to come?

That was how I came to be standing in those hand-made shoes, a double-breasted charcoal grey wool Gaultier suit, twinned with a spear-point white shirt and hand-painted tie, outside a little local gym, amid a line of very young, very spaced-out kids who looked at me as if I was from another planet. I was on the wrong side of the river for me, the wrong side of twenty-one for them, and definitely in the wrong sort of attire for this place. We managed to whisk ourselves to the front of the queue and in through the door by pulling a little rank. Then, as we entered this tiny, cramped corridor draped with white cloth, like a junior school grotto at a Christmas fête, laden with condensation and perspiration, and turned into the main room, it flew at me with a rush, or maybe it was a shoom; I knew at once it was all over. I can't say that my life flashed before my eyes or I saw the future laid out before me. But like first hearing Lonnie Liston Smith float across a crowded club full of wedge-head boys in plastic sandals, or first seeing the

Sex Pistols sneering from the stage while girls in full bondage pogo frantically beside you, you know when you've just stepped over the threshold of an epoch.

It wasn't just the drugs, though the place was soaked in chemicals, oozing trippy bliss from every pore and crevice. It wasn't just the music, that huge, thumping 4/4 house beat hitting you like waves, electronic melodies washing over you, but with U2, bloody U2, intoning over the top. It wasn't just the couple of hundred kids dancing endless, inchoate dances, entwined in lush group embraces or curled up on the floor in serpentine pre-coital knots. It wasn't just the clothes, shamelessly abandoned, formless and infantile, kindergarten colours and beaming logos and bits of hippy trivia, beads and bandanas thrown on and cast off in the heat. It was all of that. It was the realization, as I stepped into this pulsating, delirious room, that this was already the next enormous thing. And I hated it.

Never before in my lifetime had a trend spread with such ferocity. And never before had I waved it goodbye. Within a couple of weeks there was a massive house night at Heaven with queues of dutifully smiley-faced kids stretching round the block. Within a couple of months it had gone way beyond the confines of inner London, and 'acid house' became the only style and sound around. Every club became a house club, every kid a brightly dressed clubber. And in order to better replicate that alfresco Ibiza experience, huge outdoor raves, massive gatherings of tens of thousands of e'd-up boys and girls in baggy beach gear frolicked in the drizzle and mud of rural England to repetitive beats, before returning to their normal lives and their normal, bland high-street togs. It was weekend hippies all over again. It was everything I've ever despised.

People now talk about 1988 and the so-called 'second summer of love' as 'the start of UK club culture'. I've seen Shoom described as 'the herald of global dance culture'. It did indeed rush far and wide, born on an overwhelming, homogenizing wind, which meant that whether you went out in Bolton or Berlin, Rimini or Goa, the clothes and the music were cut from the same template. The very term 'dance music', a generic catch-all, was the Gap and Starbucks of youth culture, a brand which everybody can easily slip into, consume and enjoy in the way you enjoy a skinny latte or a pair of beige cargo pants. Club culture, undemanding, stylistically uncreative, had become mass culture. And in the same way as high-street chains wipe out interesting, unusual little shops and cafés, so this scene eradicated everything. Even the past.

I'm forced to chuckle a little when the house generation talk about club culture as if they invented it. I wonder what Lee Davis's brother doing the stomp and the block in his John Stephen bum-freezer at the Scene would think about that. Or Horace and Clive Clark spinning and dipping at Crackers in Smiths jeans and cap sleeves on a Friday lunchtime. I think of Louise's and the Roxy, Billy's and the Blitz, I think of the Beat Route with its coruscating 'HARD TIMES' soundtrack and tattered apparel to match, and all the pioneer warehouse parties, and dapper dandies amid the rubble of Thatcher's revolution. When I hear people saying that club culture began in the late 1980s, I chuckle. But I also know that in some ways they're absolutely right.

What I first saw and heard and felt at Shoom that night was a complete break with all that had gone before. The drugs weren't new, the music was only a slight variation, and the clothes were largely a rehash of the sixties peace and love reliquary. But the mindset was different: inclusive, easy-going, all-embracing, it had none of that exclusive Soho élitism, that restless, agitated creativity and narcissism, that tribal competitiveness or stylistic urgency. Clothes didn't matter. This was club culture with the razor creases and abrasive edges rasped away, with all traces of mod taken out of it. It wasn't sharp or cool, these kids didn't care for sharp or cool. It was a mass-market, milky coffee of a youth culture, with the sloppy gear to match.

At the height of the dance music explosion in the early nineties, concerned British newspapers would regularly state that there were more than a million young people in Britain going to clubs, dancing to house and taking ecstasy every weekend, and for once I don't suppose they were far wrong.* But it wasn't the drugs which neutralized and neutered everything. It was the fact that there was now one all-pervasive, all-encompassing scene, one size and style fits all, which perfectly suited a generation which had grown up on the overpowering, unchallenged dominance of global brands from Microsoft to Madonna, Nike to Sony. This was the time of super-brands, supermodels and superstar DJs, in cavernous super-clubs like the Ministry of Sound. This was a massive, faceless enormo-dome of a nighterie, which successfully marketed itself as a global brand, with clothing and merchandising to match, the Hard Rock Café of clubland gone soft. And not a whistle or a tie-pin in sight.

At the Scene in 1963 or the Wag in 1983, it was the people, the faces, who were the real attraction, and their pitch-perfect attire the star of the show. That's what I'd grown up longing for, to join those driven, divinely correct kiddies who had it all and wore it well. That's why I'd pulled on all those outfits, why I'd followed every trend and dived into every scene. Now that I was grown up, it was gone. I was now a man in my late twenties who had been and seen and done all that. But perhaps *it* was finally done too. That night at Shoom in my inappropriate suit let me know in no uncertain terms that I was well and truly past it. The simple fact is I was too old. But the far more complex set of facts reveals that the

* One of the positive side-effects of this drug use was a dramatic decline in football violence from 1988 onwards. It is almost impossible to go roaring into another firm on a Saturday afternoon when you've been loved up on e the night before.

mass craze for soulless dance music and styleless clothes which was the all-powerful nocturnal pull for an entire generation of British kids wiped the slate clean. And almost nothing has been written on it since.

For far more than a decade now, the once-turbulent theatre of British street fashion, the gutter dynamo that propelled that crazy merry-go-round of youth cults, has lain dark. There are still a few punks posing for tourists or fourth-generation mods dressing by rote at revival meetings. There's even an official Edwardian society of those who wish to honour the drape and the quiff, and we've seen a resurgence of interest in the new romantic scene from a generation to whom it all appears impossibly exotic and quaint. There is still perhaps an ember flickering in the periphery, out there in the worlds of garage and drum and bass, among largely black and Asian kids who have some of that excluded, angry, joyous energy. But sadly they haven't thrown up much stylistically rather than a love of bling-bling excess and a slavish adoption of American ghetto style, where a gun is the premier fashion accessory for too many urgent, working-class inner-city youths.

This isn't really a sad ending. Britain is now more like everywhere else; more affluent and easy-going, more sophisticated and sensible, more materialistic and meritocratic, less antagonistic and divided. Less creative, less well-dressed. So many of the divisions and hierarchies, the competitive, tribal passions, the restless, obsessive desire among its young to flaunt their allegiances with silly, striking clothes, were a product of a deeply dysfunctional society. But if you were out there in the fray, dressed to kill in the regimental colours, feeling natty, looking sharp, believe me, it was fun.

EPILOGUE

WHILE WRITING this book I was also simultaneously getting that suit made, the one I told you about in the introduction. I don't know which was more trying. Shirts, trousers, jumpers, even shoes, which I love immensely as objects, enjoy holding and cleaning and smelling, are not supposed to have supernatural powers. But for some reason I invest suits, especially preposterously expensive, tailor-made suits, with some sort of alchemical ability. I always imagine that the next one I get made is going to do it all, make me look like, and what's more feel like, Paul Newman in his prime. Somehow I've convinced myself that if I get the right suit women will adore me, men will admire me and maître d's in trendy restaurants will suddenly discover tables they never knew existed.

The perfect suit is always in your head, and once it's on your back it can never be quite as good. But it's still worth trying, because it can come close. There is no feeling I know of quite like pulling on a new whistle for the first time, knowing that it has been made specifically for you, and that therefore (fingers crossed) it fits in all the right places and pushes all the right buttons. You understand why this was such a nerve-racking process.

A good tailor knows what he's talking about, or more importantly what you're talking about. It's called bespoke tailoring because you speak before he makes, and the speaking is the most important bit. Any fool with a pin between his teeth and a tape-measure near your particulars can size you up, it's grasping what you really want which is the skill. And believe me, it is a skill. A gentleman's tailor is actually an interlocutor, or perhaps more accurately a translator. He doesn't wield scissors or sew anything, he coaxes out your desires and realizes your ill-formed dreams. I talked about a late 1950s, early 1960s, grown man's look, cut pre-Italian, which means not too slim-line sharp, but then not conventional English, which can get a bit stuffy, squire. Smart but not flash, that's what I want. The kind of suit that would have been worn by the kind of man who'd have driven a Jag through Mayfair in, say, 1961. It's Sean Connery as James Bond, but on his day off. But it mustn't look retro. Now you imagine trying to turn that sort of nonsense into a piece of clothing to please an obsessive.

I'm not quite as maniacally mad on clothes as I once was. I have other things now, family and furniture and a life and stuff. But it only takes a few minutes on Savile Row, or to see and feel a really exquisite piece, and all the old fervour rushes back. Getting this new suit was like reawakening all that adolescent lust and I was fired right up. I'm a little embarrassed to admit this but I took along a book to show my tailor. I know a forty-three-year-old man shouldn't really be trying to dress up like a fictional secret spy; but there's a picture of Connery in *From Russia with Love* where he has on a suit just like the one I want. In my head the duty of this garment is to make me, now, look like him, then. The fact that Connery was one of the best-looking guys of his age, lit for a movie, manicured and coiffured to perfection, and that no matter how well the whistle turns out, I'll never get Ursula Andress types fawning all over me, was never mentioned. Tailors should be masters of discretion.

A substantial part of the appeal of this whole process is simply being able to use those words 'my tailor'. I haven't had a tailor to call my own for some time. I turned to those big-brand Italian types for a while until every footballer and his brother started wearing Prada and Gucci. Then I went Savile Row, to Kilgour, who are excellent, but I could only afford off the peg, which lacks the requisite rigmarole. Now that I was back in the fray, excited and nervous and enthused again, I made sure that I told loads of people that I was off to see 'my tailor'. I can't help it. I've always had the idea that a successfully grown man has a tailor whom he visits regularly, and pays occasionally. I guess it goes back to that suit of my brother Barry's all those years and chapters ago. I once interviewed Charlie Watts, the drummer of the Rolling Stones and a famously dapper man, who now lives most of his life on a huge estate in Devon but keeps an apartment in town. When I asked him what he does when he's up in London, he answered, 'I go and see my tailor, then I take a Turkish bath.'

My new tailor had grasped the abstract concepts I was talking about, and kept the picture for reference, so it was time to get down to specifics. The first of those was how much was it going to cost. There's a degree of negotiation involved in this part of the process, and we settled on a sum somewhere between his rack rate and my budget. It was still a lot of money, but then this is an inevitably expensive business, and although you don't have to pay the fortunes charged by the softly spoken masters of Savile Row, you can't get it done cheaply and expect to get it done well. And besides, paying top dollar is also part of the rush, it ups the stakes.

Once we'd settled on a sum acceptable to us both, it was time to produce swatches. These are the books of cloth from which you have to select the fabric for your suit. I wanted a lightweight, light grey, so he produced some fine mohair mixes from a range of English cloths. Making gentleman's suiting is one of the things we're still pre-eminent in, so you should expect to see an English label on the book. Then you have to go through this ritual of taking the cloth between your thumb and forefinger and pretending that you can feel how it's going to feel and hang when it's swathing your body. You can't really, and you can't even get too much of a sense of the colour and texture from a bit of five by three inch, but you have to trust that your tailor can. Eventually we agreed on this ash grey, with very little sheen or shimmer in the weave. Another thing to be aware of when getting a suit made is that you can end up looking like a flash git. Of course you are a flash git for doing this in the first place, but you don't want to advertise that fact too loudly.

Only after all this comes a tape-measure, which is stuck in places which all too rarely feel the nudge of enquiring fingers. Just about every bit of your lopsided, slope-shouldered, pigeon-chested, knock-kneed body is quantified and noted. But that is only part of the job. Just as many judgements are made by eye, as you are scrutinized, judged and summed. Once all that is done, and your curves and your desires have been reduced to a few scribbles in a notebook, it's time for the fun bit.

This is where you talk details; pockets and vents and buttons and cuffs and all the stuff that dreams are made of. Again it is tempting to throw in the lot, all those fancy flourishes you've seen and noted over the years. You could opt for slanting pockets, ticket pockets, jet pockets or button pockets, flared sleeves, double buttonholes, cloth-covered buttons, bone buttons, pitched lapels, velvet collars; you could have stepped bottoms, or split seams on your trousers; you could suddenly decide you need a double-breasted shawl-collared waistcoat, a cape and scarlet shot-silk lining. Don't. If your tailor is half decent he won't let you anyway, because he knows you'll look like a spiv and it's too late in life for that. A tiny little private touch to display to friends can be fun. I asked for the bottom two buttons of the cuff to be genuine, so that I can undo one. It's a classic marker. At the end of the meeting all I had to show for all this effort was the promise of yet another session. Maybe this is what people who go to psychoanalysts feel.

It takes two to three weeks for a tailor to come up with a basic block of your new suit and for the process of fittings to commence. You have paid out extravagant sums in the hope of acquiring a suit which will make you look and feel like the matinée idol of your choice, and what you get is a bit of formless old tat, covered in chalk marks and random stitching, with bits hanging off. The trousers will have no waistband, pockets or fly, the jacket no collar or lapels, no cuffs, no lining, no resemblance to what you had in mind. You will then be asked to put this half-made, still ill-fitting thing on, and appraise it.

This is a midlife crisis suit. I know that I am no longer in the game when it comes to fashion. I keep up with the Hoxton shenanigans and smile benignly at statement haircuts, but just can't bring myself to dress like a kid. I scan through the glossy magazines now and then, but I don't need a pimply style editor to tell me what to wear, or where to get it. I refuse to countenance anything with a logo or a label on the outside, refuse to wear anything that makes me look like an advert. As a consequence I've whittled shopping down to a depressingly select few places. I wear the same kind of jeans I've worn since the holiday camp. I still own loafers and brogues, three-button polo-shirts and plain white cotton T-shirts, still think that deep down I'm a mod. I get my shoes at Fosters of Jermyn Street, my jumpers from John Smedley, my shirts from Turnbull & Asser, my underwear . . . well, you already know about my underwear. Writing this makes me sound horribly snotty, all very Gentleman of St James's, and it does worry me. There is a terrible tendency to start dressing like a Tory MP. But what is a middle-aged man who still cares passionately about clothes supposed to do?

I still occasionally prowl those super-smooth, transnational clothing corporations. It may have Gucci or Prada or Jill Sander on the side of the heavy-duty cardboard carrier-bag, but they're all the same. I'm bored with the attitude of those sterile designer shops, it's like shopping in an airport courtesy lounge. Then there's that burly fellow on the door with the charcoal suit and the earpiece. I object to the assumption that I might be trying to nick something. I don't like paying over the odds for the supposed kudos of the label. They have nice things sometimes but it doesn't feel nice buying them.

This suit is due to arrive round about my forty-fourth birthday, a present to myself, but also an acknowledgement of reaching a certain age. I recently took the rings out of my ears and consigned them to my past. I did it with enormous sadness, but a resigned recognition of the fact that they no longer looked becoming. My wife, who is always right, said, 'Robert, don't you think the earrings look somehow wrong now?' She didn't come out and say, 'You're an old man who should have a little more decorum,' but I knew that's what she meant and, even worse, I knew she was correct. I'm not as young as I once was. I've told myself that if this suit works, if it really hits the mark, then I shall wear exactly this style from now on in. Basically I'm searching for something to carry me elegantly into middle age and beyond, a definitive acknowledgement of my place in the world. This is not just a suit, it's a statement of life-long intent, a symbol of my standing. And the man standing opposite me has just pulled the bloody sleeves off.

Tailors always do that. It's one of their theatrical little flourishes, tugging the sleeves, which are only lightly tacked on, so that they come completely away, to reveal the structure of the shoulder. It's actually very educational: it shows you the way in which suits are constructed and the fact that a proper, well-made gentleman's suit, with all the facing and padding, the tucking and joining, is actually a considerable work of architecture and engineering. But it still comes as a bit of a shock. At this stage my suit doesn't have that much to recommend it, and I rather like my jackets with sleeves. The trousers are too baggy, the jacket too tight, it needs a lot of work, but the basic shape is about right and the cloth is indeed lovely, admirably understated with great movement.

One decision we've arrived at is to make the jacket about two inches longer. Egged on by James Bond, I'd gone for an authentically short early sixties length on the jacket, which means that it ends round about your wrist, almost a bum-freezer. That is perhaps four inches shorter than a contemporary suit jacket and it just looks too retro. If it had just been me making the decisions, I might have left it, because I'm something of a sucker for authenticity, but I would have looked silly and you can't glide through middle age looking silly. My tailor insisted we make it two inches longer and he's right. We arrange another fitting for a week or two later. He gives me a card with the date of the appointment on it, rather like your dentist does when you have to come back for a filling.

The second fitting of a suit should be the time when it all magically comes together, when the formless, shapeless, unfinished thing you've fretted over suddenly blossoms into the perfectly fitting, infinitely elegant garment which will transform you into the best-dressed man in town. Of course it doesn't always work like that. The trousers were near perfect. But the jacket, which is the real making of a whistle, was still a way off, and I began to suspect that it always would be. It wasn't really that Nick had done anything wrong, in fact he'd done exactly what tailors always do, he'd made it tailored. Contemporary men's suits are actually remarkably loosely cut. Up until Giorgio Armani and his loose-fitting style of the late eighties, the whole point of a suit, especially a made-to-measure suit, and even more especially an English gentleman's made-to-measure suit, was that it fitted precisely. It held your trunk straight and correct, adjusted your posture, dictated your stance. It wasn't exactly meant to be constrictive, not a corset, but not far off.

Even 1950s-style drape jackets were still full of wadding and facing, still structured to keep you rigidly in your place. This jacket, as it was based on a narrower 1960s style, was moulded to my middle-aged frame, cut close under the arms, darting into my ribcage, forcing me to pull my shoulders back and stop slouching. Keeping me erect and even making sure I pulled my protruding beer belly in. Nick agreed that we could take out a little from the centre seam, maybe loosen the underarm a fraction, but he argued with some vehemence that it fitted very well. Technically he was right. The problem is I'm not used to wearing suits which fit very well and the effort involved is considerable. No doubt this was what I'd asked for, but was it what I wanted? How in heaven's name did James Bond roll about with Russians in moving trains in a jacket like this?

Still, it was an undeniably lovely thing. The best part of a well-made suit for me is the roll of the lapel, the way it just naturally curves proud of the breast, arching in a fine long line, kept up by its own internal engineering. This jacket did that exquisitely. It also showed what fine fabric we'd chosen, as it moved beautifully, just catching the light. The other thing I became immediately aware of is that this suit would require a whole set of accoutrements to go with it.

If you step outside the stylistic paradigm of your time, you immediately have to change everything or else look plain wrong. This suit would absolutely require a tie. I rarely wear a tie these days, but I just looked scruffy without one. Yet when we tried it on with a standard contemporary tie, it was far too wide and thick, bulging out from beneath the close-fitting front of the jacket. To add to the problem, normal twenty-first-century shirts have collars too wide and deep to sit gracefully beneath my elegantly svelte suit front. Even my hair, which was spiked and ruffled in my normal style, was patently out of place with such a get-up.

We finished this slightly unsettling fitting with Nick saying he would make the 'minor' adjustments necessary and me heading off to try to track down a shirt and tie which would make my birthday suit look and feel right. I discovered that afternoon just how rigidly, even in this supposedly tolerant, anything-goes era, we are all still held by the thrall and diktat of fashion. We now live in a consumer-driven age, a time when choice is the watchword. You can find shops selling hundreds of types of mobile phones, you can choose from a baffling myriad of computer games or flat-screen TVs. Alternatively you can pick focaccia or sourdough or ciabatta, Manchego or Pecorino or Stinking Bishop. But you try to step outside of the latest fashion construct and see how you fare. All I was trying to buy was a crisp white cotton shirt with a small, but still stiff collar, cut at a slightly inclined angle, and a narrow, thin, flat-lying tie, ideally in silk. So I headed for Jermyn Street.

This thoroughfare is the apogee of English élan, and it's where I went straight from my tailor's. Tucked away in St James's, just behind Fortnum & Mason, is one of my favourite strolls in the world and the site of my greatest-ever spot of sartorial point-scoring. A dozen years ago I'd interviewed a master cobbler called Mr George Cleverley, in a small room above Lobbs, the famed bespoke shoe shop. George Cleverley, then in his nineties, was the absolute doyen of shoemakers, and had been the personal cobbler to such paragons of panache as Frank Sinatra, David Niven and Terence Stamp. A true gentleman and a craftsman extraordinaire, Mister Cleverley, still in his apron, shaping a last to the very last, had regaled me with tales of fitting Churchill with monogrammed slippers during the Blitz, while Winnie shook his fist at the Luftwaffe above. He was great, and his shoes were even better, absolutely perfect, and of course so horrendously expensive that I couldn't even contemplate a pair.

The piece went out on Radio 4, and a week or so later I got an unsolicited call from a guy who said that he had an unworn pair of George Cleverley Chelsea boots, and if they fitted me I could have them for seventy-five quid. (They would have been £1,500 new.) We agreed to meet up and he was holding a pair of exquisite, svelte, seamless, perfectly balanced black leather boots with a gorgeous almond toe and a heartbreaking pale blue silk lining. The name of their maker inscribed inside. The minute I saw them, I started to shake. I can only surmise that they were dead man's shoes, ordered by an aristo or showbiz mogul who had popped his clogs before he could pull them on. And now here I was, a ginger Cinderella, desperately hoping that the proffered slipper would fit.

It did, just. They are perhaps half a size too small, but I wasn't going to complain about a little pinching, I was now the proud possessor of a pair of the finest shoes ever made. Inevitably after a couple of years the boots began to wear, but unfortunately by this stage the great shoemaker had met his maker and so I took them back to Lobbs for a little repair. I cycled to Jermyn Street that day, attired for bike-riding, and had the precious artefacts in a supermarket carrier-bag. It's perhaps no surprise that the shop assistant in this most exalted of stores should look at me a little sniffily as I breezed in breathless and sweaty, proffering him a plastic bag. 'Could you take a look at these,' I said, and he held the bag as if I were handing him some soiled underpants to peruse. His face was a perfect picture of disdain, until, that is, he actually opened the carrier. Never in my life have I seen a man's expression change so suddenly or so completely. He didn't have to study the boots or look for the now faded signature. He knew straight away, though it took him a few deliciously long seconds to actually stammer out the words. With a face drenched in incredulity and apology, he finally spluttered, 'You have a pair of the master's shoes.' I just emitted a nonchalant yes.

They know me by name now in many of the shops on Jermyn Street, another sorry testament to a life spent spending far too much money on gear. They call me Mr Elms, with that slight nod which should make my class hackles rise, but does exactly the opposite, as it pinpoints my vanity like a guided missile. But no matter how courteous, they still couldn't sell me a bloody narrow tie. I thought it would be easy to get exactly what I needed to make my new suit work on Jermyn Street where things change more slowly than in the real world. But sadly every single tie in every single shop was a positive porker. Shirts too, all come with wide, long collars, to accommodate such gargantuan neckwear. Such is the overpowering force of fashion. I traipsed off defeated.

The suit was ready. On time, on my birthday. There was a sense of some unease when it first slipped out of the carry-case. Holding it, though, feeling how well balanced it was, watching the fabric sway and hit the light, it is immediately apparent that it's a beautiful thing. The finishing is exquisite, the top-stitching light and close, not too pronounced, all done by hand, the care and attention apparent the closer you look at every detail, the elliptical buttonholes with a knot stitch at the end, the fine, almost invisible edging on the vents and pockets. Nothing about this suit is flash. Which makes it a very flash suit indeed.

Carefully pulling it on, looking at myself alone in that little fitting-room, the trousers fit perfectly, easily, they always did. The minute I place my arm gingerly in one sleeve of the jacket, though, I am instantly aware that I am wearing a suit. As I swing it across to the second arm and shrug and wriggle my shoulders to make it all drop into place, I can feel the jacket doing its job. It's a piece of body armour, precisely cut and tailored and made to fit my body, but also to make my body fit a certain ideal. This is not a loose, contemporary, easy-to-wear, throw-it-on bit of gear. This is not a jacket you can sport half-heartedly or slouch about in, with bits of your underclothes showing like some cool ghetto kid. This is a piece of prime English engineering, almost an act of social engineering. It says I am a gentleman and I will hold myself and comport myself appropriately. And what's more, you will notice.

In order to make the jacket work I have to stand more upright than is entirely natural, push my shoulders back, my chest out a little; my nascent middle-age spread has to be contained by an act of will. When I do all that, this jacket is absolutely spot on, hitting all the right places, curving elegantly away from others, no pulls or sags, nothing extraneous or surplus. There's that wonderful crescent-shaped gap between the indentation under my ribs and the inner side of the sleeve, while the back falls straight down from my shoulders with no ruching or bunching around my odd, angular clavicles. This suit works absolutely perfectly providing I put in the work. But am I prepared to do all that?

My tailor grins a happy smile when I emerge from the cubicle. He grabs the lapels in the way they always do and tugs them a little, rearranging me. It's all show, I've already put everything in place. I ask him if he thinks it fits a little too well (I can't say, 'Is it too tight?' without impugning his craftsmanship and my physique). He gives me one of those arch tailor's stares. Were he of the old school he would now call me 'Sir' and shame me into silence. Instead he says something like, 'Robert, you wanted a suit that fits, didn't you.' And of course he's right. I came in here six or seven weeks ago with a picture of James Bond, and he has delivered exactly what I asked for. 007 never slouched. But unfortunately I have to accept that I am not a young Sean Connery, even in this suit. And what's even worse is I now know I never will be, and, chances are, no matter how many expensive suits I get made, I'll never be Paul Newman either. But I smile, shake hands and thank him. It's a great suit, correct in all details.

But it isn't the template for the rest of my life. I don't have the energy to wear this kind of uniform every day, to play the part that such a suit demands, much as part of me would like to. Theoretically I love the idea of sauntering to the corner shop for a paper, or round the pub for a pint in finest Savile Row, hearing the neighbours remark on how Mr Elms is always so immaculate, so correct. I'd enjoy that, but I can't manage it. I'm too tainted with slack modern mores.

When I first arrive home, though, I put it on with all the adornments and trimmings. I finally found my thin tie, a nice svelte charcoal number with a slab in the silk. I couldn't get one in a shop anywhere, but discovered just the job in a musty box upstairs with all the old scarves and hankies, cravats and belts I've accumulated over the years. The shirt too, with its cutaway collar, has come from my own stupidly large collection. I bring out the precious Cleverley's, silk socks,a tie-clip just above the break, silver cufflinks, silk hankie folded with a straight edge, a pin keeping it in place. I then walk around the house like an emperor, pompously studying my reflection, pulling in my belly and my cheeks, strutting about, much to the amusement and derision of my kids. It looks great but it's definitely a special occasion suit.

So I hang it in the wardrobe along with the all the others, admiring its elegant profile, acknowledging its place in the story. Then, a week or so later, a suitably special occasion proffers itself. I'm off to the theatre, a box at the Royal Albert Hall indeed, to see a flamenco show which is being promoted by my old college mate Iain Hill. Afterwards there's a party for cast and friends at a hip new night-club which has just opened to great fanfare. I haven't been to a nightclub, not a proper young people's, after midnight, loud music, flirting, posing and dancing type nightclub, for years. I haven't really been to a nightclub, not with any conviction, since that night at Shoom in a different grey suit, in a different age, maybe fifteen years before. Well, tonight I'm going to one. In my new whistle.

Chris Sullivan is going too. I haven't seen Chris for ages either, although we speak on the phone, occasionally bump into each other on the street and talk fondly of times. Chris still sends my mum a card every Christmas and she still tells smiling tales of his black plastic bags full of clobber. He has also become a writer, penning a fantastic book on the history of punk. So we hug when we meet and then break into a shared smile because he's sporting a similar suit to mine. It's a little earlier perhaps, with a check in the pattern, broader shoulders and a turn-up on the trouser, but to the untrained eye, pretty close. We both have passes for this party and so we stand by the cordoned-off entrance to the do, waiting our turn in line, chewing the fat, nattering as we get nearer. There's a young man, maybe just sneaking into his twenties, in ripped jeans and a pair of training shoes, on the door. He's the greeter and chooser, the one who decides who can come in to this supposedly exclusive place, a job Chris did for many years at the Wag club with great aplomb.

As we get to the front of the line this boy looks at us both with a faint air of distaste. You can see his mind working, tell that he thinks we're a couple of old duffers who don't belong in this supposedly funky club of his. In some respects of course he's right, but if he was even vaguely fluent in the vocabulary of street style he'd have picked up that the two suits in front of him are not of the common or garden, office-worker variety. But he didn't, he couldn't. This boy is from a generation which has consigned all that stuff, that rich, ridiculous story, to the past. So instead he sneered a little and said dismissively, 'We don't allow suits in here.' Chris and I looked at each other in deep amaze and then both burst out laughing, much to the surprise and chagrin of the training-shoe boy. When we'd finally stopped laughing Chris Sullivan, who is a big man and in shape, moved ever so slightly closer to the greeter, who was now completely confused, and said softly, 'Young man, I think you need to learn some history.'